# Media Guide

## for

# Interpersonal Communication

**Charles G. Apple**
*University of Michigan, Flint*

Australia • Brazil • Japan • Korea • Mexico • Singapore • Spain • United Kingdom • United States

**Media Guide for Interpersonal Communication**
**Charles G. Apple**



For product information and technology assistance, contact us at
**Cengage Learning Customer & Sales Support, 1-800-354-9706**
For permission to use material from this text or product,
submit all requests online at **www.cengage.com/permissions**
Further permissions questions can be emailed to
**permissionrequest@cengage.com**

ISBN-13: 978-0-534-53556-8

ISBN-10: 0-534-53556-9

**Wadsworth**
20 Channel Center Street
Boston, MA 02210
USA

Cengage Learning is a leading provider of customized learning solutions with office locations around the globe, including Singapore, the United Kingdom, Australia, Mexico, Brazil, and Japan. Locate your local office at **international.cengage.com/region**

Cengage Learning products are represented in Canada by Nelson Education, Ltd.

To learn more about Wadsworth, visit **www.cengage.com/wadsworth**

Purchase any of our products at your local college store or at our preferred online store **www.ichapters.com**

Printed in the United States of America
7 8 9 10 11 13 12 11 10 09

ED164

# CONTENTS

Contents

# INTRODUCTION

Hi. My name is Chuck Apple. I have been teaching interpersonal communication since 1983, where I created the course for the Communication Department in response to a request from Kathy Verderber in the School of Business. The course is one of my favorites. I enjoy teaching interpersonal communication, in part, because of its potential to help students to learn, to grow, and to direct their own growth. Teaching this course has also helped me to grow as a person. As a teacher, I enjoy the challenges involved in making the material interesting and helpful to the students.

One of the toughest challenges facing the teacher in any class, and especially in one on interpersonal communication, is making the theoretical concepts both interesting and relevant, or usable. I have found that I must use a variety of pedagogical tools in order to make significant progress in meeting this challenge. I use oral reports, written assignments, discussion groups, role-plays, simulations, and media.

Media is one of my favorite instructional aids. Some of my friends and colleagues tell me that I often speak in movie, by which they mean that I can quote from a wide variety of films and use either the dialogue or scene to support an argument or illustrate an idea. My friends and my students often comment that I must always have the VCR running because of the wide variety of material that I have taped off the cable system for use in class. Actually, I study the television booklet almost every week in order to find programs that might be of use in class. And I use media in virtually all of my classes – in introductory communication theory, rhetorical theory and social movements, ethics, research, speech, conflict management, small groups, and of course, interpersonal communication.

I am honored to provide this media guide to my fellow teachers of interpersonal communication. I want to thank Kathy and Rudy Verderber for giving me this wonderful opportunity. While I have many goals in writing this guide, my fundamental goal is to give you ideas, tips and/or guidelines, and motivation for the use of media in your teaching. I hope you find the guide helpful.

**Structure of the Media Guide**

The primary focus of this Media Guide will be on films as they combine the most powerful elements of mass communication: writing, visual drama, emotion, and human performance. Pedagogical suggestions will be organized around two key elements of the media selected, namely, **visually presented interpersonal communication theory in action** and **theory in literature and academic resources**. The former category includes the films and plays noted at the end of each chapter in the Interact text, plus relevant CNN segments that will be elaborated upon in this guide. The latter category includes the novels, academic books, journals, and web sites noted in the chapter ending material.

Resources will be presented in the following sequence:

**VISUALLY PRESENTED INTERPERSONAL COMMUNICATION THEORY IN ACTION**

- Movies
- Theatre
- CNN Segments

THEORY IN LITERATURE AND ACADEMIC RESOURCES

- Literature
- Academic Resources
- Web Resources

Each chapter of the Media Guide will begin with a brief statement of the material presented and a set of learning objectives that are tied to the corresponding chapter in *Interact 9th Edition.* A correlation chart to other Wadsworth Interpersonal Texts can be found on page 202.

As film is the primary focus of the Media Guide, each movie will be presented along with a brief summary of the story, the interpersonal communication concepts (IPC) illustrated, recommendations for the scenes to be used, and sample discussion questions and thoughts on how to develop the discussion.

I will also make suggestions as to how to use the media in the guide for assignments. Sometimes these will be matched to a specific film, play, CNN clip or reading, or web site. I will also include a box in each chapter recommending some generic assignments that you can adapt to your own course design and objectives.

All of the media discussed and recommended in this Media Guide are listed in the appendix by genre. In addition, an excellent web site to use for information on movies is All Media Guide at http://allmovie.com. This incredibly useful site contains full cast and story information. I recommend it very highly.

**Using Media to Teach**

To put it as simply as possible, using media to teach is deceptively easy. I say this because media can be difficult or even tricky to use in a classroom. Too often, teachers seem to think that they have little to do when using media. I'm only showing a video today. "Wrong answer Hans!" Showing a video requires as much preparation as any other type of lesson, perhaps more.

As Edmund Gwenn, star of *Miracle on 34th Street*, *Them*, etc., once commented, "Dying is easy. Comedy is hard." Well, using media is hard. It drives me crazy to walk down a hallway in a classroom building and see the lights out in a classroom because the teacher is showing a video tape. Students can sleep more easily in the dark. It is more difficult to take notes in the dark. The more material the class is shown in the dark, the less they will probably remember and be able to use or discuss.

I love movies. I believe that film represents a new form of literature. Movies work best when there is something in the story that resonates with the audience. That notion of resonance is, I believe, grounded in reality. In other words, when a film captures some aspect of reality, then it works best and we make a special connection with it.

Movies should not be viewed as being in competition with print literature. They are very different media. Print works with our mind and our emotion. I love books and I love to get lost in a book – to allow my imagination to run with the author. Film works with our emotions and with something deep inside of us that allows us to become one with the movie. We can almost become a part of the story. The concept of the Parasocial Interaction gets at this notion to some degree. We develop pseudo relationships with characters and personalities in the mass media to such a degree that we sometimes forget or lose sight of the fact that these are simply characters in a story or personalities on a TV show. Movies can trigger a kind of virtual reality experience. We can see through the eyes of an eight-year old child at Christmas, or a small child meeting a small wrinkled creature from another world. We can run away from a huge boulder carrying an ancient treasure in South America. We can feel the pain of a loved one who is aging and suffering from the changes. We can see what life is like for someone from another culture or racial group and develop some rudimentary level of empathy for the joys, pains, and barriers that the person might/must feel.

Theatre is closely linked to electronic media, I think. I have become a real theatre buff in recent years. While I love movies, there is nothing like sitting in a theatre with a live performance of the story. It can be electric. The Media Guide offers theatre suggestions for you to recommend to your students. Check, and have your students check, the various theatre offerings on your campus and in your broader geographical area. Samuel L. Jackson recently told Rosie O'Donnell that his acting career began as a result of an assignment in his speech class in college. His instructor required the class to take part in a play. He said that he did, and has acted ever since. Pretty neat!!

Using various forms of mass media can be an effective way to operationalize the concepts, dynamics, and behaviors of interpersonal theory. By seeing these concepts in mass media, students become sensitized to seeing them in action in their own lives. Media allows students to practice critical thinking in relational contexts in a safe, lab-like environment. They can observe the results of specific communication acts, and then posit alternatives that may produce more effective results. Students can rewrite dialogue, thus giving them practice in developing their own language and life script skills and their assertiveness skills.

Television can be a very rich source of useful material for an interpersonal classroom. Over the years, I have tapped into 60 Minutes, 20/20, PBS, the Discovery Channel, the Learning Channel, the History Channel, and any other television source that offers a story, interview, report, or documentary relating to interpersonal communication theory.

Of special interest is a project between CNN and Wadsworth. A number of news reports have been made available by CNN for use with the *Interact 9th Edition*. The tape segments are cited in the relevant chapter with a brief explanatory description and recommendation for their use with that chapter material. The material cited in this Guide can be found on three tapes. The tapes can be obtained by calling Wadsworth marketing at (650) 595-2350, ext. 789.

A very important aspect of this Media Guide is the topic of diversity. I have tried to include films whenever I could that offer a glimpse into diverse cultures, people, lifestyles, and groups of people experiencing unique life conditions. I take a very broad and inclusive view of diversity. I include race, ethnicity, culture, gender, gender selection, age, body size, and physical condition. I have included films on racial and ethnic diversity such as *Boyz in the Hood, Do the Right Thing, Crooklyn, Guess Who's Coming to Dinner, The Color Purple, The Perez Family, My Family,* and *The Wonderful Ice Cream Suit.* Films on aging and physical size are also included: *Driving Miss Daisy, I Never Sang for My Father, Nothing in Common, Simon Birch,* and *Ship of Fools*. Issues related to gender and gender selection are included in *Torch Song Trilogy, Tootsie, Mrs. Doubtfire, Switch, Victor/Victoria, Finian's Rainbow, Fried Green Tomatoes,* and *As Good As It Gets*. I make no claim to having amassed an all-inclusive list on these issues, or any others. I do think that these titles can be useful to suggest types of films that can be used to get at critical questions on diversity and do some consciousness-raising for our students, so that they can be more literate when they watch films of their own selection.

## Guidelines for the Use of Media in Class.

1. **Prepare, Prepare, Prepare!!!!**

    Electronic media are not easy to use, that is, to use properly. Such media can be very passive entities, requiring very little cognitive response from viewers. Students tend to sit back and put their brains on TV mode. To put this claim to the test, try a simple experiment. Tell your students that you want to show them a video. Give them any special instructions about paying attention that you wish, but do not offer them any special credit. While the video is playing, observe the behaviors of your students. Perhaps you can already predict them. Some sit up straight for a while, looking at the picture, some even take notes once in a while. Many others put their pens down, slouch in the seats, perhaps place their heads in one hand, and show about as much interest as being asked to take out the garbage. Using media in class requires that the instructor carefully prepare what media she/he will use, why it will be used, how it will be used, what specific instructions are given to students, and how it is debriefed/processed.

2. **Don't bite off more than the class can chew.**

    Allow for the average person's attention span. This is increasingly difficult to predict with the impact of MTV, etc. However, it should be clear from almost any use of media in class that student's mind will begin to wander after a very few minutes of viewing. A colleague of mine has a 10-minute rule. This is a good place to begin. Do not show a video that is longer than 10 minutes, or do not show a video in more than 10 minute segments without some processing. If you want students to watch an entire film, have them do it at home or in a video resources center.

3. **Be specific in your use of media samples.**

    Try to select the specific segment that illustrates your point or theory. If students have to watch too much set up material, they can become quickly lost. We can learn from a notion in small group theory, namely, the notion of the maturity of the group member. If you remember, this concept points that group maturity is a function of how dedicated the group member is to the task at hand, rather than to the person's chronological age or length of tenure in the group. Some students will have more task maturity than others. A group with high task maturity can be approached very differently than a group with low or average maturity. A general education course can be expected to have low to average maturity levels. Therefore, it is necessary to prepare the segment very carefully, strategically, and motivationally.

4. **Prepare your students for the media exercise.**

    Give students any necessary background that they may need to understand the segment and its relevance to the course. A segment may seem perfectly clear to you, but your students are not as involved in the learning process or in the content of the course as you probably are. Therefore, give the students the necessary analytical tools that they may need. Web site information can also be used to help students find additional resource material.

5. **Prepare, Prepare, Prepare!!!!!!!** As Lieutenant Kaffee says to Colonel Jessup in *A Few Good Men*, "Are we clear?"

**Suggestions for Assignments**

Each chapter will include a box with generic reminders of types of assignments that can be fashioned for your use of media. These assignments include the following ideas.

**In Classroom Assignments**

- Small Group Discussion
- Whole class discussion
- Role Play Exercises – the class can take the part of a character in the film and present what they believe that character is thinking, feeling, and how the character might say something differently for a more effective resolution. This will help students understand perception, self-concept, empathy, emotion, assertive, nonverbal theory, conflict, and relationship building.
- Conversation exercises – Chapter Six offers web sites that can be used to give students an opportunity to use the internet and bring the results to class to practice their conversation skill. I have noted these web sites in the chapter.

**For Homework**

- Position Papers
- Relationship Analysis Papers
- Web Exercises to supplement textbook and Instructor's Manual exercise
- Journal Entries – use media material to connect with the Journal assignment in the Instructor's Manual.

The relationship analysis assignment is one that I have used for many years. The description is below. In the past, I have listed a suggested group of films, plays, or books for the students to base their report on. For the Media Guide exercise, you might consider having the students do the report on any film, play, or novel in the Guide. They are listed in an appendix to the Media Guide.

**Relationship Analysis**

The assignment is for each student to read a book, watch/read a play, watch a film and then to write a paper of approximately 3-5 pages analyzing the relationship between the two major characters in terms of the quality of the interpersonal communication between them. The analysis should be an analysis of the concepts discussed in class and covered in your text. The analysis should be specific as to what each of the characters has done, said, etc. and its impact on the relationship. If you feel it is appropriate, you may wish to have the student focus the analysis on a major event in the story that may have had a critical effect on the relationship.

In addition, I also have a conversation exercise that I have used for about sixteen years with great success.

**Experiential Report**

The assignment is to write a paper of approximately 3-5 pages that analyzes a "new" interpersonal relationship during the semester. ("New" should be understood as a "new" relationship or a "new" phase or level of a previous relationship.) The relationship should either be a new one for you (the student) or an aspect of a current relationship that you have not explored, (such as talking to a grandparent, estranged friend or relative, etc.), one that forces you to grow, one that makes you analyze aspects of your communication behavior that you have either not examined before or that deserves further examination. The experience can be very brief (covering an hour or two) or it can take several days or weeks to develop. Consider a conversation with a stranger, a friend, or an intimate (family member, significant other, etc.), an interview (for a job, a promotion, a merit rating, etc.), or a visit to a hospital, senior citizen home, etc. Your report should accomplish the following things:

- Brief description of the experience.
- Analysis of your intra-personal communication – feelings, self-talk, visualization, shields, the influence of past experiences, etc.
- Analysis of your interpersonal communication – trust, perception, listening, self-disclosure, expression of feelings, assertiveness, conflict, climate, etc.
- In order to deal with a meaningful segment of the relationship, try to highlight a single exchange as the focus of the report. Keep the primary focus on your behavior as opposed to "other-bashing".
- Be specific when describing and analyzing. Your grade will be based on the quantity and quality of your report. Points will be deducted for shallow, overly general, or no treatment at all on any of the above points. It is generally useful to quote some of the dialogue between yourself and the other person. Good writing style is also important.

The very first time I used this assignment, a student noted that she had never been really close to her grandmother. Since it had been several months since the death of her grandfather, she decided to do the assignment with her grandmother. By the end of the conversation, they were laughing, crying, and hugging each other as they reminisced about grandpa.

**Web Exercises**

The Media Guide contains a great many web sites. I have tried to recommend some of them for use with specific exercises. Consider the chapter on self. There are excellent web sites on personality variables and assessment that add a great deal of insight into the nature of the self. For communication students, this gives additional understanding of sender and receiver variables.

**Storytelling and Journals**

The Instructor's Guide to Interact makes wonderful suggestions on storytelling and Journals. I am a huge fan of narrative theory and strongly support encouraging students to process their thoughts and experiences in journal entries. I recommend having students practice their storytelling abilities by having them see a film and then tell the story to members of small groups. This will extend the oral practice and their storytelling practice. The group can ask them questions about the story and the characters, thus reinforcing their understanding of the story and the storytelling process. I also recommend having students watch some of the films in the guide at home and make journal entries on their reactions, thoughts, and theoretical observations. This gives them an extra opportunity to think in critical and theoretical terms.

**Final Thoughts**

I have my own list of favorite films that I tend to use as much as possible. I am sure that you either already have a similar list, or soon will have one. Some films can serve you very well for multiple topics in the course. I am particularly fond of *Driving Miss Daisy, The Doctor, Breakfast Club, On Golden Pond, Boyz in the Hood, Do the Right Thing,* and *The Perez Family.*

You have to be careful that you do not overdo the use of a film so that the class does not sit back and think, Oh no! Not *Forrest Gump* again!!!!

Approach these films as suggestions. Work with them and be open to all kinds of exciting surprises emerging from your students. They are really connected to movies, but they may not have opened their eyes and minds to the kind of critical analysis that is possible. You can do them a real favor by illustrating Interact for them.

And now, **Lights!! VCRs!! Remote Controls!!!**

**ACTION!!!**

# CHAPTER ONE
# An Orientation to Interpersonal Communication

## INTERPERSONAL COMMUNICATION IN ACTION

Chapter one of the Media Guide examines and explores the nature of the interpersonal communication process as it has been illustrated in a variety of forms of mass media. The goal of this chapter is offer you ideas on how to use media to introduce interpersonal communication concepts and to increase your students' ability to understand and evaluate those relational dynamics in action. This chapter will illustrate the communication process from several points of view. *Simon Birch* introduces an unusual form of diversity, but one that affects perception, self-concept, emotion, masks, empathy, and relationships. The three *"Wouldn't It Be Loverly"* films address the ethical responsibility for helping a student achieve communication competence. *To Kill a Mockingbird* illustrates a variety of relationships each of which demonstrate a special form of dialogical interaction, listening, attending, honesty, respect, caring, and inclusion. Driving Miss Daisy introduces relationships, aging, racial diversity, anti-Semitism, and relationship building.

## LEARNING OBJECTIVES:

- Help students learn to recognize interpersonal dynamics in action.
- Raise awareness of the complexity of interpersonal processes.
- Raise awareness for the student to diversity in interpersonal communication.
- Introduce the student to ethical issues in interpersonal communication.
- Introduce the student to communication competence.

| In Classroom Assignments | For Homework |
|---|---|
| - Small Group Discussion | - Position Papers |
| - Whole class discussion | - Relationship Analysis Papers |
| - Role Play Exercises | - Web Exercises to supplement textbook and Instructor's Manual exercise |
| - Conversation exercises | - Journal Entries |

# *VISUALLY PRESENTED INTERPERSONAL COMMUNICATION THEORY*

## *IN MOVIES*

**Simon Birch, dir. Mark Stevenson Johnson, with Ian Michael Smith, Joseph Mazzello, Ashley Judd, Oliver Platt, David Straithairn, Dana Ivey, Beatrice Winde, Jan Hooks, Jim Carrey, 1998.**

**Brief Summary:** The movie is based on the John Irving best seller, *A Prayer For Owen Meany*. Even though the movie reduces the book down to some of the most basic plot elements, it does an excellent job of displaying the various relationships in the story. The story is about an unusually small young boy, Simon, and his best friend, Joe. Simon believes the reason he was created so small is so that he may fulfill a special purpose in life. He believes that ultimately completing a special task will redeem him.

The film takes us into the private world of Simon and Joe as they play, swim, and take care of each other. An important scene takes place early in the film when Joe's mother invites a new man, Ben Goodrich, over for dinner. She is a single mom who had Joe out of wedlock and has never divulged the identity of his father. In her small town world, having a child without being married is quite the scandal. Her suitor brings a present for Joe to try and make a connection with him. The interaction between Joe and Simon as they puzzle out what to make of the gift and the new man is a fascinating view of their process of communication. The gift turns out to be an armadillo, which serves as a major symbol throughout the rest of the film.

The story takes the two boys into a church service where Simon chooses to speak out on what he perceives to be the absurdity of organized religion. In total frustration with Simon, the Reverend Russell sends him out of the church to religious instruction for punishment. In this class, Simon's classmates are passing him around overhead when the teacher comes in and blames Simon for the disruption. The class is dismissed, but Simon is made to remain inside until he asks for forgiveness. Joe's mother learns of this and comes to Simon's defense and scolds the teacher. This act of caring serves to bond Simon even more closely with Joe's mother.

Simon loves to play baseball but is either made to take a walk or remain on the bench due to his remarkably small stature. At one fateful game, Simon manages to hit the ball far into the air and just off the left field foul line. Joe's mother, who is walking to the game to see the two boys, is fatally struck in the head with the ball. Even though the accident is no one's fault, Simon is crushed with guilt, and Joe with sorrow. The boys make peace with each other in a powerful series of interactions that are full of important interpersonal symbolic action.

The film reaches its powerful climax when Simon and Joe go to a winter camp with the minister and a group of younger children. During an accident in which the church bus slips into the lake, Simon learns the truth of his special purpose, and Joe learns the identity of his real father. Joe learns that the dream of his real father is not nearly as good as the reality of Ben in his life. Jim Carrey does the narration and plays the adult Joe at the beginning and the end of the film.

**IPC Concepts:** The movie illustrates the importance of such interpersonal concepts as truth and respect. The local minister has to deal with his secret past. Joe must learn how to relate to Simon after his part in a tragic accident. Simon must deal with his own self-talk and guilt after the accident. The two boys relate to each other, in part, through small micro rituals that they have developed.
Simon Birch is a very powerful film. It not only illustrates the communication process very effectively, but it also is a moving story about human differences, the power of friendship, the value of faith, trust and truth, and the need for openness. The film can be used to illustrate concepts from several chapters in Interact.

**Scenes for Use in the Classroom:** There are many scenes useful for the classroom, including Simon interrupting the Sunday sermon; Joe and Simon at their swimming hole; the introduction to the new boyfriend, Ben; the death of Joe's mom; the reconciliation of Joe and Simon; the accident that costs Simon his life; the discovery that the pastor is actually Joe's real father; and the death of Simon.

For use in Chapter One, I recommend showing the scene in which Joe's mom invites her new boyfriend to dinner. This scene is useful because it illustrates the interpersonal communication process very neatly and compactly. Consider the context of the scene. Everyone is somewhat anxious, mom is nervous about everyone's reaction to the boyfriend, the grandmother is nervous about who her daughter is getting involved with now, Joe is afraid of the new man in his life, Simon is anxiously protective of his best friend. Note everyone's introductory behavior, how they try to make small talk, and possibly the self-talk each person may be having. The gift that Joe is given by Ben serves as an icebreaker and as a powerful symbol for the balance of the film. Everyone has perceptual shields in place that shape their view of this new person.

This scene will give the class an effective introduction to the film and to the process of interpersonal communication. I recommend having the class watch the film on their own and then lead a discussion using the following questions.

**Questions for Discussion**

1. **How does this film illustrate the relational side of communication? How do the two boys behave in order to maintain the equality in their relationship?**
   With the exception of his relationship with Joe's mother, whom he adores, Simon feels very much one-down in most of his relationships with adults. Simon tries to level his relationships with others by his willingness to ask difficult questions, such as he does in church during the sermon. His own belief in his special purpose drives him to assertively ask others about it and to stand up for himself. After his mother's death, Joe must learn how to relate to the pastor, who is his real father; to his

mother's boyfriend, whom he accepts as his foster father; and to both his grandmother and Simon.

2. **How does Joe's relationship with his future foster father develop? What does this man do to slowly earn Joe's trust and respect?**

   Joe initially rejects the friendship overtures that he is offered. As time passes, he sees that this man is genuinely interested in him, treats him with honor and respect, and will give Joe unconditional love and acceptance.

   The "father" figure is always there when Joe needs an understanding adult. He is there when Joe's mom dies, when Joe is trying to figure who his father really is, when Joe gets in trouble for damaging school property, and when Simon dies.

3. **How do most of the characters in the film treat Simon? How does he tend to respond to this treatment? What does he do to earn more respect?**

   Almost everyone in the story treats Simon as a kind of freak of nature. The Sunday school teacher treats him as a nuisance. His fellow Sunday school classmates (except for Joe) treat him as a kind of toy. The pastor is regularly frustrated by Simon's independent and challenging ways. Even his own parents ignore him. Only Joe, Joe's mom, and Ben treat Simon with respect and acceptance.

   Simon retreats into the inner world of his special purpose, and into his relationship with Joe. He also accepts inclusion and love from Joe's mother.

   Simon tries to act responsibly. He tries to be a productive member of his little league team. He tries to affect the role of his church. He takes the role of supervisor to those children younger than he is.

## "Wouldn't it be loverly!"

These films deal with the idea of teaching someone to improve their knowledge and, in particular, their ability to express themselves in order to make themselves more upwardly mobile. In each case, better communication must be learned. However, as the student begins to learn and grow, they find that their former living conditions, and/or acquaintances, and family patterns of interaction present problems for them. In addition, their teachers/mentors must also confront their role and responsibility for the student's welfare as a result of their student's newfound communication competence. The three films are *Pygmalion*, *My Fair Lady*, and *Educating Rita*.

## Pygmalion, dir. Anthony Asquith and Leslie Howard. Leslie Howard, Wendy Hiller, Wilfrid Lawson, Marie Lohr, David Tree, 1938.

**Brief Summary:** The film version of G.B. Shaw's famous play. The story is an amusing one about a professor who takes a lower class young woman under his tutelage in order to instruct her on the proper way to speak, walk and conduct herself. As a result of his instruction, the woman is able to increase her ability and present herself as a member of the upper class. However, having made this transition, she feels she is unable to return to her former surroundings and associations. In this romantic comedy treatment, she confronts the professor and they ultimately develop their own relationship.

## My Fair Lady, dir. George Cukor. Rex Harrison, Audrey Hepburn, Stanley Holloway, Wilfrid Hyde-White, Gladys Cooper, Jeremy Brett, Theodore Bikel, Henry Daniel, Mona Washbourne, Isobel Elsom, 1964.

**Brief Summary:** The musical version of G.B. Shaw's play Pygmalion. The story is about a lower class young woman who is taken in by Henry Higgins, a wealthy man who works as an elocutionist. His belief is that anyone can be passed off as upper class, if not royalty, by merely altering the way that they present themselves and speak. He teaches Lizza Doolittle to speak with proper diction and grammar, and to walk and move with proper form and etiquette. The film depicts the power of language and nonverbal behavior in shaping the perceptions of others with regard to the social position of people.

## Educating Rita, dir. Lewis Gilbert. Michael Caine, Julie Walters, Michael Williams, Maureen Lipman, Jeananne Crowley, Malcolm Douglas, 1983.

**Brief Summary:** Re-creation of the stage play by Willie Russell. A modern spin, set in the seventies, on the older Pygmalion story set in England.

**IPC Concepts:** Language, nonverbal and perception. The key elements of this series of films raise some very important questions for class discussion and/or short response papers.

**Scenes for Use in the Classroom:** Each film has scenes in which the young woman is introduced to the teacher and must learn to interact with him. Each film depicts the woman learning to become a more competent communicator, and shows her difficulties in learning and in interacting with her former peers after the learning has taken place. Each film also illustrates the difficulties facing this woman as a result of her newfound competence. In each case there is a powerful scene in which the young woman confronts the teacher on the "what do I do now" question. Each of these scenes are useful in taking the class through the theoretical issues related to changes in perception as a result of increased communication competence and the ethical responsibility of helping someone to improve.

I recommend leading a discussion on the impact of learning on our lives. It has been my experience that the scenes depicted in these films are all too real in the lives of some of our students, especially if your students come from first generation college families. I have had speech students tell me that they were ridiculed for speaking strangely when they went home for weekends or holidays after learning to speak differently in their speech class. After a unit on assertiveness and language in relationships, one student spoke up and said, "Doc, people just don't talk that way in

Burton." My response for better or worse, was "Well Dennis, the world is bigger than Burton." These films can help to offer a better answer.

**Questions for Discussion**

1. **What is the ethical responsibility of those whose instruction brings about profound changes in the behavior of the student? Is there an ethical responsibility?**

   The issue here can be simple or complex. To what extent should change agents help prepare their students for the challenges that learning to communicate can entail? How much mentoring should teachers or advisors be prepared to play when their pupils experience stress, inner turmoil and/or rejection as a result of being able to communicate more effectively?

2. **To what extent does changing how a person speaks change the rest of that person's relationships, perceptions, and aspirations?**

   Clearly a central issue in the history of the study of communication. This question can raise a host of issues dealing with bilingual and multilingual cultures, diversity, culture, treatment from family members as the children return home from college, etc. As the class watches scenes in which the student in the film confronts the changes due to her education, their own experience will enable them to empathize. This question is a good way to illustrate the concepts of audience adaptation and rhetorical sensitivity in interpersonal relationships. Over the years I have used a wide variety of examples of people who are able to flex their communication styles depending on who they are talking to. I stress that this style flexibility can be done in an honest manner so that we are not merely trying to become some other persona just to blend in, or manipulate others.

## To Kill A Mockingbird, dir. Robert Mulligan. Gregory Peck, Mary Badham, Philip Alford, John Megna, Brock Peters, Robert Duvall, Frank Overton, Rosemary Murphy, Paul Fix, Collin Wilcox, Alice Ghostley, William Windom; narrated by Kim Stanley, 1962.

**Brief Summary:** Based on Harper Lee's magnificent novel, this movie tells the story of three children and the summer during which they come to face their fears about their mysterious neighbor, Boo Radley, and the realities of Southern racism.

Scout, Jem, and Dill have a summer of adventures trying to catch a safe glimpse of Boo. However, it is also during this summer that Atticus, Jem and Scout's father, is asked to defend a black man (Tom Robinson) accused of rape and assault. Though clearly innocent, based upon the evidence, the man is, nevertheless, convicted by the small-town, Southern jury. The children learn of the harsh, ugly side of what their father does for a living, and of the racist traditions of their culture. In an effort to be with her father during a very critical confrontation between Atticus and a mob of angry townspeople, Scout intervenes. The innocence of her presence, and her direct and honest words to the mob, forces the men in the group to reexamine their actions, resulting in the mob dispersing.

After the summer, Dill leaves for his permanent home and Scout and Jem go to school. Scout must learn how to dress less like a tomboy and to talk to children who are different from herself. Her lunchtime encounter with a poor boy from a nearby farm teaches Scout to consider the experience and perspective of the other person in communication. When she is teased by her schoolmates, who have heard their parents talking about the trial and the role played by Atticus, Scout must learn how to control her temper by dealing with her feelings and her self-talk. Scout flies into a fighting rage when the other children call her father names. Atticus counsels his daughter on the need to control her feelings and to not let the words of others affect her in such a manner.

The film tells of the adventurers of the children during the summer. They watch as Atticus and Sheriff Tate deal with a rabid dog. They learn of the town's reaction to the news that Atticus will defend a black man against the accusations of the white community. They also try to learn more about their mysterious and reclusive neighbor Boo Radley. There are many events in this film that can be useful in class, so you may simply have to select those that you feel most comfortable with.

As the movie moves to its conclusion, Scout finally meets Boo Radley when he comes to Scout and Jem's rescue. Scout realizes that the man's gentle, shy ways should not make him the outcast that he is.

**IPC Concepts**: This film illustrates virtually every aspect of the communication process in interpersonal relationships. It deals with trust, perception, empathy, conflict, stereotyping, listening, cultural diversity, and the development of the self.

**Scenes for Use in the Classroom:** I love this movie so much that I really want to say: just watch the whole thing. However, I do not believe in showing entire movies in the classroom, so let me recommend a few useful scenes for chapter one.

- Jem and Scout meet Dill.
- Mr. Cunningham making a payment to Atticus.
- Lunch with the Cunningham boy.
- Jem and Scout finding treasure in the tree near the Radley house.

**Questions for Discussion**

1. **Examine how Atticus responds to Bob Ewell when he spits at him outside of the Robinson home. How does Atticus respond? What might his self-talk have been?**

   The focus should be on self-talk and making a choice of how to respond. Atticus clearly struggles with the emotions that he feels to this man and his provocative behavior. His internal struggle is clear on his face. Ask the class what they might feel at such a moment and how they can talk to themselves to work to a moment of self-control such as Atticus has. It is then possible to discuss the importance of making a choice about how we will feel or behave. Atticus would understandably still feel angry, offended, etc., but he chooses to respond with self-respect and non-provocative behavior.

2. **How does Atticus build trust, respect and support into his relationship with Scout? Specifically, how did he handle Scout's distress about going to school and learning to read?**

Atticus always shows Scout respect. He speaks to her in a caring, patient manner that shows that he takes her concerns seriously and she is important to him. He never denies the legitimacy of her feelings. He speaks to her tenderly and respectfully. Two scenes illustrate this type of interaction, the lunch with Walter Cunningham and Scout's distress over not reading with Atticus anymore.

3. **Why did the African Americans sitting in the courthouse gallery stand as Atticus left the courtroom?**

This is a good question to raise to discuss diverse customs for respect, etc. Clearly, the group of citizens know that Atticus is a good and fair man who is willing to jeopardize his own social standing in order to do what is right. The reverend's comment to Scout tells her that her father is a man worthy of respect. Ask the class how their ethnic traditions might handle this situation. Compare and contrast the answers.

4. **How did Atticus explain Walter Cunningham's behavior at lunch to Scout? How does this incident reflect issues of diversity?**

This is another great opportunity to discuss diversity issues. The Cunninghams are poor southern whites. Atticus has to explain to Scout that her ways are not the only ways or customs that people might have. He explains Walter's shyness and his family's poverty to her. He lets her know that she owes him respect and tolerance when he is a guest in her home. Atticus is able to combine his respect for Scout with the lesson that she must show respect to other people.

This is a good opportunity to raise the nature of cultural diversity and the myriad of examples of such diversity. Diversity can be too narrowly considered. By examining the additional types of cultures, we can open our student's eyes. I include discussion of racial/ethnic diversity and other bases for cultures such as age, gender, gender selection, physical disability/ability, income based, etc.

## Driving Miss Daisy, dir. Bruce Beresford. Morgan Freeman, Jessica Tandy, Dan Ackroyd, Patti Lupone, Esther Rolle, 1989.

**Brief Summary:** Adaptation of Alfred Uhry's play. This is the story of the evolving friendship between an old, wealthy woman and her simple, aging chauffeur. The film adds the diversity issues of her being Jewish and his being African American. Daisy struggles through most of the story with the changes that she experiences as a result of aging and her relationship with Hoke. When her son forces her to accept Hoke, a chauffeur whom he has hired, Daisy responds with anger, resentment, and rejection toward Hoke. She slowly learns to accept his role as chauffeur, and even more slowly, his role as her best friend. Hoke must move very carefully through his interactions with the white community, and must wear a series of carefully constructed masks in order to protect himself and his livelihood. Daisy learns more about Hoke and herself through a series of encounters that include:

- A confrontation over a can of salmon
- The incident about reading the headstones at the cemetery
- Daisy's Christmas "gift" to Hoke
- Hoke's confrontation with Daisy on the way to a Civil Rights event
- Their shared experience with police harassment
- Their efforts to cope with an ice storm
- Their trip to another state
- And ultimately, a severe bout of disorientation by Daisy

By the end of the story, as her son says, she wants Hoke "all to herself."

**IPC Concepts:** Daisy illustrates a great many interpersonal and cross-cultural principles. I will raise a few here, but the film can serve as a conduit for many others. You can use this film to illustrate and discuss such concepts as self-esteem, self-talk, personality, emotion, self-disclosure, anger and conflict, diversity, masks, power in relationships and how it can change as the basis of the power changes, the life cycles and turning points of relationships, assertiveness, and the nonverbal presentation of self.

**Scenes for Use in the Classroom:** Once again, I love this film so much that I want to say just watch the whole thing. However, here are some very useful scenes for introducing the interpersonal communication process.

- Boolie meets Hoke
- Daisy meets Hoke
- Hoke trying to take Daisy to the store
- The missing can of salmon
- Daisy and Hoke stop for lunch on the road
- The closing scene at the nursing home

For a simple overview of the interpersonal communication process, show Boolie meeting Hoke, or Hoke having lunch with Daisy when they are traveling to Alabama for the birthday party.

**Questions for Discussion**

1. **How does Hoke mask his true feelings? In what ways does he learn to stand up for himself throughout the story?**

   Hoke speaks from an "aw-shucks" kind of nonverbal posture when discussing the position of chauffeur, responding to Daisy's hostility, or encouraging Daisy to allow him to "carry her." Hoke later evolves into a more forceful, yet deferential persona as Daisy begins to accept him. He is more open and honest about his feelings and experiences, such as on their trip or in the cemetery when he confesses that he cannot read. He becomes even more assertive when he must confront Daisy on the road so that he can go "make water." Finally, he relates to her as caregiver when she loses focus and can't remember where she is.

2. **How does this film illustrate the life cycle theory of relationships? What are the major turning points in the relationship between Daisy and Hoke?**

Their relationship is a magnificent example of this theory. They go through stages of initiation, testing, acceptance, dependence, trust, and maturity. There are several turning points. Clearly, one such turning point is when Hoke is able to convince Daisy to get in the car for the first time. Another turning point comes when Daisy accuses Hoke of stealing a can of Salmon. Still another, comes at the cemetery over the reading confession. Another series of turning points comes on their trip when they disclose some of themselves to each other, when they are accosted by the police, and when Hoke must go to the bathroom. Still another comes when Daisy confesses that Hoke is her best friend.

3. **How would you describe the self-image of Daisy and of Hoke? How is noise reflected in their interactions? How does their relational behavior reflect needs and exchange theory?**

Daisy is very insecure. She is very much afraid of what other people think of her. Daisy has strong control needs. She resents the increasing loss of control that she has over her life due to aging. Hoke has a strong sense of self, definite toughness of self. Hoke is able to ultimately make himself acceptable to her on the basis of what he can give her – initially in services, and later in friendship.

## I Never Sang For My Father, dir. Gilbert Cates. Melvyn Douglas, Gene Hackman, Dorothy Stickney, Estelle Parsons, Elizabeth Hubbard, Lovelady Powell, 1970.

**Brief Summary:** This movie is an excellent case to introduce the communication process. After the death of his mother, a man (played by a young Gene Hackman) must confront his relationship with his father, who is aging and in need of care after the death of his mother.

**IPC Concepts:** This movie focuses on a very specific cycle of this father-son relationship, but one that brings into focus much of their mutual emotional baggage.

**Scenes for Use in the Classroom:** A good scene from this film is the one immediately after the mother's funeral, when son and father meet to discuss the future.

**Questions for Discussion**

1. **How can the son try to ethically influence his father into accepting his role of caregiver? What can the son do to establish an honest, respectful relationship with his father at this late stage of their relationship?**

The father is a very controlling man. He has very little respect for his son, and harbors a huge sack of resentments. He is also extremely fearful of his own aging.

2. **How does this film illustrate the problems experienced by people as they age? What are their fears? How can empathy help to bridge the fear gap so that a caregiver can more effectively help the aging person?**

   The film effectively illustrates the problems, and resentments and fears that can accompany the aging process. The father's attempts to have the son move in with him, for example, illustrates the older man's attempt to hold on to some control of his life. His angry outbursts toward the son illustrate both his baggage and his fear of aging.

3. **What is the son's experience with his father? What are his resentments toward his father? His fears? How does he reflect his own self-talk? What can he do to more effectively bolster his self-esteem and to communicate more assertively with his father?**

   The film illustrates the son's sadness over the absence of his father's presence during his childhood, a dynamic that will resonate with many students. This should serve to trigger student memories that will help them empathize with the son.

## ***On the Stage***

Theatre offers a very dynamic way of experiencing literature in action. As Shakespeare said, "All the world's a stage." Kenneth Burke echoed this sentiment with his notion of the dramatistic character of language and life as symbolic behavior.

While the first four plays listed are drawn from the films noted above, each of the plays can give the student a unique experience of the interpersonal dynamics being portrayed. Shakespeare's Mid Summer Night's Dream is a wonderful and witty showcase of possible communication breakdowns, and evidence of the communication principle that once said, it cannot be unsaid.

### G.B. Shaw. (1913). Pygmalion.

### Alan Jay Lerner and Frederick Loewe. (1956). My Fair Lady.

### Alfred Uhry. (1987). Driving Miss Daisy.

### William Shakespeare. A Mid Summer's Night Dream.

**Brief Summary:** This is the story of a night when the world of humans overlaps with the world of the Faeries after a wedding feast for Hyppolyta and Theseus. After a series of misunderstandings, several characters wander into the forest, only to walk into the middle of a disagreement between Oberon and Titania – the King and Queen of the

Faeries. The resulting comic interactions serve to illustrate a wide range of communication principles, including misunderstandings, perceptions, and failures to listen effectively. The story is also filled with symbols of love and marriage.

**IPC Concepts:** Relationships, listening, perception, shields, personal bias, point of view.

## *CNN*

Television can be a very rich source of useful material for an interpersonal classroom. Over the years, I have tapped into 60 Minutes, 20/20, PBS, the Discovery Channel, the Learning Channel, the History Channel, and any other television source that offers a story, interview, report, or documentary relating to interpersonal communication theory.

CNN has produced videotapes with clips of news reports that relate to various aspects of communication theory. There are two clips that are relevant to chapter one. These videotapes can be obtained by contacting Wadsworth marketing at (650) 595-2350, ext. 789.

### Latch-key Kids, (2:23), CNN Interpersonal Communication Today, 1999, Volume 1.

This clip illustrates Shutz's notion of interpersonal needs. The clip demonstrates our basic need for human contact and inclusion. It is the lead clip on the tape.

### Bilingual Storyteller, (3:41), CNN Interpersonal Communication Today, 1999, Volume 1.

This clip works for the basic communication process and for language and meaning in human communication. It vividly illustrates the nature and importance of storytelling in communication and culture. It is the second clip on this videotape. This clip is a great way to introduce the nature and power of stories in human communication, and to encourage students to assemble and tell their own stories in class.

**Social Contact Cures Colds, (1:55), Human Communication Today Video, 1999 Volume 1.**

This clip also illustrates the basic human need for human contact. The clip presents the health benefit of human contact and interaction.

---

# *Interpersonal Communication Theory in Literature and Academic Resources*

## *Theory Illustrated in Literature*

One of the great values of using literature in a course in interpersonal communication is that it helps students to connect with the power of storytelling. Much of human experience is collected, shaped, and processed through the telling of stories. I believe that movies are in many ways just moving literature. Not only can students read novels as a way of illustrating interpersonal theory, but they can also practice their own performance skills by reading sections aloud to the entire class or to small groups.

**Irving, John (1989) *A Prayer For Owen Meany.* N.Y.: Ballantine Books.**

While this book served as the basis for the film, Simon Birch, the book is far more complex in its treatment of both, story and character development. This book is a fascinating treatment of the relationship between Owen Meany (Simon Birch) and his best friend – the narrator in both treatments.

**Lee, Harper (1960). *To Kill A Mockingbird.* Philadelphia: J.B. Lippincott Company.**

This book is a classic of American literature and frequently appears on lists of the best in American novels. It takes us through even more of the culture of the south during the 1930s. We learn and experience more about the people in the town, and about the children and their adventures. The book closes with a masterful statement on empathy when Scout stands on the front porch of the Radley home and realizes how the world has looked in the eyes of Boo (Arthur) Radley.

## Background Theoretical Material

All four of the following sources provide an excellent foundation for a dialogical approach to interpersonal communication. Buber is clearly the modern father of this approach. Cissna's article on Rogers links the next major contribution. Howe offers a classic work that extends the work of both Buber and Rogers. Arnett and Arneson bring the dialogical approach up to date with a wonderful discussion of the dialogical contributions of a number of modern scholars who have built on the foundation provided by Buber and Rogers. These concepts can expand our students' analytical tools and understanding of the nature of the communication process. I believe that the dialogical process is an inherently ethical approach to the study and practice of human communication.

### Ronald C. Arnett and Pat Arneson. (1999). *Dialogic Civility in a Cynical Age: Community, Hope, and Interpersonal Relationships.* N.Y.: SUNY Press.

This book is a necessary shot of optimism and substance for believers in dialogue. It offers an optimistic, philosophical, and practical approach to making dialogue a reality in interpersonal relationships. The richness of the book comes from their review of a wide range of dialogical voices that include: Buber, Rogers, Gilligan, Freire, Frank, Noddings, and Bellah.

### Martin Buber. (1958) *I and Thou.* Trans. Ronald Gregor Smith, 2nd Ed. N.Y.: Scribners.

A classic work on the philosophy and practice of dialogical communication. The approach is firmly grounded in both theology and practical philosophy. This is the seminal work on the modern discussion of dialogue in human communication.

### Reuel L. Howe. (1963). *The Miracle of Dialogue.* N.Y.: The Seabury Press.

Howe extends Buber's approach to the nature and application of dialogue. Even though the book is written from a religious point of view, it does an excellent job of discussing the nature of dialogue, the barriers to communication, the attitudes toward dialogue necessary from the participants in communication, and the benefits to a dialogical approach to communication and relationships.

**Kenneth N. Cissna and Rob Anderson. "The Contributions of Carl R. Rogers to a Philosophical Praxis of Dialogue," *Western Journal of Speech Communication*, 54, 2 (Spring 1990): 125-147.**

**IPC Concepts:** Dialogue, qualities for effective, growth oriented interpersonal communication and relational development.

**Brief Summary:** Cissna argues that Carl Rogers should be appreciated for being far more than a therapist – he should also be regarded as having made a substantial contribution to the nature and practice of dialogue. The article describes the contribution of Rogers as that of practical philosophy, which helps to extend the work of Martin Buber in I and Thou. The article delineates the qualities inherent in Rogers' work that are applicable to interpersonal communication. These include: contact, congruence, positive regard, and empathy.

**Use in the Classroom:** Because I feel very strongly about the value of the dialogical perspective as a central philosophy for communication theory, discussion of the material in these sources is very helpful in shaping and framing an entire course in interpersonal communication. I recommend the following assignments and discussion questions.

**Assignments:** Oral reports on select chapters or articles from these readings.
Written reports on these readings – assign a book report or an abstract report.
Assign the dialogical approach as an analytical perspective for viewing and analyzing one of the films previously discussed.

**Questions for Discussion**

1. **What is the nature of dialogical communication? How can it be defined?**

2. **What are the characteristics of dialogical communication?**

## *What's on the Web*

**COMFLE.**
**http://commfaculty.fullerton.edu/jreinard/internet.htm#INTERPER**

**Brief Summary:** A set of hyperlinks to a wide variety of topics in communication theory. This web address links to the other topics listed in interpersonal communication.

**PC Concepts:** In addition to a wide range of other communication research interests, this web site contains links on the following interpersonal topics: empathy, temperament, gender, nonverbal, and conflict. There are also good links on language and intercultural communication.

## Interpersonal Communication articles web site
## http://www.pertinent.com/pertinfo/business/communication/index.html

**Brief Summary:** This is an interesting web site that offers a variety of articles regarding communication. It provides a good overview on the communication process.

**IPC Concepts:** Self, relationships, culture, conflict, and interpersonal communication at work.

## Four Principles of Interpersonal Communication
## http://www2.pstcc.cc.tn.us/%7edking/interpr.htm

**Brief Summary:** This web site reinforces the basic principles of interpersonal communication discussed in this chapter, and offers "A Quick and Dirty Guide to Improving Communication."

**IPC Concepts:** The process of Interpersonal Communication.

# CHAPTER TWO

## Self

### INTERPERSONAL COMMUNICATION IN ACTION

Chapter two examines and explores the nature and role of the self in the interpersonal communication process as it has been illustrated in a variety of forms of mass media.

This chapter of the Media Guide differs somewhat from the organization of the Interact text. I believe that the core of effective interpersonal communication is in developing a healthy sense of self. I cover the nature of self, personality/temperament, shyness, and self-talk in my own course. I supplement lecture material with several of the books cited later in this chapter. Zimbardo's groundbreaking work on shyness is a particularly useful resource. I also use several film clips to illustrate the nature of self-concept, levels of self-esteem, and the role of self-talk in shaping, maintaining, and changing the self. *Ship of Fools* illustrates the power of self-talk both positively and negatively. *On Golden Pond* also illustrates self-talk, masks, expression of fear, and self-concept. *Mother* illustrates self-concept, self-fulfilling prophecies, and mother-son relationships. *Breakfast Club* demonstrates the power of self-concept on perception of self and others, self-talk, and self-fulfilling prophecies. *Driving Miss Daisy* illustrates self-concept and stereotyping.

## LEARNING OBJECTIVES:

- Help students learn to recognize interpersonal dynamics in action.
- Raise awareness of the complexity of the interpersonal processes.
- Raise awareness for the student to diversity in interpersonal communication.
- Introduce the student to ethical issues in interpersonal communication.
- Introduce the student to communication competence.

| **In Classroom Assignments** | **For Homework** |
|---|---|
| - Small Group Discussion<br>- Whole class discussion<br>- Role Play Exercises<br>- Conversation exercises | - Position Papers<br>- Relationship Analysis Papers<br>- Web Exercises to supplement textbook and Instructor's Manual exercise<br>- Journal Entries |

# *VISUALLY PRESENTED INTERPERSONAL COMMUNICATION THEORY*

## *IN MOVIES*

I recommend starting the discussion of the self in interpersonal communication with a clip from either *Ship of Fools* or *On Golden Pond.* I begin my lecture on interpersonal theory with three scenes from *On Golden Pond.*

### Ship of Fools, dir. Stanley Kramer. Vivien Leigh, Oskar Werner, Simone Signet, Jose Ferrer, Lee Marvin, Jose Greco, and Michael Dunn, 1965.

**Brief Summary:** The story is about a cruise ship before WWII. It involves the interaction of a series of people who are each carrying a considerable amount of emotional baggage around. The cast of characters includes a frustrated, disillusioned divorcee; a couple having an illicit affair; a drunk and angry baseball player; and a small man. Of particular interest for interpersonal communication is a scene between the baseball player (Lee Marvin) and the small man (Michael Dunn). Marvin is drunk and enraged about how his inability to hit a curve ball has ruined his career as a baseball player. In his rage, he reenacts stepping up to the plate to bat, swinging and missing a pitch, and reflects on his father's disgusted reaction. His self-talk is a powerful example of how we internalize the messages of significant others when we are children and then incorporate those messages into our own inner scripts. Dunn's response illustrates how he handles his own familial dysfunctional messages with more effective self-talk.

**IPC Concepts:** Self-image, self-talk, perception.

**Scenes for Use in the Classroom:** The above scene is one of the best from this film. As noted, it effectively focuses on the power and quality of our inner communication.

**Questions for Discussion**

1. **What is the baseball player saying to himself when he approaches the plate to bat? Is this effective self-talk? What is the effect on his performance? What did his father say to him that he has internalized?**

   Marvin tells himself that he can hear everyone talking about him. He is certain that they are all waiting in secret to throw the curve ball at him since they know that he cannot hit it. He also mentions that he can still hear his old man yelling at him, telling him that he is a bum and a loser. The subsequent effect is that he is convinced that he cannot hit a curve ball, that he is a bum and a loser, and that this has ruined his career and life. He has become an alcoholic.

2. **What does the small man say about the ball player's thoughts?**
   Dunn comments that the ball player has exaggerated the importance of this curve ball problem. He speculates that in all of his travels, there must be millions of people who have never even heard of a curve ball; therefore, the ball player has surely exaggerated the importance of it.

3. **How does Dunn imply his self-talk? How does it work for him?**
   Dunn says that his family is uncomfortable with him around, so they give him enough money to travel. His implied self-talk is reflected in the nonverbal behavior that accompanies his disclosure. He knows about his family's feelings but he does not allow that to interfere with his own self-esteem.

## On Golden Pond, dir. Mark Rydell. Henry Fonda, Katherine Hepburn, Jane Fonda, Doug McKeon, and Dabney Coleman, 1981.

**Brief Summary:** The story is about Norman Thayer (Henry Fonda), a retired schoolteacher who is approaching his 80th birthday, and about his anger and fear of the effect of the aging process on his faculties and ability to function. He and his wife, Ethel Thayer (Katherine Hepburn), are visited at their summer cottage by their daughter, Chelsea (Jane Fonda), her fiancé (Dabney Coleman), and soon to be stepson, Billy (Doug McKeon). The stepson stays with Norman and Ethel for the summer, while Chelsea and her fiancé travel to Europe. Norman and Billy teach each other a lot about fishing, conflict, and each other's perspectives on life. Billy introduces Norman to the slang of his generation (watch for "suck face"), while Norman introduces Billy to Long John Silver and fishing. Upon her return, Chelsea and Norman have a long overdue confrontation about their relationship.

**IPC Concepts:** Self-esteem, perception of self and others, self-talk, emotion, and conflict. Of particular interest is Norman Thayer's reaction to being lost in the woods. Discuss his probable self-talk. It is good way to help students understand self-talk and empathize with an older person. Also, his highly sarcastic and sometimes caustic interaction with Chelsea, Billy and Bill. Norman uses a variety of defense mechanisms to protect what he perceives as his threatened self-esteem. Also, note his disclosure to Ethel about being lost in the woods and his admission to Chelsea about his feelings toward her.

**Scenes for Use in the Classroom:** I strongly recommend using a sequence of scenes near the beginning of the film.

- Norman being lost in the woods
- Norman returning home to talk with Ethel and Charley, the mailman
- Norman's disclosure to Ethel on the porch regarding his fears of aging

This sequence clearly illustrates Norman's personality, his defense mechanisms, Ethel's way of relating to Norman, and some of Norman's self-talk – especially when he is lost.

A second sequence that I find useful for discussion of the self comes close to the end of the film when Chelsea returns from Europe and confronts Norman on the nature of their relationship. Norman brags about Billy and how fond he is of Billy. This puts Chelsea on the defensive, as Norman never shows such affection for her. Chelsea counters with her concerns about their relationship. After some tense words, Norman announces that he has successfully taught Billy to do a back flip dive into the lake. After Norman reminds Chelsea of her failure to perform this particular feat, she becomes determined to make the dive. This sequence is a terrific series of conversations. I have heard that Jane Fonda and Katherine Hepburn, without warning, changed the script somewhat in order to help Jane confront her real father, Henry. The tension and discomfort in Henry/Norman is perhaps very real. In any case, this shows the inner conflict in both characters, as they must wrestle with the relational baggage of a lifetime.

**Questions for Discussion**

1. **What is Norman's self-concept? Does he have high self-esteem? To what experiences does anyone refer that might explain how his self-concept was formed?**

   Norman is really a very insecure person. He hides his fears and insecurity behind a mask of sarcasm and callous indifference. He knows that he was an accomplished literature professor but, since his retirement, he has no sense of himself. However, his self-concept has had problems for longer than retirement. His difficulties with his daughter, Chelsea, have gone on for a very long time. He has had problems with not having had a son. Norman's only sense of competence is when he is fishing.

2. **How would you describe Billy's self-esteem? How does he handle Norman's crusty style and harsh manner.**

   Billy is young, but he has more self-esteem than Norman in some ways. Billy is exploring his world and is willing to take risks. He wants to experience new things, especially if he thinks they are potentially cool things to do. When Norman makes harsh statements to him, Billy sizes him up and thinks about it initially. His opening encounter with Norman, where Norman orders Billy to go read a chapter of *Treasure Island* is a good example of this. However, when Norman yells at him in the boat while fishing, Billy wastes no time putting him in his place with the rebuke, "who do you think you are, Long John Silver?" Billy has the self-esteem to be able to stand up for himself without holding a grudge or being deeply hurt by Norman's barbs.

3. **How would you describe Chelsea's self-esteem? How does she relate to her parents? What do these relational patterns reflect about her shifting patterns of self-esteem?**

   Chelsea has never received the warm, unconditional love from her father that she needs. As a result, her level of esteem fluctuates when around him.

Whatever she receives from him is highly conditional. She is, therefore, nervous, apprehensive, and uncertain as to what to expect from him and how to behave. She distances herself from him. She calls him "Norman," rather than father or dad. Not so with her mother, Ethel. Chelsea is comfortable, open, and relaxed around her. She calls her "mommy." They chat excitedly and spontaneously with each other about, just about everything. Ethel is very well aware of Chelsea's poor relationship with her father, and understands how much responsibility Norman bears for this bad situation. In one scene, they recall an incident when Norman and Ethel had been skinny-dipping in the lake. Norman made Chelsea go in while he got out of the water. Ethel recalls that she was so mad at him for that outburst that she made him stand in the water for a half hour while she pretended to put Chelsea to bed. Ethel gives Chelsea unconditional positive regard, and Chelsea blossoms in response.

## Mother, dir. Albert Brooks. With Albert Brooks, Debbie Reynolds, Rob Morrow, Lisa Kudrow, 1996.

**Brief Summary**: The story is about a successful writer whose marital life is a shambles. He has been divorced twice and feels that he needs help to make his social life more of a success. In an act of desperation he moves back home with his mother. As the two of them learn to cope with each other's ways, they also come to learn more about themselves. In an interesting way, this only begins to happen when they stop reacting to their past image of the other person and learn to engage the real person in the present.

**IPC Concepts:** Attending, listening actively, repeating information, separating facts from inferences.

**Scenes for Use in the Classroom:** There are several good scenes in this movie to illustrate the self-esteem, self-concept of each character.

- Mother giving her son love through food: salad and cheese
- Telephone conversation with the brother
- The son returning to his childhood room
- Mother's description of her current relationship with a man: dinner and sex
- The discovery of mother's past interest in writing
- Son's first encounter at the end of the film with a new woman

**Questions for Discussion**

1. **How would you describe the self-esteem and self-concept of the mother and her two sons?**

   When the son returns home, he does so in order to regain a measure of self-worth. His life is a mixed success. He is a successful writer, but his relationships are a dismal failure. He wants to confront his mother to some extent for not helping to give him better social skills for relationships with women. In contrast, we see his brother talking to mother on the phone. He is very successful, with a beautiful home, and an apparently successful marriage. But he is totally insecure with his mother on the phone, constantly looking for praise and attention. Mother is secure within herself and her role as a mother. She lacks self-confidence, however, when it comes to trying something new, like writing. She relates to her sons as though they have never really grown up. This gives her the security of the past without having to change the relational pattern.

2. **How would you describe the relational perception of son to mother?**
In many ways, the son still sees his mother from the perspective of a little boy. He cannot see her as another adult with needs, ambitions, dreams, and feelings. He has trouble contemplating a sex life for his mother. He is amazed that she might have ever had any other ambition than to be his mother. Even now, he still sees her primary role as one of waiting for him to come home so that she can continue to mother him. He is almost completely unaware of the imposition that his return might pose to her.

## Breakfast Club: dir. John Hughes. With Emilio Estevez, Judd Nelson, Molly Ringwald, Anthony Michael Hall, Ally Sheedy, Paul Gleason, 1985.

**Brief Summary:** A group of five high school students spend a Saturday in detention under the supervision of an angry, disrespectful, burned-out teacher. We slowly come to know their real names. We know them as the Jock (Andrew Clark, played by Emilio Estevez), the Princess (Claire Standish played by Molly Ringwald), the Delinquent (John Bender played by Judd Nelson), the Brain (Brian Johnson played by Anthony Michael Hall), and the Weirdo (Allison Reynolds played by Ally Sheedy).

While initially presented as a group of stereotyped students, they each disclose enough information to become real, flesh and blood individuals to each other and to the viewer. We see their initial interactions marked by the Delinquent's efforts to dominate and intimidate the group. He is met by resistance from the Jock, who doesn't want to appear weak, and by the Princess, who doesn't want to appear afraid of this low-class person. The disgruntled and abusive teacher (Richard Vernon played by Paul Gleason) provides the group with a common enemy. Led by the Delinquent and his self-sacrificing actions on behalf of the group, each character begins to open up and reach out to the others. The students are initially at odds with each other. They each come from a different student clique at the school. After several instances of conflict between the students, the group slowly opens up to each other. We learn about the abuse suffered by the Delinquent from his father, the pressure to succeed from the Jock's father, the social expectations placed upon the Princess, the pressure to be perfect in school placed on the Brain, and the lack of any interest by the parents of the Weirdo – as she describes her parents to the Jock, "they ignore me."

Eventually, each student finds something good in each of the other students. They each do something unique to their own abilities for the good of the group. Self-disclosure serves as the climax of the story.

This film transcends time and generations in its ability to resonate with a wide range of student age groups.

**IPC Concepts:** Sense of the self, self-esteem, self-concept, self-disclosure, relationship building, conflict, diversity, expression of emotion.

**Scenes for Use in the Classroom:** The opening sequence introduces us to the stereotypical view of each student. As the students interact with each other, we see them presenting themselves with the use of social masks. The delinquent is particularly harsh in his treatment of the other students, especially with the princess, in whom he is particularly interested. The abusive behavior of the Delinquent is vividly demonstrated during the lunch scene.

As the group interacts throughout the day, they begin to break down their masks and must present their real selves. A scene that illustrates both, the notion of self and the power of self-disclosure, is one toward the end of the film in which each student must open up and tell the others what they are afraid of, and why they are in detention.

**Questions for Discussion**

1. **How would you describe the self-concept of each of the students? What evidence is there for how these were formed? How do their individual self-concepts affect their communication with each other?**

   This is a really good question and one that can provide a lengthy discussion. Each student has a clear self-concept. The Brain is completely defined by his intellectual prowess. The Princess is defined by social status and popularity. The Delinquent is tough and abrasive. The Jock is competitive and combative. The Weirdo is withdrawn and yet colorful.

   There is abundant evidence for how each student's self-concept was formed. At various points in the film, each student discloses elements of how they were raised. During the Delinquent's most pointed attack on the Princess, he points out her spoiled upbringing as he focuses on her diamond earrings. He contrasts this gift for her with his own Christmas gift from his own father, a carton of cigarettes. He also refers to the time when his father put out a lit cigarette on his arm. The Jock notes his father's pressure to win, win, win. The Brain cries as he describes the pressure to be perfect in his grades. He describes the cataclysmic effect of an "F" in shop. Finally, the Weirdo notes that her parents ignore her. Hence her low self-esteem and attention gaining behavior.

2. **How would you describe the self-talk of each student? What evidence is there for their self-talk? How does it appear to affect their self-esteem and their communication behavior?**

   The self-talk is not too difficult to speculate about. Each student reinforces his/her self-concept in their thoughts. Also, they seem to be reflecting about how they feel about the teacher and the other students in detention.

3. **To what extent do these students illustrate self-fulfilling prophecies? What can they do to break the cycle of this behavior?**

   They behave in ways that reinforce their expectations. By behaving in an obnoxious manner, the Delinquent encourages rejection, conflict, and tension with others. By dressing strangely, eating unusual food combinations, and avoiding interaction with others, the Weirdo fosters the outcome of being ignored.

4. **What can each of these students do to improve their interpersonal communication?**

While the age of the group must be taken into account, these teenagers would benefit from a few basic things. First, they need to think before they speak. Managing their self-talk and their emotions would go far to improve their communication and their relationships. Second, they should consider the impact of their communication on the other person. Third, they could realize that they can select their reactions – that they do not have to be affected by rude behavior. This inner speech strategy would remove much of the sting of the Delinquent's defense mechanisms.

## Driving Miss Daisy, dir. Bruce Beresford. Morgan Freeman, Jessica Tandy, Dan Ackroyd, Patti Lupone, Esther Rolle, 1989.

**Brief Summary:** Adaptation of Alfred Uhry's play. This is the story of the evolving friendship between an old, wealthy woman and her simple, aging chauffeur. The film adds the diversity issues of her being Jewish and his being African American. Daisy struggles through most of the story with the changes that she experiences as a result of aging. When her son forces her to accept Hoke, a chauffeur whom he has hired, Daisy responds with anger, resentment, and rejection toward Hoke. She slowly learns to accept his role as chauffeur, and even more slowly, his role as her best friend. Hoke must move very carefully through his interactions with the white community, and must wear a series of carefully constructed masks in order to protect himself and his livelihood. Daisy learns more about Hoke and herself through a series of encounters that include: a confrontation over a can of salmon; an incident at a cemetery; a Christmas "gift," a confrontation on the way to a Civil Rights event, shared police harassment, an ice storm, a trip to another state, and ultimately, a severe bout of disorientation by Daisy. By the end of the story, as her son says, she wants Hoke "all to herself."

**IPC Concepts:** Daisy illustrates a great many interpersonal and cross-cultural principles. I will raise a few here, but the film can serve as a conduit for many others. You can use this film to illustrate and discuss such concepts as self-esteem, self-talk, personality, emotion, self-disclosure, anger and conflict, diversity, masks, power in relationships and how it can change as the basis of the power changes, the life cycles and turning points of relationships, assertiveness, and the nonverbal presentation of self.

**Scenes for Use in the Classroom:** Once again, I love this film so much that I sometimes show the class an edited version that takes about 50 minutes, thus breaking my own rule on video length. However, I only do this on rare occasion when I feel that I have a mature group.

Here are some very useful scenes for introducing the interpersonal communication process.

- Boolie meets Hoke
- Daisy meets Hoke
- Daisy denying Hoke the freedom to examine her family photos on the wall of her home
- Hoke trying to take Daisy to the store
- Daisy explaining her younger days to Hoke by insisting, "We didn't have anything"
- Daisy's experience of dementia

**Questions for Discussion**

1. **What is Daisy's self-concept? Does she have high self-esteem? To what experiences does Daisy refer that might explain how her self-concept was formed?**

 Daisy is very insecure. She is constantly worried about what others think of her. She doesn't want her neighbors to think that she is putting on airs. She doesn't want to admit that her life is financially secure or successful. She puts up a mask of being from poor roots as a way to evade her present reality. She also believes that she is at the top of the social structure, but her status is based on stereotypes and bigotry. As a result, even her social standing contributes to her insecurity. She is also afraid to accept her own aging as evidenced by her struggle with driving and her refusal to accept help in the form of a chauffeur.

 Daisy refers to her poor childhood. She is specific in mentioning a stray cat that she found but could not keep because her father said they were too poor to feed it. She sums up her childhood by saying, "We were from Forsyth Street. We didn't have a thing." Her father seems to have been a major force in shaping her self-perception.

2. **What is Hoke's self-concept? Does he have high self-esteem?**

 Hoke is secure within himself. He is a realist and understands how the world works. He is a very skilled worker capable of a wide variety of jobs – he evidences this by fixing the elevator at Boolie's place of business. Hoke has fairly high self-esteem. His principal area of embarrassment is that he cannot read. Hoke's sense of self-worth helps him function and maintain his integrity in a racist society.

3. **To what extent does Daisy treat Hoke as a stereotype of all African Americans? How does Hoke handle this treatment?**

 For much of the story, Daisy relates toward Hoke as "one of them." "They all steal you know," she says to Boolie when she thinks a can of salmon has been stolen. When she is invited to a speech that Martin Luther King is giving she assumes that all black people must know him. She fails to invite Hoke to accompany her because she says that he can hear him whenever he wants to. It is on their long road trip together that she begins to understand that they are both the objects of stereotyping.

 Hoke has learned to stay in his place and not to confront those who are in positions of higher authority. Rather than make demands or feel inferior, Hoke makes himself very valuable to his employers so that they cannot do without him. He is eventually able to finesse a raise out of Boolie because of his value to Boolie as a solution to his mother's needs.

## *On the Stage*

Theatre is a wonderful way to enrich the concepts of an interpersonal communication course. Watch the theatre venues in your area and encourage your students to attend as much theatre as possible. A class field trip is an excellent way to share the experience of theatre. However, individual attendance will still work to increase the student's appreciation for both, the wonder of the stage, and the application of interpersonal communication theory.

### Les Miserables, (1985). Play by Alain Boublil, and Claude-Michel Schonberg, Lyrics by Herbert Kretzmer.

*Les Miserables* is an outstanding example of the inner turmoil that people go through when they create false dichotomies in their lives. Both of the central characters, Jean Valjean and Javert, must resolve moral ambiguity. Their self-talk illustrates the functional and dysfunctional power of self-talk. The drama also illustrates the ethical dilemmas of speaking or not speaking.

**Brief Summary**: Set during the revolution in France in 1832, this play dramatizes the development of several relationships and gives us insight into the moral choices that these characters must make. It gives us a glimpse into their inner struggle and the corresponding self-talk. Of special interest is the self-talk of Jean Valjean in the song, "Who Am I?" and Javert's self-talk when he decides to commit suicide.

**IPC Concepts**: Perception, self-talk and self-concept by Javert, and the self-talk of Jean Valjean confronted by the wrong of being arrested for his "crime."

## *CNN*

### Eating Disorders, (2:09), CNN Interpersonal Communication Today, 1999, Volume 1.

This is a rich little clip. It examines the nonverbal behavior of young girls with eating disorders. The clip presents their distorted self-perceptions that are more reflective of low self-esteem. This is a good clip for opening up a discussion of the class's experience with such perceptions and cases of eating disorders. There are very probably students in the class with personal experience on this topic.

---

# *INTERPERSONAL COMMUNICATION THEORY IN LITERATURE AND ACADEMIC RESOURCES*

## *Theory Illustrated in Literature*

**James Baldwin. Go Tell It On The Mountain. New York: Dial Press, 1963.**

**Brief Summary:** This is the powerful story of John Grimes and his family on the occasion of his fourteenth birthday. It tells of his conversion and dedication to God, and focuses on the prayers of his mother, Elizabeth; his stepfather, Gabriel; and his aunt, Florence. The novel does a really good job of depicting John's low self-esteem, his self-perception as unattractive, and his near obsession with needing to serve the Lord in order to redeem his otherwise worthless life.

**IPC Concepts:** Perception of self, self-esteem, prayer as a form of self-talk.

**Alice Walker. (1982). *The Color Purple.* New York: Pocket Books.**

**Brief Summary:** This is the story of a poor, used and abused African American woman, Celie. She is given into an abusive marriage by her abusive father. She suffers in silence until she discovers that her husband, Mister, has been hiding letters from her sister, Nettie, who had moved to Africa with Christian missionaries. Celie finds the letters and secretly reads them whenever she can steal a few minutes between chores, or by hiding them inside her Bible and reading them at church. The husband has other women but barely knows Celie. Mister's mistress, Shug, befriends Celie, and they develop their own love relationship. As her love grows with Shug, Celie develops more and more self-esteem and confidence. She is eventually able to stand up to Mister and move out on her own. She moves to Memphis with Shug where her life improves tremendously.

**IPC Concepts:** Self perception, self esteem, impact of significant others, Relationships – need for warmth and affection, trust and commitment, conflict, diversity, culture, gender, emotion, gender and intimacy.

# *Academic Resources*

**Philip G. Zimbardo. (1977).** ***Shyness: What It Is. What To Do About It.*** **NY: Addison-Wesley Publishing Co.**

**Brief Summary:** Zimbardo's work on shyness is central to understanding this interpersonal dynamic. Zimbardo explores the types and characteristics of the shy person. He offers several cases of famous personalities (i.e. Johnny Carson) who are quite open and dynamic in public, but almost morbidly shy in private. Zimbardo explores a range of actions that shy people might employ to help overcome their shyness. He also suggests a number of things that no-shy people can do to help the shy overcome their shyness.

**David Merrill and Roger Reid. (1983). Personal Styles and Effective Performance: Make Your Style Work For You. N.Y.: St. Lucie Press.**

**Brief Summary:** This book provides an excellent introduction to the concept of communication style, and offers several useful ways to study and assess individual style. An excellent way to gain understanding into one's self and the people around us.

**IPC Concepts:** Communication Style.

**Mihaly Csikszentmihalyi. (1990).** ***Flow: The Psychology of Optimal Experience.*** **N.Y.: Harper Perennial.**

**Brief Summary:** This is Csikszentmihalyi's landmark work on the dynamic of flow, concentration so complete, that we are totally absorbed in the activity at hand. This book helps us to understand the phenomenon that has direct relevance to cognitive and behavioral theory, as well as to the experience of many people, including Michael Jordan.

**IPC Concepts:** Self, self-talk, cognition, and behavior.

**Bloch, Douglas. (1991).** ***Listening to Your Inner Voice: Discover the Truth Within You And Let It Guide Your Way.*** **Minneapolis: CompCare Publishers.**

**Brief Summary:** This is a very practical introduction to the nature and power of self-talk or inner speech. It is written in a simple, easy to understand manner, and offers the novice a reasonable introduction to this profound topic.

**IPC Concepts:** Self-talk.

## Borysenko, Joan. (1987). *Minding the Body, Mending the Mind.* Toronto: Bantam Books.

*Note: Actually, any book by Joan Borysenko is a good experience.*

**Brief Summary:** Joan Borysenko is one of those rare people who combine the world of medicine; psychology; communication; philosophy; and theology in a clear, practical, and reasonable manner. This book combines her work at Harvard and her personal experiences with some of the best theory on all of the above topics. She offers clear discussions of the theory, real life examples of its power, and simple exercises for enacting these ideas. This can be a life-changing book.

**IPC Concepts**: Self-talk, meditation, breathing, visualization, inner choice making

## Charles V. Roberts and Kittie W. Watson, eds. (1989). *Intrapersonal Communciation Processes: Original Essays.* New Orleans: Spectra Incorporated, Publishers and Scottsdale, AZ: Gorsuch Scarisbrick, Publishers.

**Brief Summary:** 24 essays dealing with the nature, characteristics, and approaches to intrapersonal communication. The articles discuss cognitive and psychological approaches, affective and nonconscious processes, and the role of listening in self-talk.

**IPC Concepts:** self-talk.

## Mihaly Csikszentmihalyi. Finding Flow. Psychology Today, 30, 4, July/August 1997, 46-48, 70-71.

**Brief Summary:** An excellent and brief discussion of Csikszentmihalyi's theory of flow – the sense of total acceptance of self, that can produce a kind of pureness of activity and energy. The article is an excerpt from his most recent book by the same title. He is also the author of two other books on flow – also cited above. Flow is highly relevant to a discussion of intrapersonal communication, in that how a person communicates within themselves will have a strong impact on how they feel about self, others, and behavior.

**IPC Concepts:** Self-talk, self, cognition, and behavior.

**Keirsey, David and Marilyn Bates. (1984).** ***Please Understand Me: Character & Temperament Types.*** **Del Mar, CA: Prometheus Nemesis Book Company.**

**Brief Summary:** Kiersey and Bates have taken the essential elements of the Myers Briggs personality assessment system and developed a test for basic temperament assessment. This book, although a little old, provides a nice introduction to personality, the Myers Briggs approach, and how to use this understanding in relationships.

**IPC Concepts**: Self and Personality.

**Otto Kroeger and Janet M. Thuesen. (1988). Type Talk: The 16 Personality Types That Determine How We Live, Love, and Work. New York: Tilden Press.**

This is an excellent, thorough presentation of the Myers Briggs personality assessment approach. It explains the assessment approach, parameters, typology system, its strengths, limitations, research findings, and a wide variety of applications. It also explains some of the psychology underlying this approach to assessment. It is an interesting extension of whatever lecture you might find appropriate to give on this aspect of understanding the self in personality development and interpersonal communication.

## *What's on the Web*

These web sites contain an excellent collection of supplemental materials for understanding the self for interpersonal communication. The first site explores the nature of the self in interpersonal communication. The second site offers several personality assessment instruments. This site is in the Media Guide and not the textbook so that the teacher can guide students visiting these sites.

Some students are skittish about even talking about personality assessment. Two points must be stressed. First, personality assessment is not like astrology. There is no sense of – what is my horoscope – about the process. Second, I encourage my students to think of the process as, understanding temperament, if they are uncomfortable about personality. I recommend having the students visit these sites, only after you have introduced them to the basics of personality that can be obtained in the above scholarly sources by Kiersey and Bates, and by Kroeger and Thuesen.

The insights that can be gained from an understanding of personality assessment are tremendous. Such assessment can provide the student with additional analytical tools for understanding both self, and others involved in various relationships.

## Great Ideas in Personality

http://galton.psych.nwu.edu/greatideas.html

**Brief Summary:** by G. Scott Acton (Northwestern U). While primarily a psychology site, Acton has a well-developed interpersonal theory section, which seems to be a major research interest. The site offers links to a wide variety of topics related to research of interpersonal theory and personality.

**IPC Concepts:** Self-concept, self.

## Personality Tests

http://www.personality.com/test.htm

**Brief Summary:** This site offers a variety of personality assessment mechanisms. The goal is to gain an understanding of your temperament character and those of the people around you. The list of tests includes: Keirsey Character Sorter, Keirsey Temperament Sorter, Draw a Pig Personality Test, Draw a Garden Personality Test, Draw a Vase Personality Test, Psychological Type Indicator, Ennegram Test, What is your E-IQ? Are you a freak? Goofy Personality Test, SmartQ Personality Test, Inner Self Personality Test. This is an interesting and potentially very useful web site if approached with caution and processing. It should not be taken as instant psychological analysis.

**IPC Concepts:** Self, personality, temperament.

## Kiersey Bates Temperament Sorter, version 2

www.kiersey.com

**Brief Summary:** Applies the basic elements of the Myers Briggs personality assessment theory and instrument. Based on Carl Jung's approach to personality theory.

**IPC Concepts:** Personality and the self.

## Association for Psychological Type.

**http://www.aptcentral.org/**

**Brief Summary:** Utilizing instruments such as the Myers-Briggs Type Indicator. This site is primarily for consultants and career counselors. The "related web sites" offer links to high quality web sites providing interpretation and application of psychological typing. There is also a link to a series of statements about the ethical use of psychological typing.

**IPC Concepts:** Personality and the self.

# CHAPTER THREE
# Forming and Using Social Perceptions

## INTERPERSONAL COMMUNICATION IN ACTION

Perception is one of the most enjoyable topics for me to teach in interpersonal communication. I love to show students that when they focus on one thing, they may be missing out on something really wonderful. I have collected twenty years of visual perception exercises that surprise, amuse, and occasionally, amaze my students. They ultimately help students to look at things from more than one perspective. However, film is a wonderful way to show students how the process of perception works and how they experience the process when they watch the films and interact with other people.

The films in this chapter are listed in order of complexity and length of usage, from brief and simple, to lengthy and more complex. *The Christmas Story* offers a really good example of seeing through the eyes of little Ralph as he approaches the throne of Santa. In *E.T.* we see how E.T. moves around the house and neighborhood by blending to the environment in a chameleon like manner. *Victor/Victoria* dramatically points out we bring our preconceptions to the people with whom we interact and create stereotypes and self-fulfilling prophecies. *Being There* also shows our preconceptions shape what we are able to see and hear around us. The entire of *The Doctor* is that how treat others is predicated on how we look at them. *Do the Right Thing* also demonstrates how our biases and preconceptions shape how we see and react to other people.

## LEARNING OBJECTIVES:

- Help students learn to understand the process of perception in interpersonal dynamics.
- Raise awareness of the influences on what we perceive in ourselves and in others.
- Raise awareness for the student to diversity in interpersonal perception.
- Raise awareness for the student to ethical issues in interpersonal perception as it relates to accuracy, fairness, and diversity.
- Introduce the student to communication competence by learning to improve perceptual accuracy.

| In Classroom Assignments | For Homework |
|---|---|
| - Small Group Discussion | - Position Papers |
| - Whole class discussion | - Relationship Analysis Papers |
| - Role Play Exercises | - Web Exercises to supplement textbook and Instructor's Manual exercise |
| - Conversation exercises | - Journal Entries |

# *Visually Presented Interpersonal Communication Theory*

## *In Movies*

**The Christmas Story. Bob Clark, dir. With Peter Billingsley, Darren McGavin, 1983.**

**Brief Summary:** Based on the memoirs of Jean Shepard about growing up in the 1940s. This is the story of a young boy's quest to get the Christmas gift of his dreams – a Red Ryder BB gun. The boy, his little brother, and their friends, have a series of adventures at school, and on the way to and from school. We also see the relationship and parenting approaches of both parents. Of real interest for perception is the scene where mom and dad take Ralph and his brother to the department store to see Santa Claus. Each child who goes up a long ramp to Santa's throne is filled with anticipation until they are in front of Santa, at which time they become terrified by the reality of this huge and strange grownup. When Ralph comes to Santa, the camera gives us the entire experience from Ralph's eyes – a wonderful opportunity to practice empathy and to apply perception theory.

**IPC Concepts:** Perception and empathy.

**Scenes for Use in the Classroom:** I recommend using this scene for both this chapter and for the chapter on empathy. The scene is the one in which Ralph's parents take him and his brother to the department store to see Santa.

**Questions for discussion**

1. **What is Ralph's experience with Santa and his elves? What does Ralph see and feel as he approaches and interacts with Santa?**

   Ralph initially fantasizes about finally making a successful bid to Santa for the gift of his dreams. Unfortunately, when he finally approaches Santa, he sees big people who are tired and impatient and who are not trying to make this a positive experience for the children. Ralph only sees their size and their unattractiveness. He is terrified by this encounter and freezes, unable to speak until he is pushed down the slide.

2. **What could the adults have done differently to help the children have a more pleasant experience?**

   The adults are tired and not concerned about the magic of Christmas or about helping to make the experience a warm and enjoyable one for the kids.

Clearly, these adults could have empathized with the children and been more patient and carrying about each child.

## E.T. The Extra-Terrestrial. Steven Spielberg, dir. With Dee Wallace, Henry Thomas, Peter Coyote, Robert MacNaughton, Drew Barrymore, Tom (C. Thomas) Howell, 1982.

**Brief Summary:** The film is about the experiences and adventures of a ten year-old boy and his younger sister who befriend a small space alien. The story takes us from their initial shock and uncertainty, to their growing friendship, to their desire to help him "go home," and finally, to their efforts to protect him from the adult world.

**IPC Concepts:** These scenes focus on the process of selective perception. We see what we expect to see, or we do not see something or someone if we do not expect to see it, or him/her. Or, we may only see what we have focused on, apart from whatever may be present.

**Scenes for Use in the classroom:** There are three really neat scenes from this film (at least) that are useful for introducing the process of perception. The first takes place when ET hides amongst the other stuffed animals in the closet, and therefore, escapes detection. The second occurs when Mom comes home and is in such a rush to get things done, and her attention is so completely focused on the refrigerator and meal preparation, that she does not even notice this little space alien wandering along at her feet with her children. The third scene occurs at Halloween when the children are going door-to-door for tricks and treats and ET is able to blend in with everyone because he looks like just another child in a costume.

**Questions for Discussion**

1. **In the scene in the closet with stuffed animals, how does selective perception explain ET's narrow escape? In what way does the expectation of what is there influence the perception of what is really there? To what extent does the rule of simplicity help us to explain this scene? Has this type of thing happened to any student in any context? In a relational context?**

   This scene is a wonderful illustration of the perceptual dynamics of attention, selection, organization, and interpretation of stimuli. The mother is clearly looking for something other than a space alien. She goes into a child's room looking through a child's toys and stuffed animals. She focuses on the toys as stuffed animals and she only sees what she expects to see.

2. **In the scene at the refrigerator, how does mom's focus on the task at hand influence her ability to see anything else? Has this type of thing happened to any student in any context? In a relational context?**

   This scene is another wonderful illustration of the perceptual dynamics of attention, selection, organization, and interpretation of stimuli. The mother is clearly focusing on kitchen and food. She does not even see the details of the little people scurrying around at, or below her waist. She is accustomed to having the children clamor around her as she works in the kitchen. Even if something seemed odd, she would probably just assume that one of the children was wearing something while at play or that there was another child visiting. In any case, nothing was able to break into her focus on kitchen. She focuses on the refrigerator and she only sees what she expects to see.

3. **In the Halloween scene, how does ET manage to pass as just another trick-or-treater? How does his minimal disguise help this to happen? Have you ever made a minor change in yourself and had people change their perception of you?**

   Once again, we see what we expect to see. Even children examining the costumes of other children will go with expectation over reality. The segment with the Yoda costume passing E.T. is especially cute, additionally, because it appears that E.T. might even think he recognizes this other alien.

## Victor/Victoria, dir. Blake Edwards. Julie Andrews, James Garner, Robert Preston, Leslie Ann Warren, Alex Karras and John Rhys-Davies, 1982.

**Brief Summary:** The story is about a gay man, Carroll Todd (Robert Preston), and a straight woman, Victoria Grant (Julie Andrews), who are struggling entertainers in Paris. The man suggests that the woman perform her normal nightclub act as a man pretending to be a woman. The con works so well that she becomes a major celebrity, and the pair attract the attention of an American gangster, King Marchan (James Garner), his mistress, Norma Cassidy (Leslie Ann Warren), and his attendant, Mr. Berstein (Alex Karras). The resolution is amusing and charming. The film is a really brilliant depiction of the role of perception in meeting, evaluating others, and how social stereotypes affect our interactions with others and with ourselves. The inner turmoil of King Marchan and Mr. Bernstein is effectively portrayed as they respond to their perceptions of Victor and Toddy.

**IPC Concepts:** Perception, stereotyping and the impact on relationship development.

**Scenes for Use in the Classroom:** While there is a fair amount of good comedy in this film, there are many scenes that illustrate the perceptual process. I will suggest a couple of them.

First, the early scenes involving Victoria and Toddy in which they discuss the possibility of a woman sleeping with a gay man, they meet Toddy's most recent companion, and Victoria's audition as a man.

Second, the scenes in which Marchan, Norma, and Bernstein meet Victor and Toddy. There are several examples of assigning meaning to the first impressions, to preconceptions, and to how our interactions are conditioned by these preconceptions. Marchan refuses to believe that this man could be a woman. Norma wants to convert

Toddy to be a heterosexual. Bernstein is filled with what turns out to be his own dissonance.

**Questions for Discussion**

1. **Why does Toddy's former companion mistake Victoria as a gay man? How does this illustrate the process of perception and stereotyping? What could/should the man have done to increase the accuracy of his perceptions?**

   Toddy's former partner does not expect to see a woman in Toddy's apartment. He therefore, sees what would make sense to him, responds with jealousy, and strikes out. Victoria inadvertently adds to the confusion by responding to defend her new friend. Clearly, Richard, the former lover, has selected specific stimuli, organized them according to his expectations, and interpreted them accordingly.

   Since Richard responded with passion and not thought, the simplest thing to do to change what happened would be to check his perception, which would give him more accurate information. This is one of the best techniques for our students to learn.

2. **How do the preconceptions of Marchan, Norma, and Bernstein affect their interactions with Victor and Toddy?**

   Marchan becomes defensive and insecure when he is attracted to, and aroused by, "Victor," and so, he tries to prove that "he" is a fraud. His distress leads to temporary erectile dysfunction (ED, thanks to Bob Dole) and several embarrassing situations for Marchan. It is difficult for him to accept any level of romantic and/or physical attraction between two men.

   Norma is very honest about her reaction. She is pleased by Victor's deception, partially because it confused Marchan. She is distressed by Toddy's announcement that he is gay (the queer/gay exchange between them is amusing). She is also pleasantly challenged by the prospect of converting him back to women.

   Bernstein experiences dissonance. Because we do not know anything about this character's past, we assume that his distress is due to his inner turmoil over whether or not he might also be gay. As events unfold, we learn that he is gay, but still in the closet.

## Being There. Hal Ashby, dir. With Peter Sellers, Shirley Maclaine, Melvyn Douglas, Jack Warden, Richard Dysart, 1979.

**Brief Summary:** Peter Sellers plays Chance a.k.a. Chauncey Gardener, a simple man who serves a wealthy man as his gardener. When the wealthy sponsor dies, Chauncey is put out on his own. The people he meets consistently misinterpret his quiet, simple, innocence as politically profound wisdom. An expression such as: "I like to watch," is given political undertones and satirical quality in the minds of the Washington in-crowd. Chance is ill equipped to be on the street. His whole world has been shaped by a few rooms, his garden, and most of all, by television. Chance moves from his old house, through the streets of Washington, to his new sponsor without any apparent awareness of where he is or of what is really happening. When he meets his new sponsor, they are taken by the apparent simplicity of his remarks. Believing that he must mean something much deeper (since everyone in Washington always means something other than what they say), they reconstruct his statements so that they make sense.

The film is an interesting study in how our perceptions and mind-sets condition how we listen and think.

**IPC Concepts:** Perception, stereotyping, listening.

**Scenes for Use in the Classroom:**

- His encounter with the attorneys for the "old man's" estate
- His encounter with Ben and Eve Rand at dinner
- His meeting with the President

**Questions for Discussion**

1. **Considering the material in Interact, how can you explain the behavior of those with whom Chance speaks? In other words, why do they make sense out of his meaningless comments as they do?**

   Almost every person who speaks with Chance has some personal agenda to advocate. They are caught up in the complexity of Washington and cannot accept anything said at face value. They either trust Chance and look for a positive interpretation of his metaphoric statements, or they do not trust him and look for darker motives in him. They organize his statements in such a way that gives them a plausible explanation that supports their view of the topic. Only Rob, the Doctor, is able to look at Chance and see him for the kind, simple person that he is.

2. **Why do Chance's gardening comments lend themselves to so much interpretation from others?**

   Gardening is a wonderful metaphor for this film. It allows the listener to attend to different elements within the metaphor, select specific features, organize them into an image that fits an application to policy or politics, and interpret the metaphor for the point of view held by the listener.

## The Doctor, dir. Randa Haines. With William Hurt, Christine Lahti, Elizabeth Perkins, Mandy Patinkin, Adam Arkin, 1991.

**Brief Summary**: This film is based on Dr. Ed Rosenbaum's book *A Taste of My Own Medicine*. This reality base can add a degree of credibility to the film. William Hurt plays Jack, a doctor who believes that he must maintain distance from his patients so that he can remain objective and efficient. When he develops throat cancer, he discovers what it is like to be a patient and deal with hospital bureaucracy. June is a young female cancer patient who helps him learn how to empathize with patients and to cope with his own illness. He slowly wakes up to the kind of treatment that he wants from the doctors treating him. He develops an innovative approach to the training of his interns.

**IPC Concepts:** Attending to patients, paraphrasing, listening critically, language, relationships, message clarity, jargon, ethics.

**Scenes for Use in the Classroom:** The best scenes for the discussion of perception occur in two parts. First, show the class how the doctor perceives his patients and his residents early in the film. Second, show the class how the doctor must interact with the hospital staff when he is just another patient.

After the doctor comes to terms with his illness and changes his perception of the role of the doctor, show the class the changes in his discourse to his residents as he requires them to undergo the tests that they will prescribe for their patients in the future.

**Questions for Discussion**

1. **How does the perception of hospital staff change when he is just another patient?**

   The hospital staff regard him as just another number for them to handle. They do not give him any special status or treatment, and they see him more as a civilian than as an officer in the corporation.

2. **How does the doctor perceive patients? What does he see as his role? To what extent does his belief reflect role-based perception?**

   Initially, the doctor regards his patients dispassionately. He argues against any form of personal involvement, and goes so far as to joke in surgery and sing bawdy songs. He teases one of his surgical nurses for not being willing to laugh in surgery. After he experiences the shabby treatment of the staff and the terror of being a cancer patient, he learns to take a personal interest in each patient. When going into surgery himself, he selects the most serious and caring of the members of his staff, and the nurse whom he had previously teased.

3. **How does the doctor's status change when he becomes a patient?**

   While I confess to some distrust of this depiction in the film, based on my own experiences in hospitals, the hospital staff treat the doctor as just another patient. In other words, he receives no special treatment or priority.

## Do The Right Thing, dir. Spike Lee. With Spike Lee, Danny Aiello, Ossie Davis, Ruby Lee, Richard Edson, Rosie Perez, John Torturro, 1989.

**Brief Summary:** This is a powerful story of racial diversity, racial animosity, tension, conflict, and the value question of what is meant by doing the right thing. The film is about a hot summer in Bedford-Stuyvesant in Brooklyn. The basic plot involves a successful, white-owned pizza restaurant in an otherwise poor, black neighborhood. The owner Sal (Aiello) believes that his pizzeria owes nothing to the people of the neighborhood, except to serve excellent pizza. And yet he does not want to leave the neighborhood as he has watched many of the residents grow up on his pizza. Spike Lee plays Mookie, a pizza deliverer, who, on a hot summer day, gets caught up in the middle of tension between Aiello and the community. Buggin Out (Esposito) and Radio Hakeem (Nunn) both carry their attitude around on their shoulders. As the story reaches its explosive climax, Mookie must determine what the da Mayor (Davis) means by "do the right thing."

**IPC Concepts:** Perception: of self, of others, stereotyping, self-fulfilling prophecies.

**Scenes for Use in the Classroom:**

- Mookie talking to Sal at the opening of the film and in the final scene after the fire.
- Sal talking to his sons about the role of the pizzeria in the neighborhood.
- Mookie talking to Buggin Out and Radio Hakeem.

**Questions for Discussion**

1. **How does Sal, the owner of the pizza parlor, perceive himself? How does he perceive the neighborhood and the residents in it? Is there any evidence of stereotyping in his behavior and/or comments?**

   Sal sees himself as a beleaguered white, Italian businessman in a neighborhood that has undergone tremendous ethnic and racial change. He does not believe that he owes the community other than excellent pizza and service. He view many of the residents in a reasonable honest manner, albeit through the filter of race and ethnicity. He does tend to stereotype Buggin Out and Radio Hakeem.

2. **How does Mookie perceive himself? Does he have healthy self-esteem? What are his perceptions of his boss? Of his peers?**

   Mookie has fairly good self-esteem. He is able to navigate his way through a myriad of relationships with just about everyone in the neighborhood. Indeed, he comes across as something of a community leader. He can speak to Sal as a relative equal and he will not take any sass from Vito, Sal's older son. He looks at Sal as an authority figure who tries to do his best, but who allows his temper and frustrations to get the better of him. He knows that his friend Buggin Out is looking for trouble and he tries to keep him from it, unsuccessfully.

## ***On the Stage***

**Anthony Schaeffer. Sleuth.**

**Brief Summary:** This play is a who-dunnit of sorts. It blends cues and miscues in an effort to keep the audience guessing as to the final outcome and who will survive. It is a wonderful vehicle for directing the audience's focus or attention so as to surprise the audience at several points.

**IPC Concepts:** Perception: attention, organization, simplicity, interpretation.

## ***CNN***

**Inner City Teens Talk. (2:12). CNN Interpersonal Communication Today, 1999, Volume 2.**

This clip showcases a community based in California in which teenagers from the inner city speak candidly about their concern and opinions on a variety of subjects ranging from immigration to police brutality. The performance, entitled "The Roof Is Burning," gives adults from the suburbs an opportunity to listen to the reality of inner city teenagers.

**US Reaction to Princess Diana's Funeral, (1:55). CNN Interpersonal Communication Today, 1999, Volume 1.**

The clip explores the process of empathy as Americans express their feelings about the death of Princess Diana. This tragedy functioned as a worldwide event that demonstrated Diana's power as a unifying symbol.

The clip is useful for perception since many people could not understand the worldwide reaction to Diana's death. It will offer a good class discussion on various perceptions of Princess Diana.

# *INTERPERSONAL COMMUNICATION THEORY IN LITERATURE AND ACADEMIC RESOURCES*

## *Theory Illustrated in Literature*

**James Baldwin. (1963). Go Tell It On The Mountain. New York: Dial Press.**

**Brief Summary:** This is the powerful story of John Grimes and his family on the occasion of his fourteenth birthday. It tells of his conversion and dedication to God, and focuses on the prayers of his mother, Elizabeth; his stepfather, Gabriel; and his aunt, Florence. The novel does a really good job of depicting John's low self-esteem, self-perception as unattractive, and his near obsession with needing to serve the Lord in order to redeem his otherwise worthless life.

**IPC Concepts:** Perception of self, self-esteem, prayer as a form of self-talk.

**For Use in the Classroom:** Students can discuss the nature of John's level of self-esteem and its impact on his life, and on the lives of those around him. This type of application can be extended, kind of like chaining in Fantasy Theme Criticism, to other examples in the lives of the class.

The book is also a valuable aid in discussing issues of racial diversity.

**Alice Walker. (1982). *The Color Purple.* New York: Pocket Books.**

**Brief Summary:** This is the story of a poor, used and abused African American woman, Celie. She is given into an abusive marriage by her abusive father. She suffers in silence until she discovers that her husband, Mister, has been hiding letters from her sister, Nettie, who had moved to Africa with Christian missionaries. Celie finds the letters and secretly reads them whenever she can steal a few minutes between chores, or by hiding them inside her Bible and reading them at church. The husband has other women but barely knows Celie. Mister's mistress, Shug, befriends Celie, and they develop their own love relationship. As her love grows with Shug, Celie develops more and more self-esteem and confidence. She is eventually able to stand up to Mister and move out on her own. She moves to Memphis with Shug where her life improves tremendously.

**IPC Concepts:** Self perception, self esteem, impact of significant others, Relationships – need for warmth and affection, trust and commitment, conflict, diversity, culture, gender, emotion, gender and intimacy.

**For Use in the Classroom:** Walker's book is even more powerful than the excellent film they made of it. There are several good ways to use the book in class. A book report in which the student uses communication theory to guide the analysis is a good exercise. The book can be used in conjunction with the film so that students can not only increase their awareness of interpersonal dynamics, but they can also increase their media literacy by noting how the film changes and omits elements of the book. The book can be used in order to enhance student performance ability. Students can role-play a character from the book, and a group of students can perform dramatic reading.

### Annie Murphy Paul. Where Bias Begins: The Truth About Stereotypes. Psychology Today, 31, 3, May/June 1998, 52-55, 82.

**Brief Summary:** A discussion of the psychology of bias and its development, which focuses on how stereotypes can develop unconsciously. This is a good discussion of the process of perception and the process of stereotyping.

**IPC Concepts:** Stereotypes, perception.

## *What's on the Web*

### Perception web site
### http://www.perceptionweb.com/percsup.html

**Brief Summary:** On line journal dealing with perception from a psychological and physiological point of view. It contains journal article abstracts, and abstracts of papers presented at various conferences.

**IPC Concepts:** Perception.

### A Great Stereotype Breaker
### http://www.suite101.com/discussion.cfm/relationships/25876

**Brief Summary:** This is a really neat description of an individual's son and how he works to avoid and overcome stereotyping. His approach includes this rather clever thought: I still put people in boxes, but now I let them out.

**IPC Concepts:** Perception.

## Constructive Love: The Lesson by Thom Rutledge
## http://www2.scescape.com/support/lesson.htm

**Brief Summary:** A really good reinforcer for a discussion on who is in charge of our beliefs, feelings, and actions. This reinforces Ellis' theory of the ABC process in self-talk and emotion.

**IPC Concepts:** Perception, choice, relationships.

# CHAPTER FOUR
# Using Language to Construct Messages

## INTERPERSONAL COMMUNICATION IN ACTION

Chapter four of Interact examines language in interpersonal communication, including the nature of language, meaning, diversity and gender, clarity, and appropriateness. This chapter of the Media Guide will suggest films that illustrate effective language usage in relationships, ineffective language usage, and analysis of language behavior in relationships. The films are useful in illustrating aspects of language usage in interpersonal communication. George Carlin manages to weave an excellent little primer on language into an hour-long monologue. He attacks the overuse of euphemism and jargon. *The Doctor* makes a strong case for speaking in language that patients can understand when communicating with their doctor or other healthcare personnel. *My Fair Lady* illustrates the effect of language competence on a person's life and previous relationships. *Blade Runner* posits a possible view of language in the future where multicultural and multiracial interaction may create a language that is a mixture of several language systems.

## LEARNING OBJECTIVES:

- Sensitize students to the role of language in relationships.
- Illustrate the need for more effective language usage in relationships.
- Introduce students to the need for language skills.
- Introduce students to skillful language usage.
- Raise student awareness to the nature and power of meaning through words.

| In Classroom Assignments | For Homework |
|---|---|
| - Small Group Discussion | - Position Papers |
| - Whole class discussion | - Relationship Analysis Papers |
| - Role Play Exercises | - Web Exercises to supplement textbook and Instructor's Manual exercise |
| - Conversation exercises | - Journal Entries |

# *VISUALLY PRESENTED INTERPERSONAL COMMUNICATION THEORY*

## *IN MOVIES*

### George Carlin: Doin' It Again. 1990.

**Brief Summary:** This is a one hour-long stand-up routine that Carlin did before a live broadcasted on HBO. While not a film, per se, it has some excellent ideas and examples of the overuse of jargon and euphemisms. There are two primary sections of interest and value on these topics, at the very beginning of the tape and at the end. The material in between is merely Carlin's standard shock humor.

**IPC Concepts:** Euphemisms, jargon, doublespeak. Carlin offers excellent examples of the extremes of misuse of both types of language. In so doing, he makes the argument that such language takes the humanity out of life and hides reality. Ultimately, Carlin's routine is a plea for the ethical treatment of language. Carlin's opening attack on language that hides reality is an excellent opportunity to incorporate doublespeak into the course. The books below by Lutz provide a clear, concise, and cogent discussion of this form of language misuse.

**Use in the Classroom:** This video was originally aired on HBO as part of its comedy series. Carlin has done a number of these performances. The entire video is approximately one hour. However, much of it is not appropriate for the classroom unless you are analyzing humor, taste, or the First Amendment. When I use this video (and I use it often), I use the opening several minutes in which Carlin offers examples of language that is overused. The examples tend toward jargon that has become popular, and serves to distance us from the reality in question, or cover it with pretty words and images. I then move to the last several minutes of the tape in which Carlin takes off on the euphemism. His examples are excellent in that they are humorous, provocative, and sometimes worthy of rebuttal. For example, he defends using the term "cripple" instead of "those in need of assistance" or "challenged." He argues that the Bible says that Jesus healed the cripples and that there is no shame attached to the word in any dictionary. His argument rests on denotative meaning and overlooks connotative meaning. This is a good opportunity to discuss language and appropriateness, relational context, diversity, and sensitivity to the needs of others. Since this is George Carlin, you must screen it before showing any part of it and make your own choices of the amount to show. I deeply believe it to be an effective piece of material and have used these two segments for the past nine years.

**Questions for Discussion**

1. **What is a euphemism? What are the values of euphemistic language? When are euphemisms misused?**

 It seems clear that the euphemism can be a useful tool for softening the blow of painful information. It is used to clean up something otherwise unpleasant or disgusting. It is used to take some of the sting out of painful information such as a death, natural disaster, or other tragedy. However, the euphemism can be overused so that we do not adequately describe the harsh reality of the world around us. As such, euphemisms can be used to hide the truth or to mislead others.

2. **What is jargon? What are the values of jargon? When is jargon misused?**

 Jargon is the specialized language of a professional or technical group. Jargon can be very useful when people with similar interests and/or backgrounds need to speak with word economy. Doctors, scientists, lawyers, teachers, politicians, and many others use jargon in order to communicate a lot of information in a short time. Jargon can also help to insure the privacy of a conversation and can protect in-group members from those who do not need to know what is being discussed. However, jargon can also be misused when it blocks information from being communicated to those who do have a need and a right to know. Members of relationships, work teams, etc. need to have information communicated in clear and understandable language.

3. **Is Carlin's use of the word cripple fair? Why do we shy away from calling people cripples? Are euphemistic substitutions for cripple effective uses of language?**

 I will repeat what I stated above. Carlin defends using the term "cripple" instead of "those in need of assistance" or "challenged." He argues that the Bible says that Jesus healed the cripples and that there is no shame attached to the word in any dictionary. His argument rests on denotative meaning and overlooks connotative meaning. On the one hand, expressions like physically challenged offer a more positive perception of the condition. This is a good opportunity to discuss language and appropriateness, relational context, diversity, and sensitivity to the needs of others.

## The Doctor, dir. Randa Haines. With William Hurt, Christine Lahti, Elizabeth Perkins, Mandy Patinkin, Adam Arkin, 1991.

**Brief Summary:** This film is based on Dr. Ed Rosenbaum's book *A Taste of My Own Medicine.* William Hurt plays Jack, a doctor who believes that he must maintain distance from his patients so that he can remain objective and efficient. He tells his residents that it is their job to go in, cut, and get out without any emotional involvement that might interfere with their surgical skill. He is fond of joking and singing off-color songs while conducting surgeries. He and his partner (who is accused of malpractice) tease one of the surgical nurses because she refuses to join in the joking or singing. When he develops throat cancer, he discovers what it is like to be a patient and deal with the hospital bureaucracy and uncaring doctors. He meets June, a young female cancer patient who tells him about her condition. He lies and says that his father treated many of those conditions with no problem. She later confronts him with this deception, exclaiming that she is dying and he should not waste her time. They eventually become friends and she helps him to learn how to empathize with patients and to cope with his own illness. In the course of determining his own treatment, he chooses the most caring and sensitive doctor from the staff. He also learns to appreciate the surgical nurse whom he had previously made fun of, for her caring attitude and inability to joke in surgery. He develops an innovative approach to the training of his interns by insisting that they speak plain English to their patients and learn to empathize with them.

**IPC Concepts:** Language, relationships, message clarity, jargon, ethics.

**Scenes for Use in the Classroom:** The opening sequence is useful. While it is a setup for much of the subsequent relationships, it does a good job of showcasing the doctor's attitudes and normal behaviors. In the sequence of scenes, we see the doctor joking and singing in surgery, teasing the nurse, teasing another doctor who is warm and caring with his patients, and giving his residents the advice about being an efficient, uncaring, objective surgeon.

The doctor's interactions in the oncology department are very good scenes. Here he encounters the staff's attitude toward patients, the young cancer patient, and begins to experience his own fear of cancer.

The doctor's conversations with the surgical staff prior to his surgery are interesting for interpersonal dynamics. He discusses his needs with the compassionate surgeon. As he is being taken into surgery, the compassionate nurse reassures him.

A scene close to the end of the film has the doctor introducing his residents to his new approach to caring treatment. He assigns each of them to undergo a battery of unpleasant medical tests. His explanation is that they must learn to empathize with their patients and that they must understand what the tests they prescribe are like for the patient.

**Questions for Discussion**

1. **How does the doctor's use of language distance himself from the reality of his occupation, and from the pain of his patients? What, if anything, is the problem with what he does?**

   They use a variety of techniques to distance themselves from reality: humor, sarcasm, sing bawdy songs. Interestingly, when an operation goes badly, they drop the humor and get serious. Then they go right back to being silly.

   His language is insensitive, overly informal, and inappropriate. He does not treat others, especially his patients, with proper respect. After a patient expresses her anxiety about the scar from surgery, he makes a joke about her looking like a Playboy centerfold with the staples to prove it.

2. **In what way does the doctor suffer from the abuse of language when he is a patient? What does this experience do to him as a patient?**

He is treated with the same uncaring attitude that he has given his own patients. The ENT who diagnoses his throat problem is direct, brusque, and unsupportive. The staff members who receive him for his biopsy are equally uncaring. Whenever he wants special treatment, he must make concessions that are dehumanizing and humiliating. He is offended by the casual, careless comments of those around him and by their assumption that he is not a living, thinking person. His own doctor tells him that he has a tumor without any cushioning of the blow.

3. **How does the doctor prefer to be treated after his bout with cancer? How does he change his own approach to teaching his residents?**

Jack want to be treated like an individual person. He wants to be treated with care, understanding, support, and inclusion in the treatment process. He learns to respect those health care professionals who treat their patients with respect and a caring attitude. He learns to talk to his patients during surgery even though they are under general anesthetic. In the beginning of the film, he does not believe that this makes any sense. He makes fun of the doctors who do. However, he realizes that speaking to the patient adds an extra degree of care and support and he begins to believe that the patient can hear what goes on in surgery at the unconscious level of the mind. He learns to appreciate the importance of gentle, supportive words and touches.

## My Fair Lady, dir. George Cukor. Rex Harrison, Audrey Hepburn, Stanley Holloway, Wilfrid Hyde-White, Jeremy Brett, Theodore Bikel, 1964.

**Brief Summary:** The musical version of G.B. Shaw's play Pygmalion. The story is about a lower class young woman who is taken in by Henry Higgins, a wealthy man who works as an elocutionist. His belief is that anyone can be passed off as upper class, if not royalty, by merely altering the way that they present themselves and speak. He teaches Lizza Doolittle to speak with proper diction and grammar, and to walk and move with proper form and etiquette. As her training progresses, she is taken for a Hungarian princess of royal blood. The film depicts the power of language and nonverbal behavior in shaping the perceptions of others with regard to the social position of people.

**IPC Concepts:** Language, nonverbal, and perception. For this chapter, *My Fair Lady* demonstrates the power of language in social interaction, social class, and upward mobility.

**Scenes for Use in the Classroom:** The scene in which Professor Henry Higgins meets Lizza is a good one for showcasing the linguistic differences between them. The famous "rain in Spain" sequence is also useful for illustrating the approach of the Professor to training Lizza in proper elocution. The scene in which Lizza makes her debut and is taken for royalty shows how she has learned to fit in.

**<u>Questions for Discussion</u>**

1. **How does language reflect social status in *My Fair Lady*? How does language reflect social status in society today?**

In the world of Henry Higgins and Lizza Doolittle, language is a defining quality. Higgins indicated that he can place a person in the social strata of London within a small margin of error. English society had little forgiveness or tolerance for someone who did not speak with the correct diction and style.

It seems clear that today's society is changing on these issues. On the one hand, we have a definite departure from public speaking and oratory, partially due to the rise of mass communication. On the other hand, it still seems evident that mainstream success depends on speaking standard American English.

2. **What effect does her new language skills have on Lizza's life? Are the changes for the better?**

Prior to Higgins' instruction, Lizza comes from the lower classes of London society. She fits in with her father's group of friends and is able to move from street corner to street corner selling her flowers. After her schooling, she finds that she no longer fits into her former world. Her former associates cannot adapt to her new level of communication competence. She also finds that she does not know how to fit into the world of Higgins. Her brief speech to Higgins the morning after the triumphant ball speaks to this point. Once she resolves her relational problem with Higgins, a new world opens up to her. On her own, however, she had little chance of fitting in.

## Terms of Endearment, dir. James L. Brooks. Shirley MacLaine, Debra Winger, Jack Nicholson, John Lithgow, Jeff Daniels, Danny DeVito, 1983.

**<u>Brief Summary</u>:** The story of a young woman who marries a college English teacher. She has an unusually close relationship with her mother, Aurora Greenaway. They seem to know when the other one is in need. They have ritualistic conversations that sometimes occur at inopportune moments for the daughter. Aurora is highly judgmental of everything that her daughter does. Aurora is particularly critical of her son-in-law, Flap. About midway through the film, Emma Greenaway contracts cancer. Her very domineering mother forces her to continually struggle to keep her own identity secure. Prior to developing cancer, she has an affair, partially in response to her husband's infidelity. Her mother takes charge of her health care and must contend with the husband, the children, and her own relationship needs. Two scenes stand out in terms of language and interpersonal language usage. The first involves a confrontation between the young woman and her husband's mistress. The second takes place between her mother and a doctor who is treating the cancer.

**<u>IPC Concepts</u>:** Medical jargon and relationship jargon.

**Scenes for Use in the Classroom**: There are a number of scenes that can work for the class. One involves Aurora talking to the doctor about her daughter's condition. As the doctor dances around the issue and tries to bury her in "medicalese," Aurora explodes in frustration asking him to speak English.

Winger's husband, Slap, is having an affair with a grad student. When confronted by Winger, the paramour counters with the statement, "there is nothing that you are feeling that I couldn't validate." The use of psychobabble feels irresponsible, cold, and almost silly. A good example to get the class talking about these relational issues.

**Questions for Discussion**

1. **How could the doctor speak more clearly to Aurora in the first scene?**

   The scene in question is a good example of the problems with doctor-patient relationships. Anyone who has ever had to see a doctor for an explanation of a medical condition has experienced this type of incomprehensible language. This type of language problem also occurs when the patient is highly anxious and not able to think as clearly as necessary. Doctors (and nurses, technicians, etc.) need to look at the exchange from the patient's viewpoint and speak as though the patient knows nothing about the topic. A former colleague introduced me to an acronym which I use to make this point. It is the COIK phenomenon, which stands for "Clear Only If Known." The information is so loaded with jargon that the patient must virtually be a health care professional in order to understand what the doctor has said. The Interact material on speaking with precision and clarity is very relevant for this problem.

2. **How could the husband's mistress have responded so as to come across in a more genuine manner? Could she have? Should she say anything at all?**

   This is a good one for class debate. Be prepared for some disagreement with all aspects of the scene. Some students will claim she spoke properly. Others will argue for saying nothing. Others will offer a neutral or slightly empathetic statement. In any case, this scene can spark some good class discussion on appropriate language.

## Blade Runner, dir. Ridley Scott. With Harrison Ford, Rutger Hauer, Sean Young, Edward James Olmos, Darryl Hannah, Joanna Cassidy, 1982.

**Brief Summary:** This is a futuristic, science fiction story in which Harrison Ford plays a policeman who searches for deviant robots. The city of the future is depicted as dark, crowded, polluted, and overrun by technology. Ford encounters people on the streets of Los Angeles who speak a language that blends words from English, Spanish, and Japanese.

**IPC Concepts**: Language and Diversity. This film presents a possible language of the future as a blend of English, Japanese, and Spanish. This is based on linguistic history in which languages mix and merge. What does the future hold for linguistic interaction as a result of increasing cultural diversity?

**Scenes for Use in the Classroom:** The primary scene for use occurs very early in the film. The scene involves Ford moving around the streets of L.A. seeking information. He stops at street vendors, gets dinner, and collects information. The language that he encounters makes for a very short, interesting example of diverse linguistic behavior.

**Questions for Discussion**

1. **How does Ford handle the street language? How is it similar and different from today's street talk?**

   Ford understands the street without necessarily speaking it. It is unclear if he might be fluent in street talk, but he can understand it. This is evident from his two encounters on the street, one with the street food vendor and the other with the fellow who takes him in. In terms of today's street talk, it is only different in terms of the extent of the language blended. Street talk today may blend English with Spanish, or with Black English resulting in Spanglish or Ebonics. The impact of Asian languages on American English is as yet difficult to determine.

2. **How does this language blend work? Could this type of linguistic merger occur in our society?**

   Without claiming linguistic credentials, I speculate that the speaker uses a mixture of vocabulary from all three-language systems, plus a variety of colloquialisms from all three languages.

   Of course this kind of mixture could occur in our society. The magnificent PBS series *The Story of English* and the companion text, documents how this kind of blending has happened to English for centuries, across many cultures, and with many language systems.

## *On the Stage*

### William Shakespeare. Romeo and Juliet.

**Brief Summary:** Virtually any play by Shakespeare will showcase language in interpersonal communication. Shakespeare understood human emotion, romance, and relationships very well, and used language in a creative and insightful manner. This is very clearly demonstrated in Romeo and Juliet. The language of their tragic love story is a part of our relational language.

**IPC Concepts:** Language in relationships.

**For Use in the Classroom:** For the role of language in loving relationships there is nothing like Romeo and Juliet. Actually, just about any of Shakespeare's relationship plays will do nicely to give students a dynamic experience of words in action. Ask students to see this play and to try to experience the power of Shakespeare's use of language.

## *CNN*

### Black English, (2:32). CNN Interpersonal Communication Today, 1999, Volume 1.

This clip is an excellent vehicle to introduce and focus the debate over diversity and language. The clip presents the debate over Ebonics and cites multiple points of view. This can be a multifaceted discussion for an interpersonal communication class. Allow me to suggest some of the directions that are possible.

- Bilingual education. This is the obvious topic based on the controversy.
- Black English and Ebonics. This is also an obvious point for discussion.
- A bi-lingual society. This is an interesting topic for Americans. We are very insular when it comes to language ability. Many students think that English is the only language needed for communication and that the world should just speak our language. Any international experience should shake this opinion into question. The British Empire also felt this way and while it did spread English around the world, it suffered from being mono-lingual. With the United States increasing in ethnic diversity, languages such as Spanish, Japanese, and soon Chinese emerge as very useful second and third languages. Consider showing students a clip from Harrison Ford's film Blade Runner in which he interacts with street vendors who speak a blend of English, Spanish, and Japanese. It would be useful to ask your students how many languages they speak. I have found students who speak as many as six or seven different languages. These students are typically those from another country who have traveled extensively and learned first hand the utility of being multi-lingual.

### Lost Language, (2:11). CNN Interpersonal Communication Today, 1999, Volume 1.

As large, "modern" cultures expand into remote areas of the world, what happens to indigenous languages? This question is implicit in this clip. A teacher teaches a language that was captured on audiotape over 70 years ago. This is not a unique story. Languages like Irish or Gaelic have experienced a renaissance in recent years as both a new generation of the Irish and an international interest in things Celtic have reawakened an interest in this primarily oral language.

# *Interpersonal Communication Theory in Literature and Academic Resources*

## *Theory Illustrated in Literature*

**Dashiel Hammett. (1965). The Maltese Falcon. New York: Knopf.**

**Brief Summary:** Sam Spade, the private detective at the center of the story, loses his partner on a late night assignment. Sam is then given the job of helping a mysterious woman who is caught-up in a search for the "stuff that dreams are made of"– the Maltese Falcon. Hammett has a wonderful way of creating and conveying colorful, memorable characters, and embellishing their interactions with equally colorful language. In this mystery and in the Nick Charles mystery – The Thin Man – the argot of the criminal underworld and the police world is cleverly interwoven into the story.

**IPC Concepts:** Language of the lower class of New York in the 1930s. The film does an excellent job of showcasing the argot of police work, the private eye, and the criminal underworld

**Aldous Huxley. (1965). Brave New World & Brave New World Revisited. New York: Harper & Row, Publisher, Incorporated. (Original work published in 1932)**

**George Orwell. (1949). 1984. New York: Harcourt, Brace.**

**George Orwell. (1946). Animal Farm. New York: New American Library.**

**Brief Summary:** I recommend all three of the above books for students to read within the context of language and relationships. Each book offers useful perspectives on the power of language manipulation. This is especially useful in an age where political discourse pretends to be relational through its use of mass mediated "conversation" ads for candidates, or on issue advocacy.

Huxley's brilliant depiction of the world of the future in which social interaction is controlled by test tube births, pills to control emotions, consumerism over religion, sex without relationship, and rigid social class based on scientific or genetic distinctions that are artificially created at birth.

One test of Orwell's impact can be found in the adoption of the expressions "1984" and "Big Brother" in colloquial speech. 1984 contains a bundle of expressions that have found their way into mainstream discourse.

These works are useful for book reports or journal entries, or to bridge interpersonal communication and mass mediated political communication.

**IPC Concepts:** The language of social interaction, control by science and advertising as propaganda.

## *Academic Work*

**William Lutz. (1981). Double-Speak: From "Revenue Enhancement" To "Terminal Living." N.Y.: HarperCollins Publishers.**

**Brief Summary:** Lutz has studied language misuse for many years. He tracks the misuse in any area where he can find it. His book is a rich collection of the misuse and overuse of jargon, doublespeak, gobbledygook, and euphemistic language in medicine, law, advertising, government, and everyday life.

**IPC Concepts:** Language misuse, need for message clarity.

**George Lakoff and Mark Johnson. (1980). *Metaphors We Live By.* Chicago: University of Chicago Press.**

**Brief Summary:** Examines the way in which metaphors and all language interacts with how we think, feel, and act. This is a very useful book to gain insight into how people feel and what they may really be saying by listening to their use of language.

**IPC Concepts:** Metaphor, self, relational language.

## *What's on the Web*

**How To Express Difficult Feelings**
**http://www.DRNADIG.com/feelings.htm**

**Brief Summary:** This web site examines the nature and function of language in expressing emotion. The site includes guidelines on language use when in conflict, the difference between thoughts and feelings, and detailed directions on "I" language. There are links to listening and conflict management with this site.

**IPC Concepts:** Language and conflict.

## Human Communication Research Centre
## http://www.hcrc.ed.ac.uk/Site/site_home.html

**Brief Summary:** The home page of the Human Communication Research Centre (HCRC), an interdisciplinary research centre at the Universities of Edinburgh and Glasgow. They focus on spoken and written language, as well as communication in other media - visual, graphical, and computer-based.

**IPC Concepts:** Language in human communication.

## Assertiveness prepared by Organizational Development and Training, Department of Human Resources, Tufts University.
## http://www.tufts.edu/hr/tips/assert.html

**Brief Summary:** A really good introduction to the nature of assertiveness, especially on "I" language, with specific instructions and examples that supplement the discussion on both language and influence very nicely.

**IPC Concepts:** Language and respect.

**For Use in the Classroom:** I recommend this web site to complement the textbook discussion of language specificity, clarity, and precision. The site has excellent exercises for students to complete.

# CHAPTER FIVE
# Communicating Through Nonverbal Behaviors

## Interpersonal Communication In Action

Chapter five of the Interact Text focuses on the role and power of nonverbal behavior in interpersonal relationships. This chapter of the Media Guide will offer aides to illustrate and analyze nonverbal communication in relational contexts. The films will examine the role and power of nonverbal behavior in relational interaction, gender representation and understanding, expression of attitude and feelings, reinforce meaning, and express meaning.

The films in this chapter illustrate the centrality of nonverbal behaviors in personal identification, especially in terms of establishing authority and gender. A Few Good Men is virtually a case study in how to establish authority via posture, tone of voice, gestures, and facial expressions. The three films developed in I Enjoy Being a Girl illustrate how our society associates certain with female behavior versus male behavior. This fact can offer an excellent opportunity to discuss the fairness and propriety of such behavioral enculturation.

## LEARNING OBJECTIVES

- Help the students better appreciate the nature, the types, and the power of nonverbal behavior.
- Sensitize students on how to decode nonverbal behavior.
- Reinforce the elements of paralanguage and give them practice in decoding its message meaning.
- Illustrate ways for students to improve the messages they communicate through their nonverbal behavior.
- Raise awareness of gender-based nonverbal behavior and stereotypical views of gender-based nonverbal behavior.

| In Classroom Assignments | For Homework |
|---|---|
| - Small Group Discussion | - Position Papers |
| - Whole class discussion | - Relationship Analysis Papers |
| - Role Play Exercises | - Web Exercises to supplement textbook and Instructor's Manual exercise |
| - Conversation exercises | - Journal Entries |

## *VISUALLY PRESENTED INTERPERSONAL COMMUNICATION THEORY*

## *IN MOVIES*

### A Few Good Men, dir. Rob Reiner. Jack Nicholson, Demi Moore, Kevin Bacon, Kevin Pollak, 1992.

**Brief Summary:** After a death at the Marine base in Cuba, a cocky naval lawyer, Daniel Kaffee (Tom Cruise), is assigned to the defense of a pair of marines accused of the murder. He arrogantly dismisses the idealism of his superior officer, Joanne Galloway (Demi Moore), and the realism of his partner, Sam Weinberg (Kevin Pollack). The trio meets Colonel Jessep (Jack Nicholson), the colonel in charge of the base. He is even more arrogant than Kaffee, in addition to being openly sexist. Kaffee is the type of person who goes with the flow, takes very little seriously (except for baseball), and is quick to take the shortest path to resolving a case. He has a reputation for plea-bargaining. True to that reputation, he has never been in a courtroom in his nine-month tenure in the Navy. He must now learn to get more involved in the details, issues, and personnel of a case involving murder, powerful personalities, high stakes, honor, and conspiracy.

The ensuing investigation and trial bring Kaffee face to face with himself, his choice to become a lawyer, and respect for his position as a naval attorney. The confrontation between Kaffee and Jessep is, not only one of the truly great scenes in movie history, but it also illustrates a variety of communication concepts in a very powerful manner.

**IPC Concepts:** Nonverbal – posture, facial, gestures, clothing, vocal tone, social standing. Kaffee's character moves through a wide range of postures. He is initially very casual, nonchalant, and laid back. He becomes intensely focused, determined to get the facts, and even explosive toward his clients and his partners. He also demonstrates a phenomenal ability to stay in control as he very deliberately turns up the pressure in his interrogation of several witnesses, including and especially, Colonel Jessep. In the confrontation sequence in the final scene, the eye movements, posture, and paralanguage of both Kaffee and Jessep make for a classic case in each area.

**Scenes for Use in the Classroom:** This movie is a tour de force in nonverbal behavior, especially in the ways in which posture; gestures; eye movement; and vocal tone can add to a person's power; stature; psychological size; immediacy; and influence.

I would start with the first meeting between Kaffee and Jo. She is crisp and business-like, while Kaffee is casual and uninvolved.

I would then recommend using the scene in which Kaffee and company visit Jessep on the Marine base on Cuba. The luncheon scene showcases the amount of power assumed by Jessep, the quiet deference shown to him by his subordinates, the efforts to appease him by Kaffee, and the consequences of challenging him when done by both Jo and Kaffee.

As previously indicated, the climatic confrontation between Kaffee and Jessep is a must, even if you use no other scenes from this film. Each character uses the opening sequence of questions as preparation for the inevitable clash. Jessep's show of disgust and disdain for Kaffee and the Judge demonstrates his own egoism. Kaffee's rebuke of the Colonel demonstrates his own final decision and commitment to the dangerous climax. As the two move in for the kill, each assumes a posture that demonstrates confidence and authority. Kaffee, even more than Jessep remains in control of his posture. Under pressure of cross-examination, Jessep falters when he has given conflicting testimony and realizes that Kaffee is boxing him into a corner. The resulting stress, dissonance, and anger build up in Jessep so much, that he blurts out the very confession that Kaffee wants. It is a confession that he had hoped for, but never expected to receive, as evidenced by the shocked look on his face when he has received it. Focus discussion on the eye movements, facial movements, postural movements, and vocalics in this clash of powerful personalities.

**Questions for Discussion**

1. **What message does Kaffee communicate to Jo at their first two meetings? Does his demeanor change at all during either of these meetings?**

   He takes everything as a big joke or a game. He is sarcastic, overly casual, flip, and disrespectful. He refuses to take anything seriously. He makes jokes about the case and places his softball practice above his legal responsibilities.

   His attitude changes slightly when he clarifies a couple of facts about the case during their first meeting on the softball field. His vocal tone is even, staccato, crisp as he spits out the facts.

2. **What cues does Jessep send during the luncheon questioning to indicate his attitude toward the investigation, the investigators, and himself?**

   Jessep does not take the investigation seriously. He conveys an attitude of quiet tolerance. He will go through the motions of cooperation without doing anything of substance to advance the investigation. He believes that the investigation is a farce because he believes the code red action is essential to discipline.

3. **How does Kaffee approach Colonel Jessep at the trial? How would you describe his nonverbal behavior during the opening of his interrogation of the colonel? How does Jessep respond? Be specific in noting his nonverbal behavior.**

   During their first meeting on the base in Cuba, Kaffee treats Jessep with the same approach that he seems to use with all authority figures. He maintains the minimum level of respect that gives an official mask to his real desire to be buddies, good old boys, with those in charge. He tries to reassure Jessep that he will not be a source of any more annoyance than necessary and that the investigation is just a formality.

At the trial, Kaffee begins with the same sense of calm, quiet, non-threatening deference. He wants Jessep to relax and let his guard down. He knows that Jessep is arrogant and cocky. Kaffee is also arrogant and cocky. Daniel also knows that to confront Jessep directly into the cross-examination would only serve to provoke him and keep him on his guard. He must slowly irritate Jessep so that the Colonel will completely lose his temper.

4. **Describe the interaction between Colonel Jessep and the judge when Jessep gets up to leave the courtroom just prior to Kaffee's final attack on the colonel. What does each man communicate? How do they each communicate their message?**

Jessep really believes himself to be superior to those around him. He is rising up the chain of command and treats anyone with disdain who does not treat him with complete respect and deference. When Kaffee seems to be wasting his time, he immediately transfers his disgust with Kaffee to the court, the trial, and the judge. His vocal tone is arrogant, angry, accusatory, and filled with contempt. His final comment that "I think I've earned it (respect)" is filled with sarcasm and arrogance.

The judge is in control of his own anger at Jessep's arrogance and disrespect. The Judge corrects Kaffee for his breach of protocol, but reprimands Jessep for his own breach. He adds a comment that matches Jessep's final comment and reasserts his authority in the Courtroom when he says, "I'm quite certain that I've earned it." Jessep has been put in his place in a respectful, authoritative manner.

5. **What does Kaffee do to rile Colonel Jessep? Why does this strategy work (apart from the fact that it is written into the script)? Does this seem true to reality? Why? Why not?**

Kaffee knows that Jessep does not handle cockiness well at all. He wants deference, groveling, subservience, etc. from all who speak with him. Kaffee has a gift for cocky arrogance. He has also laid the foundation for possibly having a surprise for Jessep with the two airmen from the airport sitting in the back of the courtroom. He now begins by slowly annoying Jessep. He stares him down. He stands very erect. He begins a line of questions, frustrates Jessep's efforts to answer them, and moves to another topic. He slowly challenges Jessep's word, competence, and judgment. By the time that Kaffee begins to shout at Jessep, he has turned up the heat so slowly that Jessep has been brought along at every point and is losing control of his temper and his judgment.

The strategy works because it is very possible to provoke a person into losing their temper and say things that they would never say without such provocation. In a real courtroom it is highly improbable that this would ever happen. However, for interpersonal interactions, it can certainly be true to reality. We may be on the receiving end of someone trying to goad us into an argument or a lapse of judgment. This segment can be a good case from which to learn how to break the process of agitation with effective self-talk.

## I Enjoy Being A Girl

These three films treat the topic of men trying to understand what it means to be a woman. In each case the men must learn how to behave like they think a woman would behave, including posture, walking, gestures, eye movement, voice, hand shakes, etc.

## Tootsie, dir. Sydney Pollack. With Dustin Hoffman, Jessica Lange, Teri Garr, Dabney Coleman, Charles Durning, Bill Murray, Sydney Pollack, Geena Davis, Estelle Getty, 1982.

**Brief Summary:** The film is about Michael Dorsey, a man who has trouble finding work as an actor due to his dominating and demanding personality. As a solution, he poses as a woman named Dorothy Michaels in order to get a job on a television soap opera. He initially embarks on this charade in order to prove a point to his agent, George, but soon discovers that he has been so convincing in the impersonation that his characterization of Dorothy has become successful both, on the soap opera and in his own private life. He/she even receives a marriage proposal from Les, the elderly father of the real target of his affections, Julie, the star of the Soap. This successful portrayal of the woman, both on and off camera, leads him to discover things about himself that he did not know were there. As Michael Dorsey puts it late in the film, he was "a better man as a woman."

**IPC Concepts:** Self-presentation, perception, and stereotyping based on nonverbal behavior. Dorsey initially self-presents by running around out of control, exploding and abusing anyone who gets in his way. He has little respect for Sandy, his girlfriend. He pushes his way around and, when desperate, is either hopelessly arrogant, or ineffectually submissive. When he assumes the persona of Dorothy, he begins to act according to his stereotype of what a woman is supposed to be like. As his role-play continues and becomes more complex, his understanding of his role deepens and becomes more complex. His conversation with his roommate Jeff reflects this complexity. Dorothy is in a hurry to change and go to Julie's apartment to read lines. "She" is frantic as "she" tries to find something to wear. Jeff's joking behavior serves to inflame "her" frustration and panic. Dorothy describes "her" frustration with not having a bigger wardrobe, since "she" cannot afford to be seen in "her" day wardrobe or in something that will accentuate "her" hips or butt. Dorothy's role-play demonstrates a wide range of male/female behaviors, and is a really good way of raising discussion and awareness of male/female nonverbal behavior.

**Scenes for Use in the Classroom:** Depending on time available and your course strategy on gender and diversity, you might begin with the opening sequence in which Dorsey goes from audition to audition trying to get work, and his confrontation with his agent over his inflexible approach to work.

It is then useful to move to his audition as Dorothy. The comedy in this sequence is very good for maintaining class interest and for helping to point out areas for discussion. For example, when they ask if the camera can move further back, someone remarks, "How about Cleveland?" as a way of making a comment on her less attractive features. Discussion of society's high standard for female beauty (far different than for men) can come from this one remark.

Dorothy's interactions with her and Michael's friends offer good material for class discussion. However, some of the best material comes when Dorothy must fend-off unwanted advances from men, such as the older male doctor. Of equal power are her conversations with her costar Julie and with Michael's girlfriend Sandy. Dorsey/Dorothy must learn about the inconsistencies of his behavior as a man and as a woman.

**Questions for Discussion**

1. **How does Michael initially approach imitating the behavior appropriate for a woman? Do you think he does a convincing job? Does he get better at it as the film goes on? What behaviors are convincing? What behaviors are not convincing? Are any essentially just stereotypes?**

   Because Michael begins the charade believing that this will just be a very temporary part to play, he only prepares for brief impressions. He alters his voice, posture, facial expressions, eye contact, and types of touch. He does not try to change his thinking to try to reflect the way a woman might approach a problem, especially in male/female exchanges. He does a convincing job for the early stages of the film, and he gets even more convincing as the film develops. However, it is a good idea to see what students think. Our society has undergone many changes on the question of gender and it is a fascinating exercise to see what classes think today. For example, a film like *Breakfast Club* seems to be almost timeless. Whenever I show clips from it, there is virtually no loss of impact due to its age. This also occurs with *On Golden Pond.* I have students cry with various clips. *Terms of Endearment* does not have this timeless quality which is why it must be shown carefully and with very specific objectives in mind. Because there have been several male/female switch films, their impact will be less than it once was. However, it may take on a different quality as homophobic behavior becomes less acceptable and the humor of these depictions either takes on a different basis or dissolves into some kind of historical, cultural artifact.

2. **How does Dorothy communicate with Lange differently as a woman than as a man might communicate with her? What are the nonverbal behaviors in question? How does Michael behave differently with Sandy as a man than as a woman might communicate with her? What lessons does Michael/Dorothy learn from these interactions?**

   As a woman, Michael is willing to sit and discuss, listen, probe gently, and be supportive. As a man, he cuts to the answer, tells her what he thinks she wants to hear (which gets him a glass of wine thrown in his face at a party), and is much more self serving. As he observes the actions of other men interacting with women, he begins to realize just how manipulative, dishonest, and abusive he has been to the women in his life.

3. **Dorothy receives unwanted sexual advances. How does she handle these advances? Is the interaction credible? Why or why not? What does Michael learn from this experience?**

Dorothy responds both carefully and aggressively when assaulted with sexual harassment. Dorothy allows the advance to play itself out and then responds with clear and decisive action. She may slap the aggressor. She may give the man a stern and belittling lecture.

Michael learns just how ugly, burdensome, and bothersome this kind of behavior can be. He learns that he has some real work to do on himself as a man.

4. **Dorothy's concern about what to wear when she visits Lange is amusing, but is it based on reality?**

The assumption in this scene is that women pay considerably more attention to appearance and fashion when getting together with a friend than do men. This can spark an interesting class conversation on whether this true and why or why not.

## Mrs. Doubtfire, dir. Chris Columbus. With Robin Williams, Sally Field, Pierce Brosnan, Harvey Fierstein, Polly Holiday, 1993.

**Brief Summary:** The film is about Daniel Hillard, a man who has trouble finding work as an actor and, as a result, he is limited as to how often he can see his children after he and his wife separate. He desperately wants to be with his children more often. As a solution, he poses as Mrs. Doubtfire, a matronly, British woman, and gets the job as the children's nanny. He so completely becomes the Doubtfire persona, that both his wife and his children are taken in. His successful portrayal of an older woman leads him to discover things about himself that he did not know were there.

**IPC Concepts:** Self-presentation, perception and stereotyping based on nonverbal behavior. The film also raises age as a related topic.

**Scenes for Use in the Classroom:** Show the first scene in which Mrs. Doubtfire applies for the job as nanny. Then show her interacting with individual children.

**Questions for Discussion**

1. **How does Daniel initially approach imitating the behavior appropriate for a woman? Do you think he does a convincing job? Does he get better at it as the film goes on? What behaviors are convincing? What behaviors are not convincing? Are any essentially just stereotypes?**

This film will mirror somewhat the same issues of *Tootsie*. Because of Robin Williams' ability to play comedic characters, there will be a level of believability that will get bundled up in the comedy. One way to get around this problem is to turn the sound off and have the class focus on the nonverbal behavior exclusively. Again, with Williams this can still be a problem since his humor also embraces slapstick and broad physical humor. Without sound, the class can at least focus on action without distracting vocal comedy.

2. **Daniel has serious problems with personal and relational responsibility. How does he learn about responsibility as Mrs. Doubtfire?**
   By role playing the nanny, Daniel discovers what it means to be in a position of responsibility. As Dad, he could always dodge the responsibility by making Mom the bad person or the killjoy. As nanny, it is her/his job to be responsible. He undergoes a series of events that make him accept this role, and he matures accordingly.

3. **Daniel ( Robin Williams) tries several different female personae before settling on the elderly woman for Mrs. Doubtfire. These are humorous, but are they accurate or merely comic stereotypes?**
   For purposes of establishing the character of Daniel, the film allows for Robin Williams to playfully go through some of his own improvisational style. This makes for effective humor and allows the character of Mrs. Doubtfire to be more restrained and subdued.

## Switch, dir. Blake Edwards. With Ellen Barkin, Jimmy Smits, JoBeth Williams, Lorraine Bracco, Tony Roberts, Perry King, 1991.

**Brief Summary:** A sexist, philandering man is shot and killed. He immediately returns to earth as a woman and must learn to interact with his/her former friends as a woman.

**IPC Concepts:** Self-presentation, perception and stereotyping based on nonverbal behavior.

**Scenes for Use in the Classroom:** This film is more of a comedy/who-dunnit so it does not lend itself to as much formal analysis as Tootsie and Mrs. Doubtfire. However, if you use a couple of interesting scenes you can get a good set of class reactions, and set up an interesting compare and contrast exercise for all three films.

Show the first series of scenes where our new woman is learning how to be a woman. In some ways this is a more honest portrayal of how difficult it would be to try to cross over to the other gender.

**Questions for Discussion**

1. **How effectively does Barkin imitate a man trying to learn to be a woman? Is her behavior appropriate for this switch to a woman? Does she get better at it as the film goes on? What behaviors are convincing? What behaviors are**

**not convincing? Are any essentially just stereotypes?**

Barkin's actions reveal how the man within the woman is having trouble trying to behave according to what society says a woman's behavior should be. She walks in a very funny way. Stands in a "masculine" manner. Even uses some vocal mannerisms that are associated with male behavior. The point is that the character is telling us to let go of such gender restraining perceptions.

2. **After showing the class clips from all three films, break the class into groups according to your own preferences—all male, all female or mixed gender. Ask each group to evaluate the depictions of female behavior (or in Switch both male and female).**

## *On the Stage*

### William Shakespeare. The Tempest.

**Brief Summary:** This is one of Shakespeare's most memorable and influential plays. Prospero, who has fled from civilization in order to protect himself and his daughter, utilizes the help of a magical character named Ariel. The interaction between Prospero and Ariel depend on the gestures and facial expressions of each character. Further, Ariel only communicates via gestures and facial expressions when around other characters in the story. This is a wonderful dramatization that cleverly draws our attention to nonverbal actions.

**IPC Concepts:** Gestures.

## *CNN*

### Baby's First Words. (2:44). CNN Interpersonal Communication Today, 1999, Volume 2.

This clip focuses on how deaf children develop their understanding of language at the same pace as hearing children, with the exception that deaf children express their language with their hands. The piece provides an excellent reinforcement of the role of gestures and communicating meaning. It also helps students understand how learning to communicate fits into the developmental process of children.

**"Weight Hate: Tipping the Scales." (5:25). CNN Interpersonal Communication Today, 1999, Volume 2.**

The clip focuses on the problem of discrimination against heavy people. It makes the point that weight hate is one of the last bastions of "legal" discrimination. Support groups are discussed which try to help their members lose weight and deal with unfair reactions to their weight problem.

**"The Ugly Bill: Hobbit House in Manila." (2:18). CNN Interpersonal Communication Today, 1999, Volume 2.**

This clip examines the phenomenon in Manilla of discrimination against short and unattractive people. One "haven" for such people is the Hobbit House, named for J.R.R. Tolkien's book The Hobbit. All of the employees in this establishment are under four feet. The clip examines a new bill in the Philippine legislature to give legal protection to people who are physically less attractive. The bill has received some ridicule in the legislature, hence, the name "The Ugly Bill." Its passage is still an open question. The clip makes the point that attractiveness is very important to the Philippine people.

**"Eating Disorders." (2:09). CNN Interpersonal Communication Today, 1999, Volume 2.**

This clip looks at the problem experienced by many young girls of denying themselves proper food in order to have a thin body according to social standards. This clip presents the power of nonverbal images in shaping the perceptions and values of these young women.

---

## ***Interpersonal Communication Theory in Literature and Academic Resources***

## ***Theory Illustrated in Literature***

### Ernest Hemingway. (1952). The Old Man and The Sea. New York: Scribner.

**Brief Summary:** This is Hemingway's story of Santiago, an old Cuban fisherman who has not caught a fish for over eighty days. His young friend Manolin tries to help him as best as he can, given his own poverty. Santiago goes to fish and catches a large marlin.

As the fish toes him further out to sea, Santiago must survive until the fish tires and he can tie it to the small boat. As he returns to his home, he must defend his catch from sharks. Hemingway does a masterful job of describing this man's actions; reactions; and feelings, as this largely, non-dialogue story unfolds.

**IPC Concepts:** Nonverbal – gestures, posture, facial expressions, cultural variations.

**For Use in the Classroom:** Hemmingway is a good source of human narrative material. Students might read this fairly short book and make journal entries about how Hemmingway describes the behaviors and thoughts of the old man. They might also reflect on how this translates to their own experience, either for themselves, or with older people in their lives.

## *Academic Resources*

Both Hall and Leathers offer excellent theoretical background material for a more in-depth discussion of nonverbal behavior in human relationships. Both are useful in broadening our understanding of diversity in customs and meanings associated with nonverbal behavior. Assigning chapters as outside reading, and short written summaries are one way to get the material across. Students can make oral reports on the readings, and/or use the findings in doing an analysis of the films they might be assigned to watch outside of class.

### Edward Hall. (1966). The Hidden Dimension. Garden City, NY: Doubleday & Company.

**Brief Summary:** Spatial zones generally are drawn closer for women than for men. Women approach more closely, and seem to prefer side-by-side conversations. The latter may explain differences in use of space – men prefer more face-to-face conversations, and people are generally more aware of space to the front than to the side.

**IPC Concepts:** Nonverbal communication, especially proxemics.

### Dale Leathers. (1997). Successful Nonverbal Communication: Principles and Applications. 3rd. ed Allyn & Bacon.

**Brief Summary:** Leathers does an outstanding job of reporting and discussing research findings on all categories of nonverbal communication. The book is highly readable and very useful. His material on culture, nonverbal behavior, and communication is excellent.

**IPC Concepts**: Nonverbal communication, intercultural communication.

**Dale G. Leathers and Ted H. Emigh. Decoding facial expressions: a new test with decoding norms. The Quarterly Journal of Speech, 66, 4, 1980. 418-436.**

**Brief Summary**: This is an interesting article for anyone studying nonverbal communication, in that it not only presents the statistical results of the study, but it also provides the actual facial photographs used in the Facial Meaning Sensitivity Test. This provides you with an opportunity to look at the actual test being used to collect data, and possibly, to replicate the study at a basic level.

**IPC Concepts**: Nonverbal – facial expression.

## *What's on the Web*

**Nonverbal Communication.**
http://cctr.umkc.edu/user/jaitken/nonverbhome.html

**IPC Concepts**: Nonverbal communication – all areas.

**Brief Summary**: Nonverbal Communication Textbook is a wonderful website developed by Roy Berko and Joan Aitken. A password is required to get to the most interesting material. Other links to nonverbal communication sites are available without a password.

**The Center for Nonverbal Studies (CNS).**
**http://members.aol.com/nonverbal2center.htm#Center for Nonverbal Studies**

**http://members.aol.com/doder1/bodymov1.htm**

**Brief Summary**: "a private, nonprofit research center located in Spokane, Washington, with a site for conferences and seminars in La Jolla, California. The Center is committed to the idea that, for a deeper understanding of 'who we are' and 'what it means to be human,' more attention should be paid to our nonverbal nature."

**IPC Concepts:** Areas of special interest include body movement, gesture, facial expression, adornment and fashion, landscape architecture, mass media, and consumer-product design. All the senses – of balance, hearing, smell, sight, space, taste, time, and touch – are channels for nonverbal cues.

## Gender differences in nonverbal cues
## http://www2.pstcc.cc.tn.us/~dking/nvcom2.htm

**IPC Concepts:** Eye contact, facial expressions, gesture, posture, touch, and gender as the guiding variable.

**Brief Summary:** A summary of claims regarding gender differences in interpreting the above categories of nonverbal behavior. It is an interesting way to isolate and summarize some of these claims. However, no sources are cited for research on these claims, except for one reference to Hall's book.

## Nonverbal Behaviour Nonverbal Communication
## http://zen.sunderland.ac.uk/~hb5jma/1stbersn.htm

**Brief Summary:** A really nice site that allows you to look up information on several categories of information on nonverbal behavior and research: people, journals, articles, books, videos, and a miscellaneous category that includes: (1) Test Your Nonverbal Communication Skills, (2) Nonverbal Semiotics, (3) Special Interest Groups, (4) In The French/German Body, (5)WAIS - Search Engine ANU-Gesture-L, (6).Facial Analysis. This site has interesting links. The page is put together by a Spanish, psychology student named Jaume Masip.

**IPC Concepts:** All categories of nonverbal behavior.

## Notes on 'The Gaze.' Chandler, Daniel (1998).
## http://www.aber.ac.uk/~dgc/gaze.html

**Brief Summary:** An online article on eye behavior. In the introduction, Chandler defines the Gaze. "'The gaze' (sometimes called 'the look') is a technical term which was originally used in film theory in the 1970s but which is now more broadly used by media theorists to refer both to the ways in which viewers look at images of people in any visual medium and to the gaze of those depicted in visual texts. The term 'the male gaze' has become something of a feminist cliché for referring to the voyeuristic way in which men look at women (Evans & Gamman 1995, 13). My aim here is to alert students to existing material and frameworks that may assist them in their own investigations of the issue of the gaze in relation to media texts. Chandler is a lecturer in media theory at the University of Wales, Aberystwyth. An interesting site for students who are interested in the role of "looking" at people, things, harassment via staring, and/or potential linkage to film.

**<u>IPC Concepts</u>:** Eye movement and contact.

# CHAPTER SIX
# Holding Effective Conversation

## INTERPERSONAL COMMUNICATION IN ACTION

Chapter Six of Interact explores one of the most common interpersonal communication situations, namely, having a conversation. We all have numerous conversations during the course of each day. The only problem is that no one ever shows us how to have a good conversation. Some people are shy and do not know how to initiate, maintain, or close a conversation, even if it is their job to do so (employment interviewer). Many people either simply sit there and say very little, or dominate the conversation and refuse to let the other person get a word in.

This chapter of the Media Guide will look at conversation by suggesting films that get immersed into the topic. *Diner* and *My Dinner with Andre* are two of the better films for showcasing conversation.

In addition I will suggest other media that has much to offer to this topic. Plays by Coward and Shaw are excellent vehicles for the deeper appreciation of conversation.

## LEARNING OBJECTIVES

- Give students a deeper understanding of the nature of conversation by showing them interesting conversations in action, or by showing them conversations that flop.
- Increase student understanding of conversational rules by allowing them to apply these rules in evaluating laboratory examples in films.
- Increase student understanding of the conversational principle and its maxims by illustrating these concepts through media examples.
- Increase student understanding of conversational skills by illustrating effective skills through media examples.
- Increase student understanding of turn-taking in conversations.
- Increase student understanding of the nature and importance of Johanessen's characteristics for ethical dialogue.
- Sensitize students to cultural variations in conversation.

| **In Classroom Assignments** | **For Homework** |
|---|---|
| - Small Group Discussion | - Position Papers |
| - Whole class discussion | - Relationship Analysis Papers |
| - Role Play Exercises | - Web Exercises to supplement textbook and Instructor's Manual exercise |
| - Conversation exercises | - Journal Entries |

# *VISUALLY PRESENTED INTERPERSONAL COMMUNICATION THEORY*

## *IN MOVIES*

**Diner, dir. Barry Levinson. With Steve Guttenberg, Daniel Stern Mickey Rourke, Kevin Bacon, Timothy Daly, Ellen Barkin, Paul Reiser, 1982.**

**Brief Summary:** A terrific case study for the analysis of conversation. A group of friends meet regularly in a Baltimore diner and discuss their lives, the problems of growing up, the fun they have had, and their concerns about life. The group includes Eddie (Guttenberg), Shrevie (Stern), Boogie (Rourke), Tim (Bacon), Billy (Daly), Modell (Reiser), and the almost member Beth (Barkin), Shrevie's wife.
It is a good vehicle for studying conversation techniques.

**IPC Concepts:** Conversation – control, turn taking, conflict, disclosure, relationship development, conversational rules, ethical dialogue, and the cooperative principle.

**Scenes for Use in the Classroom:**

- Any scene in which the whole group of young men are gathered around their table at the diner.
- Any of the dyadic scenes at the diner.

**Questions for Discussion**

1. **How do the conversations of the group facilitate group bonding, venting, and phatic arguments?**

   The six young men have a great deal in common. They went to high school together, dated or at least knew the same young women, and shared a number of adventures together. When they are all together, their conversations have a great deal of ritual about them. Each person teases some of the others. Shrevie and Modell argue over whether Shrevie will finish his food without Modell asking directly for the leftovers. Rourke makes wagers, while Eddie obsesses over his wedding and Tim acts wildly. Their arguments are over trivial matters and simply give them something to focus their energy on.

2. **Discuss the extent to which real disclosure occurs in dyadic conversation rather than in the full group. Why do you think this occurs? How does this reinforce the basic guidelines for self-disclosure?**

   Real disclosure and conversation over life concerns only occurs in dyads. The group is too much about image, self-image, and being one-up. In dyads, the individual young men can allow themselves to be vulnerable and in need of counseling from their friend.

Self-disclosure guidelines advocate a safe context in which what a person says can be confided without fear of ridicule or manipulation. The dyadic context is clearly the appropriate setting for the characters in the diner to disclose their fears.

## My Dinner with Andre, dir. Louis Malle. With Andre Gregory, Wallace Shawn, 1981.

**Brief Summary:** Shawn and Gregory discuss their life experiences – especially Gregory's particularly colorful and sometimes strange experiences. The result is a fascinating opportunity to look at the conversation of others. The film portrays characteristics of conversation, rules, cooperation, the need for balance, politeness, and credibility. This may not be the most exciting film ever made, but for the student of conversation it is not to be missed.

**IPC Concepts:** Conversation structure, topics, balancing speaking and listening, rules. This film illustrates the ups and downs of the conversational process, of sharing free information, and of the difficulty in balancing speaking and listening. The film is occasionally less about dialogue than monologue.

**Scenes for Use in the Classroom:** Rather than suggest any specific scene in the film, I recommend that you either find a favorite of your own, or simply show a couple of segments at random and have the class watch and critique based on the concepts in Interact. Give them the opportunity to identify conversational strengths and weaknesses and recommend how to handle the weaknesses. The film can thus become a case study in conversation. I also recommend the following discussion questions as possible starting points for a class debriefing or as the start of a paper on the film.

**Questions for Discussion**

1. **How does the conversation between Shawn and Gregory demonstrate the pros and cons of free information?**

   Neither man really knows much of substance about the other. The lengthy conversation can take place in large part due to free information. Much of the information is inconsequential, disclosing little of importance. Some of it suggests some strange obsessions especially with Gregory.

2. **How does their conversation illustrate turn-taking behavior? How can you tell when it is the other person's turn to talk? Do they ever have to break in and take a turn?**

   Gregory is sometimes reluctant to let go of his turn as speaker. Shawn has to listen patiently and wait for a chance to break in. Consequently, he has little chance to direct the conversation to his own topics.

3. **How does the film illustrate the need for balancing speaking/listening? Do you observe any problems in the conversational balance as it is depicted in the film?**

Shawn appears to feel somewhat out of the conversation as he seems to be trying to be keeping up with Gregory.

## How to Make an American Quilt, dir. Jocelyn Moorehouse. With Winona Ryder, Ellen Burstyn, Anne Bancroft, Maya Angelou, Kate Nelligan, Jean Simmons, Alfre Woodard, Kate Capshaw, Claire Danes, 1995.

**Brief Summary:** The movie adaptation of the novel by Whitney Otto. Finn (Winona Ryder), a young woman who is engaged to be married and is writing her master thesis for the third time – she keeps on changing her mind about the topic – goes to her grandmother and great aunt's home for the summer. Her grandmother, Hy (Ellen Burstyn); her great aunt, Glady Jo (Anne Bancroft); and five other women – Anna (Maya Angelou); Sophia (Loius Smith); Em (Jean Simmons); Constance (Kate Nelligan); and Marianna (Alfre Woodard) form a quilting group. The women's next project is a quilt to be given to Finn as a wedding present. The theme of the quilt is: where love resides. Each woman is to make a square that depicts where their love resides. Anna, who is the coordinator of the quilt and the group, explains that her job is to bring them – each piece of the quilt – together in a balanced and harmonious design – which is also the metaphor for the movie. Throughout the movie Finn learns the stories of each of the women's love stories and past as they disclose their stories to her.

**IPC Concepts:** Conversational characteristics, types, principles; disclosure, friendship, communication barriers,

**Scenes for Use in the Classroom:**

- Opening scene. Finn narrates and explains the set-up of the story.
- Finn's grandmother and her great aunt tell Finn about her grandmother's affair with her great aunt's husband and the consequences of that incident on the relationship of the two sisters.
- Any of the scenes of the women telling Finn their particular stories.
- After the storm when Glady Jo finally tears down the wall in the laundry- room, breaking down the barrier between her and her sister after all the years of resentment.

**Questions for Discussion**

1. **How do the conversations in this film meet participant needs?**

In many ways the primary character in this film is Finn, but each of the other characters plays a vital role in helping Finn grow. As a result of helping Finn, their conversations each resolve a problem or meet a personal need.

Finn learns how to achieve the focus and purpose that her life has lacked. She learns how to value her fiancé and discipline herself for her work.

Hy and Glady Jo finally communicate clearly with other about Hy's infidelity with Glady Jo' husband many years before. As a result Glady Jo is able to forgive Hy.
Anna learns that her love resides in her granddaughter, Marianna, rather than in any of the men in her life.

Em and Constance parallel Hy and Glady Joe to some degree. They resolve their own dispute and Em learns that she really does love her husband.
Finn helps to remind Sophia of who she is.
Marianna realizes that her love resides in her soul mate in Paris.

**2. How do the conversations in this film build relationships?**
Every character in the story is helped in their relationships as a result of their conversations in making the quilt. Hy and Glady Jo reestablish their relationship. Anna becomes even closer to her granddaughter. Em and her husband realize the depth of their love. Em and Constance are reunited. Sophia is finally able to recognize and express the positive qualities in Finn.

## ***CNN***

### Teen Roundtable. (4:32). CNN Interpersonal Communication Today, 1999, Volume 1.

This CNN clip is loosely structured as an interview between a CNN correspondent and four teenagers of different racial and ethnic groups. What actually occurs is an interesting conversation on race, interracial dating, generational reactions to race, etc. The teens are candid in their opinions and about their experiences.

## ***On the Stage***

Both of the following plays are wonderful studies in the use of conversation by the playwright. Both Coward and Shaw use conversation very effectively in order to advance the point of their work.

### Noel Coward. (1925). Easy Virtue.

**Brief Summary:** Shaw's critique of the hypocrisy of the English upper class is made through a series of conversations between the major characters of this play as they interact with the new wife of the son of a wealthy family. A superb example of ethical concerns in conversations masks that people wear to hide their true feelings, and games that are played in conversational interactions.

**IPC Concepts**: Conversational types, purposes, rules, real and false politeness, quality of information, ethical issues.

### G.B. Shaw. (1939). In Good King Charles' Golden Days.

**Brief Summary:** This is the story of Charles II of England and his conversations with an array of fascinating contemporaries, such as, Isaac Newton, George Fox, Nell Gwynn, Duchess of Cleveland, James Duke of York, Godfrey Kneller, and Queen Catherine of Braganza.

**IPC Concepts:** Conversational types, purposes, turn-taking, quality of information.

---

## *INTERPERSONAL COMMUNICATION THEORY IN LITERATURE AND ACADEMIC RESOURCES*

## *Theory Illustrated in Literature*

### Mitch Albom. (1997). Tuesdays with Morrie: an old man, a young man, and life's greatest lesson. New York: Doubleday.

**Brief Summary:** This is the powerful account of columnist Mitch Albom with his old college mentor and professor, Morrie Schwartz. Albom recounts the structure and content of many conversations as he reestablishes his relationship with Morrie after many years. Morrie is dying, and Albom takes us through the topics and pathos of each conversation. There is a lot to learn about conversation and life.

**IPC Concepts:** Conversation and disclosure, humor, quality information, speaking, and listening.

### Studs Terkel.

Just about any of Terkel's books will work for this topic. His work is based on conversations that he has had with many, many people from various walks of life. While his books are primarily the end product of these conversations, they illustrate in somewhat dramatic fashion just how effectively he is able to put people at ease, ask good questions, listen to them on several levels, and generate loads of high quality free information. His interviewees self-disclose their dreams, frustrations, work experience, life experience, and feelings on life.

**Studs Terkel. (1980). *American Dreams: Lost & Found.* New York: Ballantine Books.**

**<u>Brief Summary</u>:** Terkel reports the experiences of many Americans regarding their life dreams and experiences. He reports these conversations by grouping them according to several different contexts: city life, country life, immigrants, dreams of wealth, dreams of a quiet life, upward mobility, public and private life.

**<u>IPC Concepts</u>:** Conversation, free information.

**J.R. Tolkien. (1966). *The Hobbit.* Boston: Houghton Mifflin Company. See Chapter V, "Riddles in the Dark."**

**<u>Brief Summary</u>:** This is a delightful fantasy about how the little people called Hobbits help to fight the evil Dark Lord Sauron. It begins with our introduction to Bilbo, the Hobbit, and his adventure, in which he finds the magical ring of power. While traveling with Gandalf, the wizard, and twelve dwarfs, Bilbo becomes separated and is lost in a labyrinthine of underground tunnels. There he finds a small gold ring and meets the strange character of Gollum. The two engage in a fascinating conversation in which a battle of wits takes place. They end up playing a game of riddles in which the stakes for Bilbo mean passage to safety, and for Gollum, lunch. Their conversation is a wonderful example of sharing some highly guarded free information while they try to understand the other party. There is good balance in speaking and listening.

**<u>IPC Concepts</u>:** Conversational games.

## ***<u>Academic Resources</u>***

**Alan Garner. (1980). Conversationally Speaking: Tested New Ways to Increase Your Personal and Social Effectiveness. N.Y.: McGraw-Hill Book Company.**

**<u>Brief Summary</u>:** Examines how to listen so others will respond, handle criticism and anxiety in social interactions. Suggests ways of gaining free information, and giving compliments.

**IPC Concepts:** Conversational types, purposes, rules, speaking and listening, quality of information.

### Tannen, Deborah. (1990). You just don't understand: women and men in conversation. New York: William Morrow and Company, Inc.

**Brief Summary:** Tannen discusses patterns of interaction and conversation between men and women, and between women and women. She describes the manner in which each gender structures topics, organizes information, approaches problems, and the purposes for engaging in conversation.

**IPC Concepts:** Conversational topics and gender-based behavior, quality of information.

### Elizabeth E. Graham, Michael J. Papa and Gordon P. Brooks. (1992). Functions of humor in conversation: conceptualization and measurement. Western Journal of Communication, 56, 2, 161-183.

**Brief Summary:** This is an interesting article on conversation and using humor to achieve a variety of communicative functions. The article documents a variety of approaches to the study of humor, and uses humor measures to validate the functions that had been identified. The functional approach is helpful when learning how to use humor in interpersonal encounters.

**IPC Concepts:** Conversation – rules, techniques.

## *What's on the Web*

### VanDruff, Dean & VanDruff, Marshall (1995), Conversational Terrorism: How Not to Talk
**http://www.vandruff.com/art_converse.html**

**Brief Summary:** This web site describes negative, non-assertive behaviors that can be experienced in conversation. This site presents and discusses several categories of behavior that are defensive, aggressive, and monological in nature. The categories are Ad Hominem, Sleight of Mind Fallacies, Delay Tactics, Question as Opportunity ploys, General Cheap-Shot Tactics, and Irritants.

**IPC Concepts**: Conversation rules, balancing, speaking, and listening.

## Love Test
## http://www.lovetest.com/

**Brief Summary**: A fun and somewhat silly exercise that can put students in the mood or mind-set to discuss various attraction variables in relationships.

**IPC Concepts**: Sources of conversation topics based on attraction variables.

## The Marriage Toolbox
## http://www.marriagetools.com/betweenus/index.htm
## Paul Michael, Publisher

**Brief Summary**: An excellent group of topics and questions to initiate conversations regarding intimate relationships.

**IPC Concepts**: Conversation about relationships.

# CHAPTER SEVEN

# Listening Effectively

## Interpersonal Communication In Action

Chapter Seven in Interact takes a practical look at the process of listening. It focuses on the nature of listening, the three parts of the process, and how to become a better listener. This chapter of the Media Guide will support this approach by suggesting movies that illustrate problems with listening, poor listeners, good listeners, and specific elements of the listening process.

*As Good As It Gets* takes us through different listening and communication styles, dramatizes the perils of being a poor listener and some of the benefits of being a good listener. *Ordinary People* vividly reinforces what can go very wrong in relationships when we fail to attend and properly evaluate the comments of those around us. Abbott and Costello's *Who's On First* is not only a classic comedy routine, but it also serves as an excellent vehicle for illustrating breakdowns in the communication process, especially in the need for active listening. Imagine how quickly the comic premise of the entire routine would disappear if either Bud or Lou tried a little paraphrasing. While we may not want them to be better listeners, the short does make the point for the rest of us. *The Doctor* takes us to one of the most difficult interpersonal communication situations, namely, doctor and patient. Anyone who has ever felt that the doctor paid virtually no attention to what was said, or who felt so overwhelmed by what the doctor said and couldn't think of any questions until much later, can relate to the message of this film. While most of our students are probably not pre-med majors, everyone else can benefit from the shot in the arm that the film offers for active listening in the doctor-patient dyad. Oh, yes, and sorry for the bad pun.

## LEARNING OBJECTIVES

- Increase the student's understanding of the listening process by observing it in action.
- Increase awareness of the importance of attending to the other person in the listening process.
- Give students practice in active listening through selected scenes from films in which a character needs to understand what the other person is really saying.
- Help students better understand and evaluate the process of making inferences.

| In Classroom Assignments | For Homework |
|---|---|
| - Small Group Discussion | - Position Papers |
| - Whole class discussion | - Relationship Analysis Papers |
| - Role Play Exercises | - Web Exercises to supplement textbook and Instructor's Manual exercise |
| - Conversation exercises | - Journal Entries |

# *VISUALLY PRESENTED INTERPERSONAL COMMUNICATION THEORY*

## *IN MOVIES*

### The Doctor, dir. Randa Haines. With William Hurt, Christine Lahti, Elizabeth Perkins, Mandy Patinkin, Adam Arkin, 1991.

**Brief Summary**: This film is based on Dr. Ed Rosenbaum's book *A Taste of My Own Medicine*. William Hurt plays Jack, a doctor who believes that he must maintain distance from his patients so that he can remain objective and efficient. When he develops throat cancer, he discovers what it is like to be a patient and deal with hospital bureaucracy. A young female cancer patient helps him to learn how to empathize with patients and to cope with his own illness. He develops an innovative approach to the training of his interns.

**IPC Concepts:** Attending to patients, paraphrasing, listening critically, language, relationships, message clarity, jargon, ethics.

**Scenes for Use in the Classroom:** The opening scene in which the main doctors in the film are completing surgery is a good one to illustrate the basic attitude of these medical professionals. Two of the doctors are of the attitude that you should get in and out and remain uncaring about the patient. The surgical nurse is established as a serious, caring person who is uncomfortable about any kind of joking in surgery. We soon meet the third doctor who is also serious and caring, and the butt of some cheap-shot jokes by the smart aleck crowd.

The scene in which the Jack receives his diagnosis of throat cancer is useful. He must try to understand what it all means despite his own dissonant feelings. His doctor does not attend to his needs or try to answer his questions in a caring manner. She is more concerned with staying on schedule than showing any personal concern for her patient.

When the doctor goes in for radiation treatment, he encounters both the coldness of the bureaucracy and another patient. His encounter with the staff person is a good point of discussion as she illustrates Buber's I-It perspective. His encounter with the other patient earns him a stiff rebuke later on in the film. He tries to appease her by glibly saying that her type of cancer is easily treated and curable, despite the fact that he knows otherwise. His attitude is uncaring, and denies her the right to her own fear. He fails to attend to her in any meaningful manner.

**Questions for Discussion**

1. **What do you think of the doctor's basic attitude toward patients? Is he right? Should a doctor be attentive to his patient as a whole person, or**

**should he/she remain aloof and objective so that no emotion clouds judgment during surgery?**

The film makes the argument that doctors and other healthcare professionals should be caring, concerned, and involved with the overall welfare of their patients. Play devil's advocate to force some discussion and even debate over whether or not there is a place for neutral, dispassionate medical professionals who can look at the facts of a case in order to make objective decisions.

2. **How much does the doctor change in his listening behavior during the film? What does it take for him to begin to attend to what others say to him? Does he attend to his wife?**

Jack initially behaves in a superior, I'm important manner. He tries to pull rank in order to receive special, preferential treatment. This doesn't work in the admitting room, or at radiation treatment, or when receiving a room for a biopsy. Jack receives the kind of thoughtless treatment from hospital personnel that many viewers can identify with. His doctors are not concerned about his input or understanding of his condition.

After undergoing poor interpersonal treatment from his ENT doctor, his radiation doctor, and hospital staff, Jack has still not seen the light. He begins to understand what should occur when he meets June, a cancer patient in radiation therapy with him. He treats her like a child who will believe anything. When she challenges his story about one of his father's cancer patients, he begins to understand that he is as guilty of an uncaring attitude as the rest of the healthcare system. He makes an immediate gesture of reconciliation with June. They begin developing a special friendship.

Another turning point for Jack occurs when his ENT tells him that his cancerous tumor has gotten larger. She says this without even looking at him, and she throws it out assuming that he already knows about the negative change. She also reflects out loud that she had had hopes for better results given an 80% success rate with radiation. She is completely unaware of her behavior or of its impact on her patient. Jack is horrified by the news and traumatized by her careless, callous behavior.

As Jack prepares for surgery, he realizes the importance of caring personnel. He changes doctors and picks a colleague whom he had previously ridiculed for being a caring person. He also requests the surgical nurse who was embarrassed to sing in surgery.

Post-op, Jack begins to train his residents to be attentive and caring. He also treats his own patients very differently.

Jack has a serious relational problem with his wife as a result of his illness. He responds by closing her out of his life. He has to learn how to handle his own emotions. June helps him to understand this. Gradually, he opens up to his wife.

3. **What experience have you had with each type of doctor? How do you believe the appropriate role to be for a doctor, objective or involved?**

This is a good question for open discussion. It gets at role-based behavior. It also opens the door to how certain types of professionals should behave, and how we should be able to communicate with them. You can also incorporate relational theory at this point. Should we be one up with the doctor, or one down, or one across? Also note the content/relational components in doctor-patient communication. We can be informed, even instructed by the doctor, but we do not have to feel inferior in the basic relationship.

## Ordinary People: dir. Robert Redford. With Donald Sutherland, Mary Tyler Moore, Judd Hirsch, Timothy Hutton, Elizabeth McGovern, 1980.

**Brief Summary:** This story is about a seriously dysfunctional family and its efforts to deal with the death of the elder son and the attempted suicide of the younger. Both parents lack effective listening skills, but the father, Calvin (Sutherland), makes a serious effort and eventually gets it right. The mother, Beth (Moore), is an angry woman who refuses to deal with the death and makes the younger son, Jared (Hutton), the target of her anger and grief. Jared is trying to put his life back together by seeing a psychiatrist, Dr. Berger (Hirsch). The father tries to avoid conflict and plays the role of peacemaker. By the end of the film, he learns the value and necessity of active listening to the world around him, and the need to deal with the conflict in a more proactive manner.

**IPC Concepts:** Attending, listening actively.

**Scenes for Use in the Classroom:**

- Scene in which Jared first talks with Dr. Berger.
- Beth surprising Jared by coming home unexpectedly.
- Beth and Conrad discussing what to do for the holiday.
- Final confrontation between Beth and Conrad..

**Questions for Discussion**

1. **Does the mother ever really listen to anyone? What effect does this have on the family?**

   Beth is a real mess. She so loved her older son that she placed too much importance onto his life. His death sent her into a downward spiral from which she cannot get out. She listens only to superficial details so that her responses can be polite but uninvolved. She does not listen to the pain of her husband or the pain of Jared. His suicide attempt is an obvious sign of pain and cry for help. Beth seems more ashamed of the public embarrassment than the pain of her son.

   There is little warmth in the family. Calvin is a very warm, caring, sensitive person. It seems clear that Jared gets his sensitivity from his dad. Beth is removed, cool to cold, and uninvolved in the lives of either father or son.

2. **How would you characterize the father's behavior? When does he seem to really begin to listen?**

   Calvin is clearly warm and caring. He is involved in his son's day to day activities. He counsels him on getting counseling. He is genuinely pleased and positive when he learns that Jared has seen Dr. Berger. However, Calvin seems to be taken in by his wife's coolness. He does not recognize her behavior as a form of game playing in order to avoid and deny her own pain. He only starts to listen to her when she demonstrates her almost total lack of concern for Jared.

3. **How would you describe the listening style of Dr. Berger? How does he make a positive impression on Jared?**

   Dr. Berger is an expert at reflective listening. He does not force Jared to engage in counseling. He does not react to Jared's defensive behavior or reluctance to accept him as counselor. He works with Jared on the basis of whatever he says and helps Jared to feel comfortable and safe to open up to him.

## Who's On First in *Naughty Nineties*. Jean Yarbrough, dir. With Bud Abbott and Lou Costello. 1945.

**Brief Summary:** This is one of the great comedy routines of all time, and it is an effective vehicle for analyzing both the communication and the listening processes. The routine is only one segment in a feature-length film in which Bud and Lou play vaudeville entertainers.

**IPC Concepts:** Listening – barriers, bad habits, circular communication. Clearly, neither person is effectively listening to the other. They overreact to each other and increase their own emotional dissonance. Both Bud and Lou draw incorrect inferences about what the other person says and means. The need for reflective listening is very clear in this routine.

**Scenes for Use in the Classroom:** The entire routine takes about ten minutes. It is worth showing the entire bit and then discussing the communication theory embedded in it. You might also consider showing the entire routine and then playing it back a second time, only interrupting it as significant things happen.

**Questions for Discussion**

1. **I always begin by quizzing the class on the nine players. Just ask: name the nine players by their position. You might help out by taking the class through each position. First base? Who. Second base? What. Third base? I don't know. Shortstop? I don't care. Pitcher? Tomorrow. Catcher? Today. Left Field? Why. Center Field? Because. Right Field? Not mentioned.**

   This is a good exercise for discussing the role of memory cues. Many students are familiar with the positions on a baseball team, thus the player names go with the position. The names are repeated so many times that they are strongly reinforced. Finally, there may be motivation to remember them as we want to help Lou get it right when we listen to the routine.

2. **How would reflective listening change this routine? Would there even be a routine if they had used reflective listening techniques?**

As John Ford once said, if we did it that way, there wouldn't be a movie. Okay, so real reflective listening would probably remove the humor from the skit, but the skit still offers students some good practice in correcting poor communication. Take the class through the routine two or three times. Also, consider making a transcript of the routine or of parts of the routine so that the class can write reflective responses for either Lou or Bud. You can also make the point that as Lou gets frustrated by his inability to get the names of the players, his ability to listen goes down with the increase in his blood pressure. See the book by Lynch, *The Language of the Heart: The Human Body in Dialogue,* listed below for more discussion of this critical physical relationship.

## As Good As It Gets, dir. James L. Brooks. With Jack Nicholson, Helen Hunt, Greg Kinnear, Cuba Gooding, Jr., Shirley Knight, 1997.

**Brief Summary:** This is the story of three people whose lives become increasingly interdependent. As they become connected to each other, they come to like and love each other. Melvin Udall (Jack Nicholson) and Carol Connelly (Helen Hunt) must learn to listen to others more carefully and openly. Carol does a pretty good job of this, but she has blinders when it comes to Melvin because he is so caustic. Melvin, in particular, must learn to open up to others in order to overcome his bundle of phobias. Initially an obnoxious, homophobic individual, he must learn to give other people a chance and to take risks of his own. Rather than simply rejecting others out of hand, he learns to pay attention to what they say, listen to their body language, to ask questions and even to pay them compliments.

**IPC Concepts:** Attending, listening actively, listening critically.

Of the fascinating cast of characters in this film, Melvin is perhaps the most interesting for the study of communication. He is a person almost without concern for others. As an obsessive-compulsive personality, his rituals are the only things that matter or have intrinsic value to him. He responds to the rest of the world, almost without exception, from Buber's I-It perspective. Other people are like things, sometimes with utilitarian value to him (i.e. getting him his breakfast, processing the business dimension of his books), almost always annoying. He does not stop to think of the effect of his statements on the other person, indeed he seems incapable of it unless almost forced to do so. When he does try to really attend and respond appropriately, you can almost see the wheels turn in his mind, as he must work through each small step of the process. He would seem to have been so completely caught up in his own little world, that it takes a major effort of will to make even a small gesture to consider the feelings of others.

Carol exemplifies the overtaxed, stressed out single parent, who has only so much energy to devote to anything other than taking care of making a living and caring for her family. She functions from a more dialogical perspective than Melvin, but her willingness to make the effort is limited by the demands of her stressful life.

Simon Bishop is another interesting character, in that he probably works from a more open, trusting, and dialogical perspective than any other character in the film. His gay life choice brings him far more unnecessary abuse than the others, and his very openness and gentle spirit leaves him vulnerable to vicious physical and verbal assault.

**Scenes for Use in the Classroom:** There are numerous scenes that show Melvin's character flaws. His opening interactions with Simon and his dog are clear demonstrations of his I-It point of view. Other evidence of his point of view come in with his treatment of the other people in his favorite restaurant, his comments to the receptionist at his publishing company, and to one of his neighbors.
There are several good scenes in which Melvin tries to change his ways.

- After Carol scolds him for his comment about her son
- Melvin's efforts to be nice to Simon. Start with his rude comments after Simon comes home from the hospital and then Melvin bringing the Chinese soup.

**Questions for Discussion**

1. **How would you describe Nicholson's listening style in this film? What is it at the beginning? How does it evolve?**

   Melvin's character is a classic I-It monological person. He is only interested in what he wants and places no value on anyone else, except in very self-serving, utilitarian terms. He only listens to another person when forced to do so, as when Cuba Gooding confronts him and succeeds in terrifying him. As his need for Hunt intensifies, due to her absence, he must make adjustments in his behavior or risk losing contact with her completely. He slowly learns to be more attentive to other people. He must pay attention to nonverbal cues. He must take the other person's response into account and be concerned about them before proceeding.

2. **How would you describe Simon's listening behavior? Why does it eventually work with Melvin?**

   Melvin is a patient, empathetic listener. He cares deeply about the feelings of others. It is his sensitive nature that gets him into trouble with the thugs who rob and beat him. He is willing to treat Melvin as a genuine person with real individual needs. Melvin is so accustomed to people rejecting him so completely that he eventually warms to the idea that Simon cares about him in a non-sexual manner. Ultimately, Melvin accepts him as a friend as he says, "if that did it for me, I'd be the luckiest guy in the world."

## Mother, dir. Albert Brooks. With Albert Brooks, Debbie Reynolds, Rob Morrow, Lisa Kudrow, 1996.

**Brief Summary:** The story is about a successful writer whose marital life is a shambles. He has been divorced twice and feels that he needs help to make his social life more of a success. In an act of desperation he moves back home with his mother. As the two of them learn to cope with each other's ways, they also come to learn more about themselves. In an interesting way, this only begins to happen when they stop reacting to their image of the other person from the past and learn to attend to the real person in the present.

**IPC Concepts:** Attending, listening actively, repeating information, separating facts from inferences.

This film does a superb job of presenting a set of people who tend to see each other in the past, and who make all of their current perceptions through this filter. The two brothers see each other as if they were still small children. They both see their mother from the point of view of a child. Mother responds as the mother. She still sees her sons as her little boys.

**Scenes for Use in the Classroom:** The scene in which the son comes home and mother insists on feeding him is a good one for a start.

**Questions for Discussion**

1. **How do the perceptions of each character affect their ability to listen to each other? Do they really attend to each other?**

   Mother still sees her sons as her little boys. She makes some changes in what she talks about with them, such as when she tells Brooks that she has a male friend with whom she goes out to dinner and has sex. However, she still regards her son as someone who needs a mother's care. The scene with the cheese and salad when Brooks first returns home is reflective of this perception.

   Brooks also sees his mother as unchanging. He responds to her disclosure of having sex with the discomfort of a child.

   Both mother and son attend to an image of each other based in the past. Neither really looks at the real person until they each have a turning point.

2. **To what extent would indexing and dating their responses help mother and son open up and be more honest? More patient? More attentive?**

   Both mother and son would benefit greatly from such qualifying techniques. They both see each other as they did when the son was a little boy. By placing beliefs or behaviors in their proper time and place, it would allow both people to think in the present.

3. **What habits are apparent in their speaking and listening when they reunite? How do these patterns change as the story goes on?**

   In the beginning, both mother and son are caught up in their own thoughts and problems. The son is especially caught up in his own sense of personal failure and he tends to place the blame at the feet of his mother. He comes home so that he can work through his childhood with her. She, on the other hand, has no real interest in reliving the past just to be blamed for the pattern of her son's life. She is willing to take him back into her home because she loves him.

   After they have spent time together, they each slowly change how they relate to each other. The discovery of Mom's past interest in writing opens the son's eyes to the reality that his mother is more than he ever knew. By learning to attend to her son in the present, Mother helps her son learn to take personal responsibility for his life.

## *CNN*

### Inner City Teens Talk. (2:12). CNN Interpersonal Communication Today, 1999, Volume 2.

This clip showcases a community based in California in which teenagers from the inner city speak candidly about their concern and opinions on a variety of subjects ranging from immigration to police brutality. The performance, entitled "The Roof Is Burning," gives adults from the suburbs an opportunity to listen to the reality of inner city teenagers.

### Sibling Rivalry. (7:24). CNN Interpersonal Communication Today, 1999, Volume 1.

This clip focuses on family conflict where siblings war with each other. It makes the point very clearly that better attending skills will help these siblings get along better with each other and with others.

## *On the Stage*

### James Lapine and Stephen Sondheim. (1985). Sunday in the Park with George.

**Brief Summary:** This is a wonderful musical about artist Georges Seurat (George), and his relationship with his mistress, Dot. In one memorable song from the libretto, she sings out in anguish, "Hello George. Remember me George. I'm here George." George is so consumed by his work that he almost totally failed to attend to her, or to her needs. This failure eventually leads to the end of their relationship.

**IPC Concepts:** Listening, attending, bad habits, and poor listening.
George has come to take his model/partner so much for granted that he fails to attend to anything that she says. His failure as a listener forces her to eventually accept the love of

another, even though she is still in love with George. Listening is one of the central dynamics in this fascinating play about a major piece of art.

---

# *INTERPERSONAL COMMUNICATION THEORY IN LITERATURE AND ACADEMIC RESOURCES*

## *Theory Illustrated in Literature*

**Harper Lee. (1960). To Kill A Mockingbird. New York: Harper Collins Publishers.**

**Brief Summary:** Harper Lee's magnificent novel tells the story of three children and the summer during which they come to face their fears about their mysterious neighbor, Boo Radley, and learn about the realities of Southern racism. Scout, Jem, and Dill have a summer of adventures trying to catch a safe glimpse of Boo. However, it is also during this summer that Atticus, Jem and Scout's father, is asked to defend a black man (Tom Robinson) accused of rape and assault. The children learn of the harsh, ugly side of what their father does for a living, and of the racist traditions of their culture. When Scout goes to school in the fall, she must learn how to talk to children who are different from her, and how to control her temper by dealing with her feelings and her self-talk. As the novel moves to its conclusion, Scout finally meets Boo Radley when he comes to Scout and Jem's rescue. Scout realizes that the man's gentle, shy ways should not make him the outcast that he is.

**IPC Concepts:** This novel illustrates virtually every aspect of the communication process in interpersonal relationships. It deals with trust, perception, empathy, conflict, stereotyping, cultural diversity and the development of the self. It is especially effective in illustrating the value of listening in the relationship of Scout and Atticus.

## *Academic Resources*

**Andrew Wolvin and Carolyn Gwynn Coakley. (1996). Listening 5th Edition. Boston: McGraw-Hill.**

**Brief Summary:** This book provides a thorough introduction to the listening process. It goes into depth on the nature of the process, analysis of barriers to listening, and techniques for improving listening ability.

**IPC Concepts:** All aspects of the listening process.

### Lynch, James J. (1985). *The Language of the Heart: The Human Body in Dialogue.* New York: Basic Books Inc., Publishers.

**Brief Summary:** This is a fascinating discussion of the physiological side of the impact of communication on health. Of particular interest is the relationship between tension, listening, speaking, and blood pressure.

**IPC Concepts:** Physiological nature and impact of listening.

## *What's on the Web*

### Tips on Effective Listening
### http://www.DRNADIG.com/listening.htm

**Brief Summary:** This web site examines the nature and function of listening in effective communication. The site reviews the nature of listening, sources of difficulty for both – speaker and listener, listening modes, levels of communication (cliché, facts, etc.), and tips for effective listening. This is an excellent supplement to the discussion in the text. There are links to expressing emotions and conflict management.

**IPC Concepts:** Attending, understanding, remembering, evaluating.

### The Active Listening Exercise was prepared by the New England Regional Leadership Program.
### http://crs.uvm.edu/gopher/nerl/personal/comm/e.html

**Brief Summary:** This site provides a lengthy explanation of active listening. The document is provided by the Center for Rural Studies, a nonprofit, fee-for-service research organization, based in the College of Agriculture and Life Sciences at the University of Vermont. There is an excellent, extensive discussion of active listening, and a good, active listening exercise.

**IPC Concepts:** Remembering, evaluating.

## Harmonious Assertive Communication.
## http://front.csulb.edu/tstevens/c14-lisn.htm

**Brief Summary:** Tom G. Steven's methods to create understanding and intimacy provide a web-based explanation of empathetic listening. This web site provides something more than lecture notes or a single chapter, but it is not book-length either. Steven is a psychologist for the Counseling and Psychological Services at California State University Long Beach. He is the author of a recent (1998) book, *You Can Choose To Be Happy: "Rise Above" Anxiety, Anger, and Depression* (he has an online version of this book available at his web site).

**IPC Concepts:** Attending, understanding.

# CHAPTER EIGHT

## Interpersonal Communication and Emotion

### INTERPERSONAL COMMUNICATION IN ACTION

Chapter eight takes a somewhat different approach in the Media Guide than it does in the textbook. The Interact text discusses empathy in chapter eight. The Media Guide will blend empathy into a media based discussion of emotion in interpersonal communication. I have included readings in this chapter to supplement the discussion of empathy in Interact. I have spent many years learning about the nature and power of emotion in interpersonal relationships. I frequently conduct in-service training workshops on the role of emotion, self-talk, and how to respond to difficult people and situations. A central idea to grasp about emotion is that we have the power to choose what we want to feel. Too often we simply react from habit or from the life scripts of significant adults who raised us, or from patterns learned from our current partners and friends. We can gain tremendous personal freedom by learning to check our perceptions and choose how we want to respond and feel with a specific person or in a specific situation. I have tried to make this point in a chapter in my article "Freedom of Choice: Intrapersonal Communication and Emotion," published in, p. 319-337. Roberts and Watson, Intrapersonal Communication Processes.

## LEARNING OBJECTIVES

- Increase the student's understanding of the nature and power of human emotion in interpersonal communication.
- Help students understand the power of making choices about which emotions to experience, rather than be controlled by other people and stimuli to whom we respond from habit.
- Increase the student's ability to describe their emotions more accurately and effectively.
- Provide students with visual examples of emotional expression and empathy.

| **In Classroom Assignments** | **For Homework** |
|---|---|
| - Small Group Discussion | - Position Papers |
| - Whole class discussion | - Relationship Analysis Papers |
| - Role Play Exercises | - Web Exercises to supplement textbook and Instructor's Manual exercise |
| - Conversation exercises | - Journal Entries |

# *VISUALLY PRESENTED INTERPERSONAL COMMUNICATION THEORY*

## *IN MOVIES*

**To Kill A Mockingbird, dir. Robert Mulligan. Gregory Peck, Mary Badham, Philip Alford, John Megna, Brock Peters, Robert Duvall, Frank Overton, Rosemary Murphy, Paul Fix, Collin Wilcox, Alice Ghostley, William Windom; narrated by Kim Stanley, 1962.**

**Brief Summary:** Based on Harper Lee's magnificent novel, this movie tells the story of three children and the summer during which they come to face their fears about their mysterious neighbor, Boo Radley, and the realities of Southern racism. Scout, Jem and Dill have a summer of adventures trying to catch a safe glimpse of Boo. However, it is also during this summer that Atticus, Jem and Scout's father, is asked to defend a black man (Tom Robinson), accused of rape and assault. Though clearly innocent, based upon the evidence, the man is convicted by the small-town, Southern jury. The children learn of the harsh, ugly side of what their father does for a living, and of the racist traditions of their culture. During a very critical confrontation between Atticus and a mob of angry townspeople, Scout intervenes in an effort to be with her father. The innocence of her presence, her directness, her honesty, and her words to the mob, forces the men in the group to reexamine their actions, and the mob disperses.

After the summer, Dill leaves for his permanent home, and Scout and Jem go to school. Scout must learn how to dress less like a tom-boy, and to talk to children who are different from herself. Her lunchtime encounter with a poor boy from a nearby farm teaches her to consider the experience and perspective of the other person in communication. When she is teased by her schoolmates, who have heard their parents talking about the trial and the role played by Atticus, she must also learn how to control her temper by dealing with her feelings and her self-talk. Scout flies into a fighting rage when the other children call her father names. Atticus counsels his daughter on the need to control her feelings and to not let the words of others affect her in such a manner. As the movie moves to its conclusion, Scout meets Boo Radley after he comes to the children's rescue. Scout realizes that the man's gentle, shy ways should not make him the outcast that he is.

**IPC Concepts:** This film illustrates virtually every aspect of the communication process in interpersonal relationships. It deals with trust, perception, empathy, emotion and conflict, stereotyping, listening, cultural diversity and the development of the self.

**Scenes for Use in the Classroom:** The set of scenes to show first is the one in which Scout gets into a fight at school and must talk with Atticus about what took place, why, and how she should handle it in the future. These scenes address how we can handle our emotions when we are in a conflict situation.

The scene in which Scout explodes over Walter Cunningham pouring syrup over his lunch also illustrate the need for Scout to learn how to handle her emotions. Again, Atticus discusses the problem with her.

A powerful example of handling emotion occurs when Bob Ewell confronts Atticus outside of the Robinson home and spits in Atticus' face. We have every reason to believe from the story that Atticus could probably beat him silly. Ewell is a coward who only attacks those weaker than himself. Atticus does not respond with open anger. He clenches his face, walks past Ewell, and climbs into his car.

One final scene to use occurs toward the end of the story, just after Scout and Jem have been attacked on their way home. Scout is introduced to their rescuer, Boo Radley. Instead of reacting with fear and superstition (like Jem would have done), Scout looks up at him with interest, acceptance, tenderness, and affection as she takes his hand.

**Questions for Discussion**

1. **How does Atticus counsel Scout to handle her emotions? Why does he say it is important and necessary to do so?**

   Atticus tells Scout that some people don't have very much and have different ways from those that Scout knows. He also tells her that she has to be tolerant and understanding when she has guests in her home. He says that sometimes you have to let people talk even if what they have to say might hurt.

2. **How does Atticus handle his emotions when Ewell spits in his face? What would be his probable self-talk? What would you have done in a similar situation? What would be the likely outcome of expressing your anger to Ewell?**

   Atticus knows that there is no victory in fighting Ewell. The humiliation and frustration are better than lowering himself to Ewell's level. A fight would make Ewell a victim of the smart-talking, high-minded lawyer who would betray his own kind.

## I Enjoy Being A Girl

These three films treat the topic of men trying to understand what it means to be a woman. The set of films has also been developed and presented for use in chapter five on nonverbal communication. I also strongly recommend their use for the discussion of empathy and emotion. The core concept to illustrate is the differences between men and women on how each gender approaches the experience and processing of emotion. The films portray one person learning how to experience life from the point of view of a woman. For this set of films, I will present the classroom use somewhat differently. I will present the three films, suggest scenes, and then recommend processing questions for all three films at once. Obviously, you can decide whether you want to use only one of these films or some combination of the three.

**<u>The Films</u>: *Mrs. Doubtfire, Switch,* and *Tootsie.***

**<u>Scenes for Use in the Classroom</u>:** I recommend showing the class one scene from each film before doing any debriefing. You might have the class watch each film at home prior to the class discussion.

**<u>Questions for Discussion</u>**

1. **What does each central character learn about what it means to be a member of the opposite sex? Do they learn to empathize? How do they handle emotion?**

2. **Do men and women handle emotion differently? If so, how? What effect does this difference have on relationships?**

**<u>Assignment</u>:** Have the class write their responses in a short reaction or position paper and then have them discuss their observations, conclusions, and beliefs in small groups. Both of these questions are open questions. I do not believe that the answers, such as we have, are absolute or completely understood, so there is room for healthy discussion and debate. However, be prepared for some real dogmatic approaches to these questions.

## Mrs. Doubtfire, dir. Chris Columbus. With Robin Williams, Sally Field, Pierce Brosnan, Harvey Fierstein, Polly Holiday, 1993.

**<u>Brief Summary</u>:** The film is about a man who has trouble finding work as an actor and, as a result, he cannot see his children. As a solution, he poses as a matronly woman and gets the job as the children's nanny. His successful portrayal of an older woman leads him to discover things about himself that he did not know were there.

**<u>Scenes for Use in the Classroom</u>:** Show the scene in which Mrs. Doubtfire applies for the job as nanny.

## Switch, dir. Blake Edwards. With Ellen Barkin, Jimmy Smits, JoBeth Williams, Lorraine Bracco, Tony Roberts, Perry King, 1991.

**<u>Brief Summary</u>:** A sexist, philandering man is shot and killed. He immediately returns to earth as a woman and must learn to interact with his/her former friends as a woman.

**<u>Scenes for Use in the Classroom</u>:** Show the first series of scenes where our new woman is learning how to be a woman. In some ways this is a more honest portrayal of how difficult it would be to try to cross over to the other gender than occurs in the other films.

## Tootsie, dir. Sydney Pollack. With Dustin Hoffman, Jessica Lange, Teri Garr, Dabney Coleman, Charles Durning, Bill Murray, Sydney Pollack, Geena Davis, Estelle Getty, 1982.

**Brief Summary:** The film is about a man who has trouble finding work as an actor due to his dominating and demanding personality. As a solution, he poses as a woman in order to get a job on a television soap opera. His successful portrayal of the woman, both on and off camera, leads him to discover things about himself that he did not know were there. As Michael Dorsey puts it late in the film, he was "a better man as a woman."

**Scenes for Use in the Classroom:** Depending on time available and your course strategy on gender and diversity, you might begin with the opening sequence in which Dorsey goes from audition to audition trying to get work and his confrontation with his agent over his inflexible approach to work.

It is then useful to move to his audition as Dorothy. The comedy in this sequence is very good for maintaining class interest and for helping to point out areas for discussion. For example, when they ask if the camera can move further back, someone remarks, "How about Cleveland?" as a way of making a comment on her less attractive features. Discussion of society's high standard for female beauty (far different than for men) can come from this one remark.

Dorothy's interactions with her and Michael's friends offer good material for class discussion. However, some of the best material comes when Dorothy must fend off unwanted advances from men, such as the older male doctor. Of equal power are her conversations with her costar (Lange) and with Michael's girlfriend (Garr). Dorsey/Dorothy must learn about the inconsistencies of his behavior as a man and as a woman.

## Trading Places, dir. John Landis. With Eddie Murphy, Dan Ackroyd, Ralph Bellamy, Don Ameche, Denholm Elliot, Jamie Lee Curtis, 1983.

**Brief Summary:** Louis Winthorpe III (Ackroyd) works for major stockbrokers who toy with people's lives as a hobby. He has been raised in a world of wealth and privilege. Billy Ray Valentine (Murphy) plays a poor, slum raised thief and con artist. The Duke Brothers (Bellamy and Amechie) are the wealthy, manipulative stockbrokers. They place a bet to see what would happen if Winthorpe and Valentine had their circumstances reverse. Winthorpe is rejected by everyone who has previously cared about and for him. He winds up in desperate straits on the street and is befriended by a prostitute, Ophelia (Curtis). After trying to turn the tables on Valentine, Winthorpe tries to take back his own life. He is rescued by the timely arrival of Valentine who has just learned of the bet by the Dukes. After reuniting Winthorpe with his servant, Coleman (Elliot) and his home, the foursome set out to gain their revenge and set things right. The resulting comic interactions effectively dramatize the value of supportive behavior, empathy, and friendship.

**<u>IPC Concepts</u>:** Treating people as having intrinsic value and being worthy of respect vs. treating them as objects, ability to empathize, supporting behavior.

**<u>Scenes for Use in the Classroom</u>:** I recommend using a mixture of shots to set up each character, such as:

- Winthorpe and Ophelia shortly after they first meet talking on the street.
- Valentine's first day on the job when the Dukes explain their business to him.

**<u>Questions for Discussion</u>**

1. **How does Winthorpe change from his new life position?**

   Winthorpe is a more real, down to earth person. Prior to the switch he was an arrogant, uncaring twit. After the betrayal by the Dukes, he appreciates what he has and the people around him. He also has a more profound appreciation for the relationships in his life, including his friendship with Valentine and Coleman, and his affection for Ophelia. He also learns to be more genuine in his interactions with others. Instead of the stilted person from Harvard, he can now do the impression of the fellow from Camaroon.

2. **What does Valentine learn as a result of being in another person's shoes for a few days? What emotional experience is it for him to see the old life style contrast with the new on eat his "party" for the bar crowd?**

   Valentine has probably always wanted to improve himself, but he had no idea as to how to do it. After he sees that he can behave differently, he comes to respect some of the aspects of his new life. He realizes that the furnishings of his new home are worth protecting and caring for. He also realizes that his former crowd do not have the same attitude and he does not want to live like that anymore.

## Quantum Leap, television series, presently in syndication.

**<u>Brief Summary</u>:** The core of this series is that the central character must assume the persona of many different people from different times, places, and of different genders, races, and ages. In order to effectively "become" these people, he must learn to look through their eyes and walk in their shoes. An excellent ongoing presentation of the value of empathy.

**<u>IPC Concepts</u>:** Empathy. The whole point of this highly creative series is that the central character must learn who he is to become and how to behave and feel in his persona as that other person.

**<u>Use in the Classroom</u>:** I recommend asking the class the following question about almost any episode in this imaginative series.

**Questions for Discussion**

1. **What does Bakula learn about his new persona from walking around in the person's skin in each episode?**

    The main character must learn what made the person in question tick in order to fulfill his mission. It is a good illustration of the nature of empathy.

# *On the Stage*

## Burton Lane and E.Y. Harburg. (1960). Finian's Rainbow.

Whether you assign the play or the film version of this wonderful story, it is an excellent vehicle for dramatizing the importance of empathy.

**Brief Summary:** The play is a musical fantasy about racial injustice. This story is set in the south in the 1940s. An Irish immigrant, his daughter, their leprechaun, a pot of gold, and two young southern men run afoul of a wealthy, old, white aristocrat. As the story unfolds, one of the wishes granted by the pot of gold turns the old man into a black man. He then experiences what life is like for black people in the south. His newly discovered empathy gives him a unique perspective for the resolution of the play.

**IPC Concepts:** Empathy and diversity.

# *CNN*

## US Reaction to Princess Diana's Funeral, (1:55). CNN Interpersonal Communication Today, 1999, Volume 1.

The clip explores the process of empathy as Americans express their feelings about the death of Princess Diana. This tragedy functioned as a world-wide event that demonstrated Diana's power as a unifying symbol.

## Prozac For PMS, (1:38). CNN Interpersonal Communication Today, 1999, Volume 1.

This clip examines a report on the benefits of taking Prozac by some women who have very serious bouts with PMS. For one woman who is profiled, Prozac helps her to be able to control the emotional difficulties of this monthly hormonal swing. As she puts it, "I just felt like myself again." The clip helps to make the point that emotions are bio-chemical in nature. Our minds and our thoughts play the major role in controlling, selecting, changing, and handling our emotions. However, sometimes it can be helpful to use some modern chemistry to balance the emotional equation.

---

# *INTERPERSONAL COMMUNICATION THEORY IN LITERATURE AND ACADEMIC RESOURCES*

## *Theory Illustrated in Literature*

**John Howard Griffin. (1976). Black Like Me. Updated with epilogue for the author. New York: New American Library.**

**Brief Summary:** This is one of the most important books to emerge from the American Civil Rights Movement of the 1950s and 1960s. John Howard Griffin, a white man, had his skin pigmentation darkened so that he could pass as an African American and experience what life was really like for black people as he traveled around the south. His experiences present a fascinating discussion of what empathy can be like.

**IPC Concepts:** Empathy and diversity.

**Tim O'Brien. (1991). "The Things They Carried." *In Lives & Moments: An Introduction To Short Fiction*, Ed by Hans Ostrom. Fort Worth: Holt, Rinehart and Winston, Inc. pp. 583-596.**

**Brief Summary:** The story follows a small unit of soldiers in Vietnam. It focuses on their inner thoughts as they struggle to play their part in the war. They each manage to carry very few personal items with them into combat – items that remind them of their humanity, individuality, and hope for survival and peace. The items also serve as metaphors for the inner baggage that they carry.

**IPC Concepts:** Emotion, empathy and self-talk.

# *Academic Resources*

The following works can be very valuable extensions of the Interact textbook. Each one of them can add a great deal of insight to the student's understanding of the nature and power of emotion, and of the need to learn how to harness that power, and if necessary, to program or reprogram our emotional responses to life and relationships.

Goleman's works are a good place to start, as he has expanded the modern discussion of emotion and placed it on a par with the development of cognitive ability. Emotional Intelligence has a decent discussion of the nature of emotion. Cameron-Bandler adds the notion of emotion and freedom of choice. Building on the work of Adler and others, this book stresses the fact that we can choose our emotions and our emotional responses to situations.

Whether you assign these books as outside reading, book reports, oral assignments, etc., they will increase the student's understanding of emotion, and in turn make true empathy more likely to occur since the student will know what it is that they might be feeling.

**Daniel Goleman. (1995). Emotional Intelligence: Why It Can Matter More Than IQ. New York: Bantam Books.**

**Brief Summary:** Goleman's work advances the argument that emotion can function similar to intelligence for human development and maturity. He argues that we can have an emotional capacity just like we have a cognitive ability, an EQ like an IQ. Goleman explains that EQ is the inner dynamic that helps the individual develop self-control, confidence, persistence, and motivation. These capabilities can be taught when we are growing up. We can improve our EQ as we grow older as well. The concept of EQ helps us to explain why some people who are very intelligent do not seem to be able to function in life as well as people who are less intelligent. Goleman's work is filled with insight and helps balance our understanding of human development.

**IPC Concepts:** Self, emotion, self-talk.

**Daniel Goleman. (1998). Working With Emotional Intelligence. New York: Bantam Books.**

**Brief Summary:** This book further develops Goleman's theory of Emotional Intelligence by making specific application to the workplace. It is a valuable work for helping us to understand those with whom we work.

**IPC Concepts:** Self, empathy, emotion.

**Charles V. Roberts and Kittie W. Watson, eds. (1989). *Intrapersonal Communication Processes: Original Essays.* New Orleans: Spectra Incorporated, Publishers and Scottsdale, AZ: Gorsuch Scarisbrick, Publishers.**

**Brief Summary:** 24 essays dealing with the nature, characteristics, and approaches to intrapersonal communication. The articles discuss cognitive and psychological approaches, affective and non-conscious processes, and the role of listening in self-talk. Without being self-serving, I recommend my own article in this collection: "Freedom of Choice: Intrapersonal Communication and Emotion," p. 319-336.

**IPC Concepts:** self-talk.

**Cameron-Bandler, Leslie and Michael Lebeau. (1986). *The Emotional Hostage: Rescuing Your Emotional Life.* San Rafael, CA: FuturePace Inc.**

**Brief Summary:** Bandler and Lebeau offer a solid discussion of the nature of emotion as it relates to personal and interpersonal choices and patterns of behavior. Their focus is on the power of the individual to change their emotional life by choosing to do so. They examine the way in which our self-talk or inner speech allows us to be trapped by dysfunctional patterns of thinking. The end result is that we feel helpless to change the circumstances of our lives. By changing this kind of dysfunctional thinking and feeling, we can learn to reprogram ourselves and live with the power of emotional choice. This is a serious academic treatment of this subject matter.

**IPC Concepts:** Emotion, self-talk.

**Andrew LeCompte. (1999). Creating Harmonious Relationships: A Practical Guide to the Power of True Empathy.**

**Brief Summary:** This is a good resource for understanding how cognitive processes affect our behaviors and interactions with others. LeCompte discusses a variety of perspectives on the importance of understanding ourselves before we tackle our understanding of others. He discusses psychological research in the communication process, and offers illustrations with teenagers and coworkers.

**IPC Concepts:** Empathy – approaches, increasing ability, responding with understanding.

**Mark V. Redmond. (1985). The Relationship between perceived communication competence and perceived empathy. Communication Monographs, 52, 4, 377-382.**

**Brief Summary:** Redmond distinguishes the relationship between empathy and communication competence. He cites four dimensions of competence: behavioral flexibility, interaction management, support, and social relaxation. He offers an interesting definition of empathy, and stresses the need to carefully define it for both, research, and understanding the process.

**IPC Concepts:** Empathy – nature, relationship to competence.

## *What's on the Web*

**Annenberg CPB Project – Personality, Thoughts and Feelings: What Makes Us Who We Are?**
**http://www.learner.org/exhibits/personality/thoughts.html**

**Brief Summary:** Focus on thoughts and feelings and their relationship to behavioral trait, cognitive and emotional traits, and their role as the basis for many of our actions. The site also discusses the function of masks to hide our real self, and the corresponding difficulty in empathizing with others.

**IPC Concepts:** Approaches to empathy, increasing our ability to empathize, interpreting empathic cues.

**Empathy: Deepening your relationships**
**http://www.igc.apc.org/PeacePark/tslskc03.html**

**Brief Summary:** An interesting discussion on the nature and importance of empathy in relationships. It also has two exercises to help illustrate empathy. Also, some interesting metaphors for, and quotations about empathy.

**IPC Concepts:** Empathy – nature, importance, and ways to increase our ability.

**Empathy**
**http://www.utexas.edu/ftp/courses/kincaid/ddye/empath.html**

**Brief Summary:** A very nice poem on empathy. It illustrates the nature of empathy as one person describes it, by using a variety of metaphors for empathy.

**IPC Concepts:** nature of empathy.

# CHAPTER NINE

# Communication Climate: Self-Disclosure and Feedback

## INTERPERSONAL COMMUNICATION IN ACTION

Chapter Nine of Interact explores self-disclosure in interpersonal relationships. This chapter of the Media Guide will present examples of self-disclosure from four films. Each of these films depicts the nature and power of disclosure in relationships, ranging from high school kids, to young men, to senior citizens, to parent-child, and that deal with issues like racial tensions, aging fears, gender and gender selection, etc. The interactions in *Breakfast Club*, for example, presents how disclosure can be beneficial in building relationships, as well as some of the cautions that should be taken when engaging in self-disclosure. *On Golden Pond* illustrates the power of self-disclosure in building relationships. This film also illustrates the kind of disclosure issues and concerns experienced by older people.

## LEARNING OBJECTIVES

- Increase the student's understanding of the nature, value, and dangers of self-disclosure in interpersonal relationships.
- Students should know the guidelines for self-disclosure and how to apply them.
- Deepen the student's ability to describe one's feelings in a relational context.
- Increase the student's ability to make an effective praise statement.
- Increase the student's ability to recognize and evaluate effective and ineffective criticism in interpersonal relationships.

| In Classroom Assignments | For Homework |
| --- | --- |
| - Small Group Discussion | - Position Papers |
| - Whole class discussion | - Relationship Analysis Papers |
| - Role Play Exercises | - Web Exercises to supplement textbook and Instructor's Manual exercise |
| - Conversation exercises | - Journal Entries |

# *VISUALLY PRESENTED INTERPERSONAL COMMUNICATION THEORY*

## *IN MOVIES*

**Breakfast Club: dir. John Hughes. With Emilio Estevez, Judd Nelson, Molly Ringwald, Anthony Michael Hall, Ally Sheedy, Paul Gleason, 1985.**

**Brief Summary:** A group of five high school students spend a Saturday in detention under the supervision of an angry, disrespectful, burned-out teacher. We slowly come to know their real names. We know them as the Jock (Andrew Clark, played by Emilio Estevez), the Princess (Claire Standish played by Molly Ringwald), the Delinquent (John Bender played by Judd Nelson), the Brain (Brian Johnson played by Anthony Michael Hall), and the Weirdo (Allison Reynolds played by Ally Sheedy).

While initially presented as a group of stereotyped students, they each disclose enough information to become real, flesh and blood individuals to each other and to the viewer. We see their initial interactions marked by the Delinquent's efforts to dominate and intimidate the group. He is met by resistance from the Jock, who doesn't want to appear weak, and by the Princess, who doesn't want to appear afraid of this low-class person. The disgruntled and abusive teacher (Richard Vernon played by Paul Gleason) provides the group with a common enemy. Led by the Delinquent and his self-sacrificing actions on behalf of the group, each character begins to open up and reach out to the others. The students are initially at odds with each other. They each come from a different student clique at the school. After several instances of conflict between the students, the group slowly opens up to each other. We learn about the abuse suffered by the Delinquent from his father, the pressure to succeed from the Jock's father, the social expectations placed upon the Princess, the pressure to be perfect in school placed on the Brain, and the lack of any interest by the parents of the Weirdo – as she describes her parents to the Jock, "they ignore me."

Eventually, each student finds something good in each of the other students. They each do something unique to their own abilities for the good of the group. Self-disclosure serves as the climax of the story.

This film transcends time and generations in its ability to resonate with a wide range of student age groups.

**IPC Concepts:** Sense of the self, self-esteem, self-concept, self-disclosure, relationship building, conflict, diversity, expression of emotion.

**Scenes for Use in the Classroom:** The opening sequence introduces us to the stereotypical view of each student. As the students interact with each other, we see them presenting themselves with the use of social masks. The delinquent is particularly harsh in his treatment of the other students, especially with the princess in whom he is particularly interested. The abusive behavior of the Delinquent is vividly demonstrated during the lunch scene.

As the group interacts throughout the day, they begin to break down their masks and must present their real selves. A scene that illustrates both, the notion of self and the power of self-disclosure, is one toward the end of the film in which each student must open up and tell the others what they are afraid of, and why they are in detention.

## Questions for Discussion

1. **The self-disclosure scenes in this film are a mixture of appropriate and inappropriate disclosure. Using the guidelines for appropriate self-disclosure in *Interact*, describe and evaluate the disclosure in *The Breakfast Club*.**

   Initial disclosure occurs due to anger and self-defense on the part of John Bender, the Delinquent. He is trying to make the others realize just how bad he has it in life. He is not the least bit interested in relationship building. His anger toward Claire seems to mask his interest in her. He wants to make her less spoiled so that she can learn to like him. As Bender has disclosed so much about his horrible relationship with his father throughout the day, he is largely silent about himself during the climatic disclosure scene.

   When the group starts to open up, they disclose some pretty private information. It is clear that they do so in order to be fair with one another. When Andrew (Jock) convinces Allison (Weirdo) to open up, he does so by telling her about himself and by showing her that he knows the right questions. He also talks to her in encouraging, sympathetic vocal tones and facial expressions.

   The disclosure from Andrew (Jock) and Brian (Brain) comes out after some pressure and in the midst of an angry eruption from each boy. Andrew reveals his own poor relationship with his father. Dad pressures him to win, win, win! He admits that he was the one who taped the fat kid's buns together. However he is ashamed of doing it, since he knows how humiliated the boy would have been when he went home and had to show his father and admit that he had been unable prevent this from happening to him. Brian reveals that he had considered suicide as a result of flunking shop.

   Claire's disclosure only comes out as a result of intense pressure from John, Andrew, and Allison. She hides behind so many masks that the group believes it to be in her best interest to be a more real, honest person. The process is hardly appropriate as they apply intense pressure to her in the form of ridicule, coercion, and humiliation.

   The group appears to give little thought to the guideline of on-going relationships. As teenagers, their thought is mostly for the moment. The one clue that they are thinking about the future comes when one group member asks if they will go back to their old patterns of relating to each other, namely, within the walls of their individual social cliques.

2. **Why does each member of the group gain acceptance and respect from the rest of the group as a result of their self-disclosure?**

Each member of the group has a superficial view of the others based on their very limited interaction during the regular school week. They look at each other as members of other cliques with no other defining or interesting features. In fact, Bender leads his attacks on each of the others based on this superficial view.

As each person discloses information about who they are and why they are in detention, a basic level of acceptance begins to develop. Bender's disclosure initially makes the group feel uncomfortable, as no one asked him to tell them such negative news. However, as he sacrifices himself for the sake of the group, they begin to respect and understand him. As the others open up, their personal pain allows the other members of the group to identify, accept, and respect them.

## How to Make an American Quilt, dir. Jocelyn Moorehouse. With Winona Ryder, Ellen Burstyn, Anne Bancroft, Maya Angelou, Kate Nelligan, Jean Simmons, Alfre Woodard, Kate Capshaw, Claire Danes, 1995.

**Brief Summary:** The movie adaptation of the novel by Whitney Otto. Finn (Winona Ryder), a young woman who is engaged to be married and is writing her master thesis for the third time – she keeps on changing her mind about the topic – goes to her grandmother and great aunt's home for the summer. Her grandmother, Hy (Ellen Burstyn); her great aunt, Glady Jo (Anne Bancroft); and five other women – Anna (Maya Angelou); Sophia (Loius Smith); Em (Jean Simmons); Constance (Kate Nelligan); and Marianna (Alfre Woodard) form a quilting group. The women's next project is a quilt to be given to Finn as a wedding present. The theme of the quilt is: where love resides. Each woman is to make a square that depicts where their love resides. Anna, who is the coordinator of the quilt and the group, explains that her job is to bring them – each piece of the quilt – together in a balanced and harmonious design – which is also the metaphor for the movie. Throughout the movie Finn learns the stories of each of the women's love stories and past as they disclose their stories to her.

**IPC Concepts:** Disclosure, friendship, communication barriers.

**Scenes for Use in the Classroom:**

- Opening scene. Finn narrates and explains the set-up of the story.
- Finn's grandmother and her great aunt tell Finn about her grandmother's affair with her great aunt's husband and the consequences of that incident on the relationship of the two sisters.
- Any of the scenes of the women telling Finn their particular stories.
- After the storm when Glady Jo finally tears down the wall in the laundry- room, breaking down the barrier between her and her sister after all the years of resentment.

**Questions for Discussion**

1. **How does disclosure play a part in each woman's story? Why is the Quilt a safe way to disclose?**

   As each woman discloses the background to their part of the quilt, they disclose something very personal. This is possible for them because the quilt serves a neutral focal point for the disclosure. Rather than feel like the individual woman is on display with her soul being open to the world, the woman disclosing can talk about the quilt almost as if telling a story about someone else.

2. **How does the disclosure help to build relationships?**

   In the case of Hy and Glady Jo, Hy's disclosure is the first time that Glady Jo has heard the real story of Hy's brief affair with her husband. Armed with the facts, Glady Jo is finally able to deal with her anger and forgive her sister. The same can be said for Em and Constance with the additional benefit that Em also learns about her husband's depth of love for her. Two different relationships benefit from the disclosure.

## Diner, dir. Barry Levinson. With Steve Guttenberg, Daniel Stern Mickey Rourke, Kevin Bacon, Timothy Daly, Ellen Barkin, Paul Reiser, 1982.

**Brief Summary:** A terrific case study for the analysis of conversation. A group of friends meet regularly in a Baltimore diner and discuss their lives, the problems of growing up, the fun they have had, and their concerns about life. The group includes Eddie (Guttenberg), Shrevie (Stern), Boogie (Rourke), Tim (Bacon), Billy (Daly), Modell (Reiser), and the almost member Beth (Barkin), Shrevie's wife.
It is a good vehicle for studying conversation techniques.

**IPC Concepts:** Self-disclosure and relationship development.

**Scenes for Use in the Classroom:**

- Eddie talking to Boogie about his fears over getting married
- Boogie talking to Beth about her marriage

**Questions for Discussion**

1. **Discuss the extent to which real disclosure occurs in dyadic conversation rather than in the full group. Why do you think this occurs? How does this reinforce the basic guidelines for self-disclosure?**

   Real disclosure and conversation over life concerns only occurs in dyads. The group is too much about image, self-image, and being one-up. In dyads, the individual young men can allow themselves to be vulnerable and in need of counseling from their friend.

   Self-disclosure guidelines advocate a safe context in which what a person says can be confided without fear of ridicule or manipulation. The dyadic context is clearly the appropriate setting for the characters in the diner to disclose their fears.

2. **How does Boogie handle Beth's disclosure about her marriage? Note how his respect for the information and her marriage helps him decide to not have sex with her.**

Boogie knows that within the group he is free to say a variety of things to each of the others. He knows that the topics of their conversations are rarely about anything really important. However, he also realizes that when he speaks with an individual alone, that the rules change and that those discussions must be held to a higher standard, to real respect and confidentiality.

## On Golden Pond, dir. Mark Rydell. Henry Fonda, Katherine Hepburn, Jane Fonda, Doug McKeon, and Dabney Coleman, 1981.

**Brief Summary:** The story is about Norman Thayer (Henry Fonda), a retired schoolteacher who is approaching his 80th birthday, and about his anger and fear of the effect of the aging process on his faculties and ability to function. He and his wife, Ethel Thayer (Katherine Hepburn), are visited at their summer cottage by their daughter, Chelsea (Jane Fonda), her fiancé (Dabney Coleman), and soon to be stepson, Billy (Doug McKeon). The stepson stays with Norman and Ethel for the summer, while Chelsea and her fiancé travel to Europe. Norman and Billy teach each other a lot about fishing, conflict, and each other's perspectives on life. Billy introduces Norman to the slang of his generation (watch for "suck face"), while Norman introduces Billy to Long John Silver and fishing. Upon her return, Chelsea and Norman have a long overdue confrontation about their relationship.

Self-disclosure plays an important role in the film in two places. In the opening sequence, Norman has gotten lost amongst his own trees looking for strawberries. After he returns, he pretends everything is fine and gives Charley a hard time. After Charley leaves, Norman angrily confides to Ethel that the reason he came back so quickly is because he was lost and afraid. He also notes that he needed to see her pretty face so that he would know that he was safe and still himself. The disclosure tightens the bond between Norman and Ethel.

Near the end of the story Norman and Chelsea discuss their feelings toward each other. This is very difficult for them, as they have a lot of baggage from their father-daughter past that interferes with closeness. Chelsea initiates the conversation and Norman responds defensively. Chelsea is shocked to hear that her father's perception of their relationship is that he thinks they just do not like each other. Norman, however, tries to make a connection by asking if she would come around more often if they got along better. He says it would mean a lot to her mother. His insecurity and baggage prevent him from being any more honest about his own desire to see more of her. Chelsea is able to see through the shield and briefly and gently touches his forearm, a significant amount of touching for the two of them.

**IPC Concepts:** Self-esteem, perception of self and others, self-talk, emotion, and conflict. Note the probable self-talk when Norman is lost in the woods. Also, note his disclosure to Ethel about being lost in the woods and his admission to Chelsea about his feelings toward her.

**Scenes for Use in the Classroom:**

- Sequence with Norman, Ethel, and Charley discussing Chelsea's upcoming visit, followed by Norman and Ethel on the porch.
- Chelsea returns from Europe and confronts Norman about their relationship.

**Questions for Discussion**

1. **Discuss Norman's disclosure to Ethel about his fear of aging and her response. How clearly did he express his feelings? How well did she handle his vulnerability?**

   Norman's intense feelings lead him to a clear statement of his fears. Normally he maintains sufficient self-control to keep his shields in place. He leaves it up to others to try to translate what he might be feeling.

   Ethel is very good at reading what her husband is feeling, having many years of marriage to instruct her. She holds him and tells him just what he needs to hear. When he ultimately responds with a joke, she jokes right back to him.

2. **Comment on Norman's inability to express his feelings clearly to Chelsea. He seems only able to express anger and sarcasm. How does Chelsea understand his real feelings?**

   Chelsea is clearly hurt by his caustic remark, but she looks at his total posture. He is looking down, pinches his eyes together to block a tear, and ever so slightly, extends his left forearm to her. Chelsea is a good listener as she listens to the whole person. Clearly his words and his actions are inconsistent. Chelsea takes the body language as the more accurate expression of his true feelings.

   Norman reflects the upbringing of many men who are not taught how to experience, manage, or express their feelings. He wanted to have a son and in a passive aggressive manner took out his frustration on his daughter. Billy has helped to fill this void and now Norman is just barely able to begin to make peace with Chelsea.

## Boyz in the Hood, dir. John Singleton. Larry Fishburne, Ice Cube, Cuba Gooding Jr., Nia Long, Morris Chestnut, Tyra Ferrell, Angela Bassett, 1991.

**Brief Summary:** This is the story of the struggle to survive in the black section of south central L.A. Fishburne plays Furious Styles who tries to give his son, Tre, the values that will help him to live a better life. The story begins with a young Tre getting into a fight at school and then moving in with his father so as to be given guidance, as his mother puts it, on "how to be a man." We follow him settling into the new home and watching his friend Doughboy being taken by the police for stealing.

After seven years, we rejoin the story with Tre attending a party welcoming Doughboy back from jail. Tre is trying to live according to his father's values amid the challenges of the violence of his neighborhood. Ricky is trying to get into college to play football, while coping with the pressures of being a teenage father. The SAT test is a major challenge to his ability to achieve his goal. Furious, Tre's father, is an advocate for community pride, integrity, and African-American culture.

An ongoing feud with a neighborhood gang leads to the shooting death of Ricky. In his rage Tre wants to shoot the perpetrator, but his father intercepts him and talks him out of it for the moment. Tre sneaks out and joins Doughboy as they hunt for the killer. Tre opts out of the car, but Darren leads his other friends and kills three gang members. Doughboy talks to Tre about staying out of the violence. His overall mood and his obvious pain tells Tre that he found and killed the killer. Doughboy's disclosure takes place on a couple of levels.

**IPC Concepts:** Self-disclosure, feelings: expressing, displaying, and withholding.

**Scenes for Use in the Classroom:**

- Tre and Rick in the car on the way to football practice. Tre discloses that he is still a virgin because he is afraid of being a father.
- Tre visits his girlfriend after being humiliated by an African American policeman. Tre explodes in anger and then breaks down crying. His demonstration of vulnerability leads to the couple having sex.

**Questions for Discussion**

1. **When Tre discloses his feelings about being a virgin, Ricky laughs at him. What effect would the laughter have on his feelings and on his willingness to disclose in the future?**

   In all likelihood, Tre would at least be reluctant before disclosing anything that personal or intimate again. Since the two young men are very close, he would certainly be willing to confide in his best friend. But both young men have been enculturated to hide their feelings. They are allowed to express feelings about sports or attractive women.

2. **What does Tre's emotional eruption after his humiliation by the police reveal about his ability to handle emotion? How does he handle his feelings? Does he express them clearly to Brandi? Does he know any more about dealing with feelings than Doughboy?**

   Tre has been taught to keep his emotions in check. Furious knows that uncontrolled emotion results in unnecessary violence and death. Tre has strong emotional reactions to the world in which he lives, but he keeps most of these feelings bottled up inside. As the neighborhood continues to eat away at him, it only takes one more insult or hurt to move him to breaking. Brandi senses this moment. She keeps out of the way as she knows that some men express emotion by shouting. Once his fury wanes, she is able to help him deal with his pain and frustration. However, because Tre has been taught to keep his feelings in, he is not much better prepared to deal with them than Doughboy. His saving grace is that he has stronger boundaries on the limits of acceptable behavior.

3. **How does Doughboy express his feelings to Tre after he shoots the killer of his brother Ricky?**

Tre can sense the difference in Doughboy's overall posture. Doughboy is normally brash, tough, even loud. Now he approaches Tre in a quiet, gentle manner. He speaks softly and with a slight glint of moisture in his eyes. Tre knows where he was going on the previous evening and recognizes the changes in his childhood friend. He has a fatalistic attitude about himself and his disclosure.

## *CNN*

### High-Tech Job Interviews. (1:47). CNN Human Communication Today, 1999, Volume 1

The segment examines the changing dynamics of interviewing in the 90s as a result of new video technology. CityBank donated a video conferencing system to over 30 universities. The bank used to spend about $1,000 per interview, due to expenses incurred while traveling to each campus. The video conferencing costs about $13 plus $60 per hour to run. Companies save $800-900 per interview.

## *On the Stage*

### Alfred Uhry. (1987). Driving Miss Daisy.

**Brief Summary:** This play, like the movie, is a powerful illustration of the role and value of disclosure in a developing relationship. At first, Daisy keeps Hoke at a great distance, not even willing to discuss family photos on the wall. As Daisy and Hoke become more familiar and interdependent, their disclosure deepens and their friendship intensifies.

**IPC Concepts:** Disclosure and masking feelings, displaying feelings; disclosure and relationship building.

# *Interpersonal Communication Theory in Literature and Academic Resources*

## *Theory Illustrated in Literature*

**William Styron. (1979) Sophie's Choice. New York: Random House.**

**Brief Summary:** This story is a powerful one, as Sophie moves from a fun-loving, carefree woman in playful romantic relationships, to the mother who has to make the most difficult choice that a mother can make. The role of disclosure in both relationships, and personal mental health and well-being, is clearly dramatized.

**IPC Concepts:** Relationships and self-disclosure, masking and displaying feelings.

## *Academic Resources*

**Lawrence W. Hugenberg, Sr. and Mark J. Schaefermeyer. (1983). Soliloquy as Self-Disclosure. The Quarterly Journal of Speech, 69, 2, 187-187.**

**Brief Summary:** This article examines the nature of disclosure in research, and argues that much can be learned about the nature of disclosure by studying its use in dramatic literature. The authors analyze the soliloquy as Shakespeare uses it in Richard III and Henry III. Good examples and an interesting argument.

**IPC: Concepts:** Self-disclosure, nature, qualities and types.

## ***What's on the Web***

### Annenberg CPB Project: Sincerity and Deception: How You Present Yourself

**http://www.learner.org/exhibits/personality/thoughts_sub.html**

**Brief Summary:** An excellent discussion of the role of masks to protect from self-disclosure. The site discusses the relationship between masks and the true self. The Johari Window is also presented and explained. This site can serve as a useful reinforcement for the class discussion of disclosure viz a viz the Johari Window.

**IPC Concepts:** Self-disclosure, masks, self-presentation.

### Interpersonal Communication: Self-Disclosure by Tim Borchers, Moorhead State University

**http://www.abacon.com/commstudies/interpersonal/indisclosure.html**

**Brief Summary:** This web site is part of a series of six web sites on interpersonal communication. This site contains an excellent and concise overview of self-disclosure, its functions, its risks, and role in the Johari Window. There is a good exercise and an excellent set of references.

**IPC Concepts:** self-disclosure: nature, functions, risks.

### The Six Steps To Self-Disclosure: A Guide For The Sender, by Marty Crouch, Pastoral Counselor.

**http://www.martycrouch.com/Disclosure.html**

**Brief Summary:** A good, simple reinforcement for some basics of the process of disclosure framed in terms of assertiveness theory. The chart offers examples of five different types of content for disclosure.

**IPC Concepts:** Self-disclosure and assertiveness, describing feelings and opinions.

**Self-Disclosure of HIV Infection to Sexual Partners after Repeated Counseling. Perry, S. W., C. A. L. Card, et al. AIDS Education & Prevention 1994; 6(5): 403-411.**
**http://hivinsite.ucsf.edu/topics/testing/2098.366e.html**

**Brief Summary**: Abstract of journal article on an important aspect of self-disclosure in relationships dealing with a serious illness or a contagious medical condition.

**IPC Concepts:** Disclosure and ethics.

# CHAPTER TEN
# Conflict Management

## Interpersonal Communication In Action

The Interact text discusses conflict in chapter eleven. The Media Guide will illustrate the dynamics of conflict and interpersonal communication by suggesting films that showcase conflict and diversity, and conflict and decision-making. Spike Lee's masterpiece, *Do the Right Thing*, dramatizes the complexity of inter-racial relations. *Guess who's Coming to Dinner* shows how superficial and decorative beliefs can be until they are genuinely put to the test when a white, liberal family in the 1960s must decide what they really believe in when faced with their daughter's announcement that she will marry a black man. The film demonstrates its depth, as it also raises the same issues from the point of view of the black man's family.

*Twelve Angry Men* is an excellent case study in conflict, interpersonal and small group dynamics. The film brilliantly presents a myriad of personalities, communication styles, and conflict issues. *Big Chill* also offers the ensemble of personality and communication styles. This group also haves considerable history dating back from their college days, but their values have changed, and they must come to terms with changes in their old friends. *The War of the Roses* offers an example of relational conflict at its worst and most destructive. *Torch Song Trilogy* explores conflict over gender selection and diversity.

Several analytical issues will be addressed with each film: types of conflict, styles of managing conflict, relevant communication skills, including compliance gaining strategies and assertiveness.

If you are pressed for time or only wish to use one or two films on conflict, I recommend *Do The Right Thing* and *Twelve Angry Men*. These are the most complete presentations of interpersonal conflict that I can recommend. They both treat issues of diversity, albeit in very different ways.

## LEARNING OBJECTIVES

- Increase the student's understanding of the nature and types of conflict.
- Increase the student's awareness and understanding of styles of responding to conflict.
- Increase student ability in recognizing and evaluating communication skills necessary for initiating and responding to conflict.
- Increase student understanding of the guidelines for managing conflict.

| **In Classroom Assignments** | **For Homework** |
|---|---|
| - Small Group Discussion | - Position Papers |
| - Whole class discussion | - Relationship Analysis Papers |
| - Role Play Exercises | - Web Exercises to supplement textbook and Instructor's Manual exercise |
| - Conversation exercises | - Journal Entries |

# *VISUALLY PRESENTED INTERPERSONAL COMMUNICATION THEORY*

## *IN MOVIES*

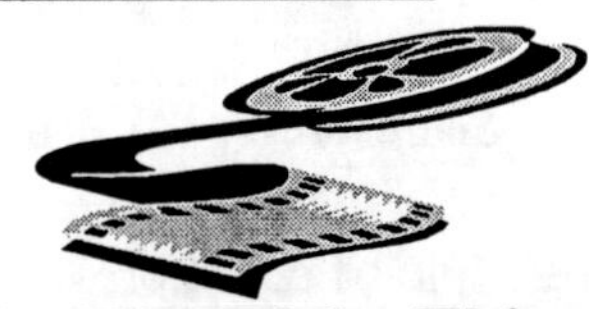

**Do The Right Thing, dir. Spike Lee. With Spike Lee, Danny Aiello, Ossie Davis, Ruby Dee, Richard Edson, Rosie Perez, John Torturro, Bill Nunn, 1989.**

**Brief Summary:** This is a powerful story of racial diversity, racial animosity, tension, conflict, and the value question of what is meant by doing the right thing. The film is about a hot summer in Bedford-Stuyvesant in Brooklyn. The basic plot involves a successful, white-owned pizza restaurant in an otherwise poor, black neighborhood. The owner Sal (Aiello) believes that his pizzeria owes nothing to the people of the neighborhood, except to serve excellent pizza. Spike Lee plays Mookie, a pizza deliverer, who, on a hot summer day, gets caught up in the middle of tension between Aiello and the community. Mookie must determine what the da Mayor (Davis) means by "do the right thing." The need for this understanding increases as Buggin Out (Esposito) keeps putting pressure on Sal. When Buggin Out recruits Radio Hakeem (Nunn) to join his boycott, the crisis quickly becomes very real.
Mookie also faces conflict from Tina (Perez), the mother of his child. Da Mayor is constantly yelled at by Mother Sister (Dee).

**IPC Concepts:** Conflict – pseudo, value, ego, styles, emotion, language.

**Scenes for Use in the Classroom:**

- Mother Sister yelling at da Mayor on the stoop of her building.
- Buggin Out arguing with Sal over the lack of African American pictures on the wall of the pizzeria.
- The final confrontation between Sal and Buggin Out and Radio Hakeem

**Questions for Discussion**

1. **Discuss the types of conflict in the film?**

   This film is a masterpiece of good writing. It exhibits all forms of conflict.

   Pseudo conflict occurs when Sal refuses to compromise with the community and put both Italian and African American and Hispanic photos on the wall. It also occurs when Sal responds with intense anger to Radio Hakeem's radio volume rather than showing respect and asking him politely to turn it down.

   Fact conflict occurs over the realities of racial differences between Sal and his son.

Value conflict occurs frequently in the film as Sal places different value on his vusiness than his older son Tito. It also occurs when Buggin Out clashes with both Sal and Mookie over the right thing to do regarding neighborhood recognition and pride.

Ego conflict occurs when Sal clashes with Buggin Out; when Tito clashes with almost everyone; when Radio Hakeem clashes with Sal.

2. **How does each character manage conflict? Which are more effective? What does their conflict style reveal about the person?**

Most characters in the story demonstrate the forcing style of conflict management. Mookie and da Mayor are definitely exceptions to the rule as they both try to collaborate, accommodate, or withdraw when appropriate. Mookie only resorts to forcing when he feels himself pushed into the corner as when his sister seems to be submitting to Sal and when he throws the trash can into Sal's window.

3. **Describe the evidence for passive, aggressive, and assertive behavior in this story.**

Sal, Tito, Buggin Out, and Radio Hakeem exhibit the aggressive style of conflict. They all have very little respect for the object of their conflict and try to run it over.

Mookie exhibits the most style flexibility. He is occasionally passive as when he puts up with the abuse from Sal on occasion. He is assertive when he asks Sal for his pay at two different junctures in the story. He is aggressive when he confronts Sal about his sister.

## Guess Who's Coming To Dinner, dir. Stanley Kramer. With Spencer Tracy, Katharine Hepburn, Sidney Poitier, 1967.

**Brief Summary:** When a young, white girl returns from Europe with her fiancé, her liberal family is thrown into chaos because the fiancé is black. Her father (Spencer Tracy) tries to mask his racial reaction under concern for practical considerations. Her mother (Katharine Hepburn), after an initial negative response, is very supportive. Even the African-American maid is opposed. The fiancé (Sidney Poitier) is an internationally recognized doctor who came from very humble surroundings. His parents also join the family for dinner. A series of conversations ensue, in which the parents try to discourage the couple from getting married. Each conversation illustrates pseudo-conflict, value, and ego conflict, styles of managing conflict, as well as approaches to influencing others, and the handling of emotion. As the climax of the film approaches, Poitier and Tracy engage in a set of conversations that make this film a classic.

**IPC Concepts:** Conflict – pseudo, value, ego, styles, emotion, language.

**Scenes for Use in the Classroom:**

- The daughter's announcement of her engagement and of her fiancé.

- Each parent's response to the engagement, including the parents of the groom.
- Each father's argument with the groom and the groom's response to his father.
- The groom's mother talking to Spencer Tracy toward the end of the film.
- Spencer Tracy's final soliloquy.

**Questions for Discussion**

1. **Discuss the types of conflict in the film. Many factual claims are made by both fathers. Are they really advancing a fact-based argument or a value-based argument?**

All four types of argument are at work in the film. There is the pseudo conflict regarding whether the couple must get married immediately. Without this conflict there would probably not be a movie. But this is a good example of a decision that does not have to be made this quickly.

A variety of examples of factual conflict emerge. Pure facts are rarely in question, but their interpretation is often challenged. What is the parental responsibility toward the children? What is the child's responsibility or debt toward the parents?

Value conflict is the most frequent type of conflict depicted in the film. The children value their relationship, their love, and their confidence in the trust they share in each other. The fathers value what is best for their children and their role as provider for, and protector of, their children. Both fathers are concerned about the problems due to racial prejudice that the marriage will face. The mothers place most importance on their children's happiness and love. They both see past the day-to-day racial problems and choose to focus on the love and closeness that the couple will share. The clash over happiness versus fear of problems becomes the central issue between the parents.

Ego conflict seems to emerge as the underlying value for the fathers. The mothers seem to understand this, especially the groom's mother. She confronts Tracy in a most eloquent speech. As a result of this speech and a conversation with the groom, Tracy seems to have a personal epiphany and he makes a speech to the entire group in which he clarifies the conflict and resolves the major issues.

2. **How does each character manage conflict? Which are more effective? What does their conflict style reveal about the person?**

The major characters are the bride and groom-to-be and the four parents. The bride is a young, idealistic, young woman, the child of wealthy liberal parents. She reflects her optimism and idealism in her choice of a husband and life partner. She cannot believe that her parents will object to her choice as they have preached racial equality her entire life. She essentially withdraws from most of the conflict with the belief that it will simply go away.

The bride's mother is initially opposed to the marriage, but she quickly changes her opinion in favor of her daughter's love and happiness. She is a good example of the accommodating style.

The father of the bride is confronted with a myriad of emotions. He is forced to face the negative side of his own liberalism and, he must choose what he really believes. Is he really this accepting of racial equality or does he really harbor racist feelings? Is he really just concerned about the happiness and safety of his daughter? Tracy's approach is a mixture of the forcing and collaborating styles. He argues his opposition to the marriage most forcefully to everyone involved. He also engages in several conversations in which he tries to problem solve and persuade the others.

The father of the groom blends forcing and accommodating styles of management. He argues with his wife, his son, and Tracy. When he seems to be losing, especially after his son confronts him in a very forceful manner, he withdraws almost completely. Only his facial anger is evident to reflect his feelings.

The mother of the groom is most concerned with her son's happiness. Her opinion is in favor of her son's love and happiness, hence, she favors the marriage. She is a good example of the accommodating style. She does illustrate the collaborating style in her final conversation with Tracy.

The groom is very collaborative in his approach. He listens to all of the others and is very respectful of their feelings and opinions. He demonstrates the accommodating style when he strikes a deal with Tracy that he will not go through with the marriage if Tracy finally objects to it.

3. **Describe the evidence for passive, aggressive, and assertive behavior in this story.**

The two passive characters in the film are the bride and her mother. While they are both respectful of the father/husband, they are not really active in advocating their position and seem content to let events take their course.

The fathers are closer to being aggressive than anyone else. They are not abusively aggressive, but they are genuinely forceful in advocating their position.

The groom and his mother are the most consistently assertive characters in the story. They advocate their own feelings while respecting those of all the others. The father of the bride finally demonstrates his own assertiveness during his closing soliloquy. While it would normally seem like an I-It type of monologue, Tracy develops each idea within the context of each relationship and with a complete sense of respect for each person.

4. **In what way does Tracy's final speech function as both an assertive effort to persuade the others and a form of self-talk to help him resolve his own feelings?**

Tracy reviews the issues in the situation in a thorough and chronological manner. He recalls the announcement and the initial responses of himself, his wife, and their daughter. He notes the changes in attitude, sometimes with humor, sometimes with a light touch of sarcasm, but always with caring concern. He reflects on his own opposition and finally on his own epiphany. This soliloquy is of interest in terms of film history as it is the final film that Spencer Tracy made before his death. He was sick during most of the filming of the movie.

5. **What would the situation be today if these two people made the same announcement to their parents? Would they still face the same opposition? On the same grounds?**

This is a good question for the class. It should tap into their feelings and possibly their experience. American society has undergone considerable changes since 1967, and yet, interracial relationships still face considerable racial prejudice and subtle opposition and harassment. Two very good friends of mine must go to emergency separately in order to be treated with prompt attention. If the white woman goes with her African American husband, she receives radically different treatment.

## Twelve Angry Men, dir. Sidney Lumet. With Henry Fonda, Lee J. Cobb, Ed Begley, E.G. Marshall, Jack Klugman, Jack Warden, Martin Balsam, John Fielder, George Voskovec, Robert Webber, Edward Binns, Joseph Sweeney, 1957.

**Brief Summary:** This is a powerful story of 12 jurors trying to determine the verdict in a murder trial. We only see the defendant once at he beginning of the film when the judge is giving instructions to the jury. We also only see the evidence through the jury-room debate.

When the jury is in the jury room, the group decides on procedures for arriving at a verdict. The foreman handles the secret ballot and the first vote is 11 guilty votes and 1 not guilty vote. Fonda is the only not-guilty vote. Fonda then leads an effort to examine all of the evidence and issues surrounding the trial. He is able to force the jury to change its perception of their responsibility, of the accused, and of each other. In the process, every person in the room is forced to examine their values, their beliefs, and their attitude toward justice. The balance of the film is about the deliberations and conflicts that eventually result in a unanimous verdict for acquittal.

This film illustrates a fascinating mixture of communicator types. It is a very rich resource for a communication course, whether the focus is interpersonal, small groups, argumentation theory, or legal communication. I have used the film to illustrate group interaction, leadership styles, decision-making procedures, value versus policy debate, etc. For interpersonal communication, I recommend examining the types of conflict, the personality variables of the group, the communication style of the group, and their level of assertiveness.

**IPC Concepts:** Every type of conflict is in evidence. Also, stereotyping, emotion, styles of conflict, styles of communication, personality, listening, etc. This is a blockbuster film for communication theory. You would think that someone wrote it just for communication classes.

**Scenes for Use in the Classroom:** This may be one of those rare exceptions to the rule, where you may want to show the entire film. I would only do this with breaks for processing. Give the class the analytical variables to use when watching and the discussion questions for debriefing and then guide their watching by stopping during and after major interactions.

- The initial episode with the knife
- The discovery of the man from the ghetto
- The "assault" on the elderly juror
- The challenge between the juror with the son and Fonda
- The group's hostile rejection of the racist, hostile man
- The review of the woman with glasses testimony, and the juror who never sweats
- The final confrontation with the juror who is angry with his own son

## Questions for Discussion

**1. Discuss the types of conflict in the film.**

There are numerous conflicts over facts in this film. The jury must determine what evidence is a real fact and what evidence is conjecture about a fact. The existence of a duplicate of the knife is a good example. The proper manner for holding the switch knife is a good example. The length of time for the elderly witness to make it from his bedroom to the door is a good example of reconstructing an event in order to determine the factual elements of the incident.

Values are a major source of conflict in this film. The hostile elderly juror does not believe in "those" people. He believes himself to be superior to the poor, to immigrants, to anyone different from himself. Fonda and the foreign juror value truth, fairness, compassion, and doing the right thing. Several of the jurors share his general value system. One juror is particularly quick to defend the kindly, elderly juror from insult or attack from two of the more rude jurors. The juror with the son is filled with anger and is opposed to any sign of compassion.

Ego plays a major role in the jury room conflict. Several jurors place a great deal of importance on protecting their egos. The juror with a son is clearly not willing to admit to being wrong about anything. The hostile elderly juror displaces any flaw in himself onto another group. The juror with the glasses who does not sweat places a great deal of importance on his ability to remember details, to having the right idea, and to knowing what is right. Fonda is also strong on ego. He champions his value system and has a great deal of ego strength to take the abuse that he is given, without giving up and withdrawing.

**2. How does each character manage conflict? Which are more effective? What does their conflict style reveal about the person?**

Several jurors are willing to accommodate or to withdraw rather than take an individual stand. The foreman, the nice juror to his left, the working man, the ghetto dweller, the baseball fan, and the advertising man.

Two jurors are clearly of the forcing style people: the hostile elderly man and the juror with a son.

The remaining jurors are primarily collaborating in their conflict style: Fonda; the kind, elderly juror; the juror with the eyeglasses; and the foreign juror.

Each person responds according to how they value their duty, how they problem solve, how they process information as part of their personality or temperament, and how much self-confidence they have.

3. **Describe the evidence for passive, aggressive, and assertive behavior in this story.**

The jurors' conflict management style pretty closely matches their passive-assertive behavior. The forcing style jurors are also those who tend to be aggressive and to show no respect for others. The accommodating and withdrawing style jurors tend to be passive in their communication style. The collaborating jurors tend to be the most assertive.

4. **Note how the 12 jurors develop relationships during the deliberations. Discuss how they move from 12 separate individuals to a series of dyads, tryads, and small groups.**

The first move toward a relationship occurs when the kind, elderly man chooses to give Fonda some support so that the group will not rush to judgment. Their friendship develops very quickly and is strong by the end of the deliberations. They are joined by the ghetto dweller juror; the working man; the foreigner; and the quiet, nice juror. The more hostile jurors hold onto support from the ad man, the baseball fan, and the juror with glasses. The foreman tends to remain neutral until he joins the acquittal group close to the end.

## Torch Song Trilogy, dir. Paul Bogart. With Anne Bancroft, Matthew Broderick, Harvey Fierstein, Brian Kerwin, Karen Young, Charles Pierce, 1988.

**Brief Summary**: This is powerful translation of the Broadway play by Fierstein about the life of a drag queen and his conflict with his mother.

Arnold Beckoff (Harvey Fierstein) is a gay, female impersonator at a gay club. Both his mother and father can't accept his lifestyle or his being gay, and treat him as if he is going through a phase and will someday straighten up.

Arnold meets Ed Reese (Brian Kerwin) at a gay bar, and the two men become lovers. Ed is bisexual, and leaves Arnold for Laurel, a woman, whom he eventually marries. After the painful break-up with Ed, Arnold is reluctant to enter into a new affair, but Alan (Mathew Broderick), a young and successful male model, pursues him, and convinces Arnold that he loves him. The two men enter into a long-term relationship, and after nine years together, decide to adopt a child – a troubled and abused gay fifteen year-old. In anticipation of the adoption, they decide to move into a larger apartment. On the evening of their move, Alan goes out to get take-out for dinner, and is savagely killed when he tries to help another man who is being beaten by a gang of gay haters.

The movie then jumps to a year after Alan's death. Arnold has gone through with the adoption of the troubled youth, David, and his old boyfriend, Ed, who is having marital problems with his wife, is back in the picture, and wants to return to Arnold and help him to raise David. Arnold's mother (Anne Bancroft), who moved to Florida after the death of her husband, is coming to Brooklyn to visit. Arnold has not told her about David, and did not tell her the truth about the manner of Alan's death. Mother and son confront each other, and the truth of their resentments surfaces. In the end, they do come to terms with each other's feelings and part on a reconciliatory note. The movie ends with Arnold symbolically embracing all of those he loves by embracing an object representing each person: David's baseball cap, the oranges his mother brought from Florida, Ed's glasses, and Alan's picture.

**IPC Concepts:** self talk, emotion.

**Scenes for Use in the Classroom:**

- The initial scene where the mom is looking for Arnold, and finds the little boy in the closet playing dress-up.
- Arnold at his dressing room getting ready for his show. His self-talk and explanation of who he is and what is important to him.
- The scene where Alan is killed and Arnold's reaction as they wheel the gurney into the ambulance.
- Arnold and his mother at the cemetery. His mother praying at her husband's grave and Arnold praying at Alan's grave, and the confrontation between the two of them.
- The final scene back at the apartment when Arnold and his mother finally come to terms with each other's differences.

**Questions for Discussion**

1. **Discuss the types of conflict in the film.**
   The story illustrates two types of conflict, fact and value. Fact conflict centers around Arnold's mother. She refuses to accept the facts of Arnold's life; his gay life, his lovers, etc. Her homophobic reactions are so strong that she cannot see the reality of her son's life. Value conflict exists between Arnold and his mother over the question of his gay life. She rejects the legitimacy of the gay life. She thinks it is evil and unnatural. He knows that his life is just as legitimate as her own and that his ability to love is just as real, natural, and deep as hers oranyone else.

2. **How does each character manage conflict? Which are more effective? What does their conflict style reveal about the person?**
   Mother responds to most conflict by withdrawing. She tends to live in a constant state of denial and avoidance regarding her son and his life. She lashes out in a forcing style when she is provoked to respond to Arnold. Arnold exhibits the accommodating style much of the time in order to get along with his parents. He does not change his life, but he does not argue with his parents as often as he might. He also exhibits the collaborative and the forcing style. He tries to collaborate with his mother by giving her information about gay living and analogies between his life and hers. He finally forces her to look at his life in a real fashion. This confrontation allows her to see his reality for the first time.

3. **Discuss the mother-son argument in this story. In what ways do they illustrate passive/aggressive/assertive behavior?**
   Mother vacillates between passive and aggressive. Mother either says nothing or attacks and rejects her son. Arnold exhibits passive and assertive behavior. He

either tries to get along or he tries to reason with his mother.

## War of the Roses, dir. Danny DeVito. With Michael Douglas, Kathleen Turner, Danny DeVito, 1989.

**Brief Summary:** This is the story of a relationship that has gone dangerously bad. The two main characters have lived together for a number of years, accumulated considerable affluence, and yet have not grown as a couple at all. Their total focus on the accumulation of wealth and property has warped their sense of what is important in life. They have built up a tremendous storehouse of angry feelings. When Barbara finally gets in touch with her desire to get a divorce, both she and Oliver have too many pent up feelings to be able to control them. They have never developed a healthy sense of self-esteem or mutual respect, and so they have no foundation for these feelings during the divorce proceedings.

The net result is an awful, violent, destructive conflict over just about everything possible. The end result is that they wind up killing each other.

**IPC Concepts:** Conflict in intimate relationships, types of conflict, methods of managing conflict, non-assertive behavior.

**Scenes for Use in the Classroom:**

- The party in their apartment to celebrate Oliver's successful litigation on behalf of the firm. The victory advances his case to become a partner in the firm, a promotion that would enable them to buy the kind of house that they want.
- Their argument in bed the night after the party.
- Her passive aggressive behavior in the kitchen the night they quarrel over the contract that she has asked Oliver to review for her new business endeavor.
- Her announcement that she wants a divorce.
- The meeting in the office of Barbara's lawyer to discuss the property settlement. This is the meeting in which the house emerges as the central symbol in the upcoming fight.

**Questions for Discussion**

1. **Discuss the types of conflict in the film.**

There are examples of all four types of conflict in Interact. Pseudo conflict is introduced early in the divorce negotiations when the Roses focus on the house as the non-negotiable element in the property settlement.
Factual claims are made by both Barbara and Oliver about their history, their needs, and each other' t actions.

Both Barbara and Oliver value material possessions over just about anything else. Oliver still places some value on his feeling for Barbara, which is revealed in their final act of mutual destruction. Value conflict is illustrated in their insistence on wanting the house. Oliver has a prized car that becomes the target of Barbara's destructive aggression.

Both Barbara and Oliver are completely caught up in satisfying and salving their egos. Neither one can allow themselves to lose any argument or concede to any loss in their vicious property settlement...

2. **Describe the styles of managing conflict by the Roses.**
   While there are miniscule examples of compromising and withdrawing, the principal form of management for both Barbara and Oliver is the forcing style. Verbal and physical attacks, coercion, and manipulation are all in evidence. Both combatants view the divorce and property settlement as a total win/lose type of conflict.

3. **Describe the evidence for passive, aggressive, and assertive behavior in this story.**
   Several supporting characters demonstrate passive behavior. The main behavior illustrated in this tragic story is aggressive and sometimes, passive-aggressive.
   Barbara and Oliver engage in terribly aggressive behavior. They use language that rips into each other, is selected to hurt the other person as much as possible, and coerce the other into submitting.
   The interesting type of behavior is the passive-aggressive. The first form of this behavior occurs when Oliver delays in reviewing the contract for Barbara's new catering business. Oliver finally starts to read the contract, but allows a fly to distract him. He kills the fly with the contract and then takes a client's phone call. Barbara is so angry that she turns on every kitchen appliance that makes noise, turns off the lights, and leaves the room. When confronted by Oliver about this, she states that she must have left something on when she left the kitchen.
   A second passive-aggressive act occurs when Oliver is taken to the hospital for an apparent heart attack. Barbara never calls him directly and never comes to the hospital. She waits until he returns home to see him. She says that a nurse told her that he was okay and she did not think her presence would be helpful.

## Big Chill, dir. Lawrence Kasdan. With Tom Berenger, Glenn Close, Jeff Goldblum, William Hurt, Kevin Kline, Mary Kay Place, Meg Tilly, JoBeth Williams, Don Galloway, 1983.

**Brief Summary:** This story is about a group of people who knew each other at the University of Michigan during their college years in the sixties. The group reunites after the suicide of a member of the group. They meet at the South Carolina home of Harold (Kevin Kline) and Sarah (Glenn Close). Harold sells running shoes. Sarah is a doctor. The other members of the group include Michael (Jeff Goldblum) a gossip columnist, Sam (Tom Berenger) TV's Magnum-type private eye, Nick (William Hurt) a drug dealer, Meg (Mary Kay Place) a lawyer, Karen (JoBeth Williams) an unhappy wife and mother, and Chloe (Meg Tilly) Alex's girlfriend. The group works through a series of issues in the process of getting reacquainted and of processing their grief over the loss of Alex.

Several scenes involving interpersonal conflict occur that dramatically illustrate the principles in Interact.

**IPC Concepts:** Conflict: types, styles of management, communication skills, and assertive influence.

**Scenes for Use in the Classroom:**

- The argument between Nick and Harold after the U of M football game and the incident with the local policeman.
- A pair of arguments within the group as they sit talking after dinner. These arguments focus on how well we really know our friends, the possible influence we have on each other's lives, the degree of self-importance that some of us construct and carry around, and our inner pain.

**Questions for Discussion**

1. **Discuss the types of conflict in the film.**

   There are few real conflicts over facts per se. There are some disagreements over how to interpret facts. For example, Nick and Sam clash a couple of times over the meaning of past events, such as why Alex held some of the jobs that he held when he had so much potential.

   The group does argue over value and ego related issues. Nick and Sam clash over the depth and quality of the friendships that they all made in college. Nick maintains that "a long time ago, you knew me for a short time. You don't know anything about me." This raises the question about how much we really know about the people in our friendships. We tend to idealize our previous relationships such as college acquaintances, but we may not have had as much depth in those friendships as we would like to think. Nick's somewhat abrasive, often, cynical style irritates several of the other people in the group, especially Sam.

2. **How does each character manage conflict? Which are more effective? What does their conflict style reveal about the person?**

   Harold tends to withdraw or accommodate when in conflict. He can, however, confront the other party as he illustrates when he challenges Nick about the direction of his life. Sarah is the classic earth mother type of character. As a doctor she extends the healing quality of her life to other areas. When Meg discloses her frustration over not meeting someone with whom she can have a baby, Sarah offers her husband, Harold, to serve as the father. Sam and Nick are both confrontational. They prefer open conflict to quietly smoothing things over, the approach of Harold, Meg, and Karen, who all prefer the accommodating style.

3. **Describe the evidence for passive, aggressive, and assertive behavior in this story.**

   Karen tends to be the passive style of communication. She has been passive with her husband, Richard, and she approaches her relationships with the group members in a similar fashion, with only occasional glimpses of assertiveness.

Meg and Chloe are also passive in the communication style. Meg describes her feelings very well, but shows virtually no evidence of confronting any of the others. Chloe, as the youngest person present, quietly sits by watching everyone else. Her major contribution occurs when she makes the comment, "I haven't seen that many happy people. How do they act?" This brings the group up short in their assumptions.

Harold and Sarah are both fairly assertive. They both show a lot of respect for themselves and others. They are patient and accepting in allowing others to be themselves. They only speak up when they are seriously provoked or shown disrespect.

Michael ranges across the passive-aggressive-assertive continuum. He shows some evidence of passive behavior when the women rebuke his advances. He can be assertive as when he tries to respond to Sam during a conversation about the grieving process. Michael tends to be aggressive in that he continually seeks to satisfy his own needs with less concern about the needs of others. He is trying to gain investment help from the entire group. He tries to hit on Chloe after the funeral, believing her to be vulnerable. He tries to hit on Sarah and Meg. He shifts style from aggressive to passive when rejected.

Sam and Nick tend to be aggressive in their communication style. They are quick to pounce on something that they disagree with, especially with each other. Both seem to be bitter about life and have lost their idealism.

4. **How much influence can we realistically expect to have in our friendships?**

This is a question based on the comment by Nick when he responds to the group by saying, "so what do you think, that you could have saved Alex if you had been there? Wake up people." We tend to think that we know our friends better than we may actually know them. This is a good question to raise a general class discussion on friendship in relationships.

## *CNN*

## Sibling Rivalry, (7:24). CNN Interpersonal Communication Today, 1999, Volume 1.

This is a good segment to use in conjunction with scenes from the film, *Crooklyn*. This clip explores families and their methods of managing conflict between siblings.

**Domestic Violence, (4:30). CNN Interpersonal Communication Today, 1999, Volume 1.**

This segment examines the problem of domestic violence and approaches to its management in both intimate and health care settings.

## *On the Stage*

**Edward Albee. (1962). Who's Afraid of Virginia Woolf.**

**Brief Summary:** Martha and George, a married couple, are unable to have children. Their coping with this fact has lead them to create a vicious, desperate, and mean-spirited relationship in which they both engage in games in order to hurt the other person. One night after a dinner party, a young couple is drawn into their games.

**IPC Concepts:** Types of conflict, especially pseudo conflict, fact conflict, and ego conflict, styles of managing conflict, and games and conflict, intimate relationships.

---

# *INTERPERSONAL COMMUNICATION THEORY IN LITERATURE AND ACADEMIC RESOURCES*

## *Theory Illustrated in Literature*

**Alice Walker. (1982). The Color Purple. New York: Harcourt Brace Jovanovich.**

**Brief Summary:** This is the story of a poor, used and abused African American woman, Celie. She is given into an abusive marriage by her abusive father. She suffers in silence until she discovers that her husband, Mister, has been hiding letters from her sister, Nettie, who had moved to Africa with Christian missionaries. Celie finds the letters and secretly reads them whenever she can steal a few minutes between chores, or by hiding them inside her Bible and reading them at church. The husband has other women but barely knows Celie. Mister's mistress, Shug, befriends Celie and they develop their own love relationship. As her love grows with Shug, Celie develops more and more self-esteem and confidence. She is eventually able to stand up to Mister and move out on her own. She moves to Memphis with Shug where her life improves tremendously.

**IPC Concepts:** Self-perception, self-esteem, impact of significant others. Relationships – need for warmth and affection, trust and commitment, conflict, diversity, culture, gender, emotion, gender and intimacy.

## *Academic Resources*

### Ellis, Albert and Arthur Lange. (1995). *How To Keep People From Pushing Your Buttons.* N.Y.: Citadel Press Book.

**Brief Summary:** This is an excellent book that explores the theories of Albert Ellis, the famous psychologist. The focus is on how we respond to conflict by allowing our emotions to run wild, rather than remaining in control of our emotions. By focusing on Ellis' ABC process, the book offers very practical advise on handling conflict more effectively. A major point of the approach is the ability of each person to freely choose what their response will be when confronted by a conflict situation. This approach dispels the notion that our reactions to provocations must be automatic. Coupled with The work on life scripts, this makes a profound contribution to the management of interpersonal conflict.

**IPC Concepts:** Conflict and the management of emotion.

### Solomon, Muriel. (1990). *Working with Difficult People.* Englewood Heights, New Jersey: Prentice Hall.

**Brief Summary:** Solomon offers an excellent source for examining specific coping strategies for communicating with specific types of problem people, and problems with people.

**IPC Concepts:** Types and causes of interpersonal conflict, strategies for handling specific types of problems with people.

# *What's on the Web*

### Interpersonal Communication: Interpersonal Conflict by Tim Borchers, Moorhead State University
**http://www.abacon.com/commstudies/interpersonal/inconflict.html**

**Brief Summary:** This web site gives an excellent, concise overview of basic components of conflict and communication, including a definition of conflict, defensive and supportive climate elements, problems in conflict management, tips, a web chat room, conflict activity, and a quick quiz. There is also a link to a reference page with 23 sources.

**IPC Concepts:** Nature of conflict, styles of conflict management.

### Jere Moorman (1999). The person centered approach to conflict transformation. Center for Studies of the Person.
**http://users.powernet.co.uk/pctmk/papers/conflict.htm**

**Brief Summary:** This is a paper posted on the Association for the Development of the Person Centered Approach web site. The paper outlines an entire approach to conflict that places particular emphasis on congruence and empathy in focusing on the person. The goal of the approach is to strive for conflict transformation, rather than conflict resolution. The author stresses that resolution demands the person's full humanity, while transformation enhances complete, fully functioning humanity.

**IPC Concepts:** Conflict, and a new approach to managing conflict.

### Conflict Resolution Resources at The School of Social and Systemic Studies
**http://www.nova.edu/ssss/DR/**

**Brief Summary:** Maintained by faculty at Nova Southeastern University, the site includes information on the school's academic offerings via distance learning. The school offers graduate degrees in dispute resolution. It describes its goal on the site: The Department of Dispute Resolution is committed to the study, practice, and research of conflict resolution as a process for achieving improved societal relations among individuals and organizations." There is an extensive list of conflict resolution resources: Internet Resources and Listserves (this is an overwhelming list of resources), Newsletters, Journals, Membership Organizations, Resource Organizations.

**IPC Concepts:** Conflict management via arbitration.

## How To Express Difficult Feelings
## http://www.DRNADIG.com/feelings.htm

**Brief Summary:** This web site examines the nature and function of language in expressing emotion. The site includes guidelines on language use when in conflict, the difference between thoughts and feelings, and detailed directions on "I" language. This site has links to listening and conflict management.

**IPC Concepts:** Language and conflict.

# CHAPTER ELEVEN

# Communication in Intimate Relationships

## Interpersonal Communication In Action

Chapter Twelve of Interact discusses intimate relationships with friends, spouses, and family. This chapter of the Media Guide focuses on intimate relationships with friends, spouses, and significant others. The films will illustrate both functional and dysfunctional relationships.

If you are pressed for time or only wish to use one or two films on intimate relationships, I recommend *Nothing in Common* and *Steel Magnolias*. These are excellent presentations of interpersonal intimate relationships. And they both treat issues of diversity, albeit in very different ways. There are many films that can be tapped on this topic. Let me just offer a short list: When *Harry Met Sally, Beaches, The Turning Point, Bridges of Madison County, Ground Hog Day, How Stella Got Her Groove Back, In and Out, Joy Luck Club, Martha and Ethel, Moonstruck, Rain Man, Remains of the Day, Smoke Signals, Tender Mercies, Jungle Fever,* and *Hannah and Her Sisters*. This list merely scratches the surface, but it should serve to illustrate the range of types of films that you might use for this chapter.

# Learning Objectives

- Increase student understanding of the nature of intimate relationships.
- Increase student understanding of the types of intimate relationships.
- Increase student awareness of problem areas in intimate relationships.
- Help students deal with destructive intimate relationships.
- Increase student awareness of the effect of gender, aging, and diversity on intimate relationships.

| In Classroom Assignments | For Homework |
| --- | --- |
| - Small Group Discussion | - Position Papers |
| - Whole class discussion | - Relationship Analysis Papers |
| - Role Play Exercises | - Web Exercises to supplement textbook and Instructor's Manual exercise |
| - Conversation exercises | - Journal Entries |

# *VISUALLY PRESENTED INTERPERSONAL COMMUNICATION THEORY*

## *IN MOVIES*

**The Color Purple, dir. Steven Spielberg. With Danny Glover, Whoopi Goldberg, Margaret Avery, Oprah Winfrey, Akosua Busia, Rae Dawn Chong, Larry Fishburne, 1985.**

**Brief Summary:** This is the story of a poor, used and abused African American woman, Celie. She is given into an abusive marriage by her abusive father. She suffers in silence until she discovers that her husband, Mister, has been hiding letters from her sister, Nettie, who had moved to Africa with Christian missionaries. Celie finds the letters and secretly reads them whenever she can steal a few minutes between chores, or by hiding them inside her Bible and reading them at church. The husband has other women but barely knows Celie. Mister's mistress, Shug, befriends Celie, and they develop their own love relationship. As her love grows with Shug, Celie develops more and more self-esteem and confidence. She is eventually able to stand up to Mister and move out on her own. She moves to Memphis with Shug. This is a powerful adaptation of Alice Walker's novel.

**IPC Concepts:** Relationships – need for warmth and affection, trust and commitment, conflict, diversity, culture, gender, emotion, gender and intimacy.

**Scenes for Use in the Classroom:**

- Scenes involving Celie and Shug. Their relationship develops due to Shug's efforts to bring Celie out of her shell and her fear.
- Scenes where Celie reads the letters from her sister. These letters reflect the degree of closeness between the two sisters.

**Questions for Discussion**

1. **To what extent does the relationship between Celie and Shug measure up as an intimate relationship? Be specific on the criteria in Interact for an intimate relationship.**

   Shug comes to Celie as one who can rescue her from the terrible abuse of Mister. Despite Mister's abusive ways with Celie, Shug clearly holds the upper hand with him. Shug shows Celie what it means to receive warmth and affection. Celie is able to give to Shug, but for the first time since she was with her sister, Celie receives affection in return. She learns that she can trust Shug. The two women disclose to each other and develop love and friendship.

2. **What does Celie learn from her sister's letters about relationships?**

Celie learns what people do in normal relationships. Her sister is a missionary in Africa. Despite the somewhat foreign living conditions, Celie is able to discern the relational conditions and behaviors between her sister and the other people with whom she lives. Celie is able to take warmth and joy from her sister's letters. When she is finally able to leave Mister, she has learned something about how she wants her life to change. She lives with some of her best friends in life when she is reunited with her sister.

## Nothing in Common, dir. Garry Marshall with Tom Hanks, Jackie Gleason, Eva Marie Saint, Hector Elizondo, Sela Ward, 1986.

**Brief Summary:** Tom Hanks' character must confront his feelings of rejection by his father when his elderly parents divorce, and his father becomes very sick from untreated diabetes. Hanks plays a silly, but brilliant advertising executive. As it becomes clear that there is no one else to be the primary caregiver for his ailing father, he must focus his life, energy, and time on being there to take care of his father. His father resists any attempts to be helped as he is in denial about the severity of his condition. Hanks has several intense conversations with both parents. He must fight with his father in order to help him face a potentially dangerous surgery to save his life. In the end, he earns the praise from his father, "I never thought you would be there for me."

**IPC Concepts:** Relationships, turning points, crises and conflict, caring, trust, commitment, warmth, and affection.

**Scenes for Use in the Classroom:**

- The scene in which Hanks learns about his parents' divorce.
- When Hanks learns that his father is sick and needs surgery.
- The confrontation between Hanks and his father over the need for someone to care for his father.
- The final scene in which Hanks is taking his father out of the hospital.

**Questions for Discussion**

1. **What is the nature of the relationship between father and son at the beginning of the film? How does it change?**

As the story opens, Hanks is a young, successful, free wheeling advertising executive who has little contact with his father. His father is a career salesman who is a fast-talking, uncaring individual who takes very little seriously. Father and son have never worked on their relationship. When father and mother decide to divorce late in life, it comes as a shock to their son who simply assumed that his parents were together for life. When dad needs a primary caregiver due to his advanced diabetes, Hanks must step up to the plate to serve his father's needs. The relationship slowly builds as a result of mutual disclosure, conflict, Hanks' responsiveness to his father's needs, and the dependability of the son.

As the father approaches a dangerous surgery, he faces up the fact that his son is really committed to his welfare and that his son really cares about him. He slowly tries to return this level of caring.

2. **What does the son do to demonstrate his commitment to his father? How does he build trust and intimacy with his father?**

The son does a variety of things to prove his commitment to his father. Initially, he tries to get his mother to return in order to be the caregiver. When she makes it clear that she can no longer do that, he makes an effort to try to get to know his father better. At first, his father behaves like he always has behaved, in a flip, superficial, joke-making manner. He keeps everyone at arm's length in order to protect himself from his own insecurity. The son confronts his father over his lack of personal attention to health care, argues with his father, forces him to take the doctor seriously, and brings him to the hospital. The son even allows his job to take a distant second place to the health care needs of his father. All of these actions demonstrate his commitment, affection, and responsibility for the father and for their relationship.

## Steel Magnolias, dir. Herbert Ross. With Sally Field, Dolly Parton, Shirley MacLaine, Darryl Hannah, Olympia Dukakis, Julia Roberts, Tom Skerritt, Sam Shepard, 1989.

**Brief Summary:** A composite story of the lives of six women, Mlynn Eatenton (Sally Field); Truvy Jones (Dolly Parton); Ouiser Boudreaux (Shirley MacLanine); Clairee Belcher (Olympia Dukakis); Shelby Eatenton (Julia Roberts); and Annelle Dupuy (Daryl Hannah). The common ground for the women is Truvy's beauty parlor. Shelby, Mlynn's daughter, is a diabetic. The women are all getting their hair done for Shelby's wedding which is to take place later that afternoon. While there, Shelby has a diabetic reaction. She confesses that a few days earlier she almost called off the wedding because of her health. She has been warned by doctors that her diabetes is so severe that pregnancy would put her live in severe jeopardy.

We get to know the six women better through their interactions both outside of the beauty salon and at the beauty salon. Shelby does become pregnant. She has a healthy little boy, but as predicted, to a great cost to her health, so much so, that she is in dialysis and in need of a kidney transplant. Her mother, Mlynn volunteers to donate one of her kidneys to her daughter. The transplant takes place, successfully, they thought. But eventually, Shelby's body rejects the new kidney and she goes into a comma from which she never recovers. After a long time in a comma with no hope of recovery, her husband signs the papers to have her taken off of life support, and Shelby dies. The women rally around Mlynn to offer their condolences and support. The story reinforces the metaphor of the title, that the women must be the members of their marriages who are strong and able to weather life's difficult times.

**IPC Concepts:** Relationship – warmth and affection, trust, commitment, gender, and intimacy.

Scenes for Use in the Classroom:

- The women at the beauty salon having their hair done for the wedding.
- Conversation between Shelby and Mlynn when Shelby tells her mother that she is pregnant.
- The six women at the beauty salon when Shelby tells the other women that she is going to have a kidney transplant the following day and that her mother is the donor.
- The scene at the cemetery when the women gather around Mlynn to offer her comfort and their support.
- Scene where Clairee apologizes to Ouiser for offering her as a sacrificial lamb at the cemetery.

Questions for Discussion

1. **When the women are getting their hair done in preparation for the wedding, how does their conversation and behavior toward each other show the depth of their comfort with each other and the degree/depth of their friendship?**

   Their communication is spontaneous, lacking any tension. It is filled with playfulness and humor as appropriate. They know a lot about each other and they demonstrate their friendship by showing that they care and are reasonably inquisitive. There is no defensiveness in the conversation.

2. **When Shelby tells her mother that she is pregnant, Shelby is hurt by her mother's reaction to the news. Has her mother broken the trust that Shelby has in her by this reaction? Why not?**

   A relationship that is characterized by what Carl Rogers would call unconditional positive regard will accept what the other person says without any kind of negative response. The response will be one of acceptance and understanding, one that tries to support and help. For the mother to immediately lash out tells the daughter that she cannot tell her mother anything but what she wants to hear. The negative reaction and the accusatory tone does break the trust level that may have been there before.

3. **Ouiser tries to put up a front as being a crusty, uncaring, cranky woman. Is this just a front? Do her friends see through this mask? In what ways does Ouiser show that she cares more than she lets on?**

   After finding out about Shelby's poor health condition, Ouiser confesses to Clairee that she is very sorry for her comment earlier at the beauty salon about wishing that her body would just wear out.

   After the funeral, as she walks behind Drum (Shelby's father), she gives him a pat on the back. The two are constantly teasing each other and never have a civil word to say to one another, yet, both know that they care about the other person.

   This film illustrates the need for a good friend or set of friends who can keep us grounded in reality by seeing through our masks and not allowing us to hide behind them anymore than is completely necessary.

4. **How does Clairee go about breaking the tension at the cemetery? What role does humor play in the friendship between the women? Has humor ever played a role in diffusing tension in your lives, with your friendships/relationships?**

Humor is an excellent way to diffuse tension if it is appropriate humor, effectively timed, and most of all, funny. Humor that is in bad taste or abusive to anyone involved would backfire and create even more tension, pain, and open conflict. Virtually everyone has experienced humor as a tension release.

## Fried Green Tomatoes, dir. Jon Avnet, with Kathy Bates, Jessica Tandy, Mary Stuart Masterson, Mary-Louise Parker, Cicely Tyson, Chris O'Donnell and Stan Shaw, 1991.

**Brief Summary:** An excellent adaptation of Fannie Flagg's novel. The film takes us through a story-within-a-story as we follow a young woman in Alabama, Evelyn (Kathy Bates), and her troubles relating to herself and to her husband. In a nursing home, Evelyn meets an elderly lady, Mrs. Threadgoode (Tandy), who serves as her mentor through her telling the story of her life and the history of the Whistle Stop Cafe in her hometown during the 1920s. We meet Idgie, Buddy, Rose, Big George, Stump, Mr. Smokey, and of course, Mrs. Threadgoode. The film rotates between 1986 and the 1930s, as it relates the past and present. In so doing, it covers issues in the relationships of the major characters, how Idgie, in particular, becomes a caring, nurturing rebel; how southern racism touches the lives of everyone in Whistle Stop; and how the people of this community work together in order to help each other make it through the depression.

**IPC Concepts:** Relationships, turning points, trust, disclosure, diversity.

**Scenes for Use in the Classroom:**

- Buddy talking to Idgie when she is a little girl.
- Idgie going to rescue Ruth from Frank Bennett, her abusive husband.
- Idgie taking Stump out of the Whistle Stop when he was shaking too much to eat his supper.
- Almost any scene that shows Idgie and Ruth running the Whistle Stop and working to help the other members of the community.
- Reverend Scroggins testifying to help keep Idgie from being convicted for the death of Ruth's husband.
- Any scene in which Mrs. Threadgoode helps Evelyn to develop more self esteem in her marriage.
- Final scene in Whistle Stop in which Evelyn invites Mrs. Threadgoode to come live with her, and finds proof that Idgie is still alive.

<u>Questions for Discussion</u>

1. **Discuss the relationship between Idgie and Ruth, as intimate friends and as members of a loving relationship.**

   These two women form a special relationship as young women. Ruth admires Idgie for her free spirit, sense of adventure, courage, and her integrity. Idgie admires Ruth for her sweet, gentle soul, and her caring attitude toward life. They grow to trust each other totally. Idgie cannot bear to see Ruth suffer at the hands of her brutal husband, so she rescues her from him. The two women live together after that episode and share everything. They run the Whistle Stop, raise Buddy together, help the community, and possibly become lovers.

2. **Discuss the relationship between Evelyn and Mrs. Threadgoode. Does it qualify as an intimate relationship?**

   Their relationship is definitely intimate. Evelyn discloses her most intimate feelings and fears. Mrs. Threadgoode reciprocates, which helps to cement the friendship. Mrs. Threadgoode gives warmth and affection freely to Evelyn, something that Evelyn has apparently not received from anyone before. She helps Evelyn in her quest for growth and self-esteem. Slowly, Evelyn comes to accept herself for who she is. Her confidence comes only after a series of humorous, and sometimes farcical adventures. She manages to change her life. When Mrs. Threadgoode needs Evelyn to help her face the end of her stay at the Home, Evelyn returns with her to Whistle Stop and helps her face the reality of what has changed. Her house has been torn down and she has no place to live. Evelyn takes her into her own home. Mrs. Threadgoode thanks her by telling her the most important thing in life, "friendship, best friends."

3. **Discuss the relationship between Evelyn and her husband. While a marriage, is it really an intimate one?**

   Evelyn does not have an intimate relationship with her husband. He has never tried to get to know her as anything other than a cook, housekeeper, and probably, occasional sex partner. I do not describe her as his lover, as I doubt that the act was ever really about anything more than physical release. Theirs is an I-It relationship according to Buber. She does try to treat him with warmth, affection, caring, commitment, and responsiveness, but he has no interest in anything more than his dinner, the ballgame, and the dependability of his home never changing from fulfilling his needs.

4. **Discuss any other relationships in this film. What characteristics of these friendships make them intimate relationships?**

   There are several relationships in the film, including Big George and Sipsey, Reverend Scroggins and Idgie, Stump and Idgie, and Buddy and Idgie. There is Smokey Lonesome and Ruth. They have a special, and essentially silent friendship. Smokey has real problems. He is an alcoholic, a drifter, hobo, and is incapable of living a normal life. Yet, he has a deep and abiding love for Ruth. He would do anything to help her. And last of all, there is the town of Whistle Stop that brings all of the people together.

## The Wonderful Ice Cream Suit, dir. Stuart Gordon, with Joe Montegna, Esai Morales, Edward James Olmos, Clifton Gonzales, Liz Torres, Sid Caesar, and Howard Morris, 1998.

**Brief Summary:** The Wonderful Ice Cream Suit tells the story of five young men: Gomez (Mantegna) the fast-talking schemer, Vamenos (Olmos) the tramp, Martinez (Gonzalez-Gonzalez) the innocent, Villanazul (Sierra) the intellectual, and Dominguez (Morales) the romantic. Gomez (Joe Montegna) spots a beautiful white suit in a department store window. The suit costs $100, but he only has $20. Gomez gathers four other men, all about the same size, and they each chip in $20 to purchase and share the suit. The suit brings out their innermost desires. It does not take long for the five men to discover that the wearer of the suit has his wishes come true. The adventures the men share and what happens to them changes their lives in hilarious and meaningful ways, and through the gift of sharing, the five men become great friends.

**IPC Concepts:** Relationships, culture, identification, self, face.

**Scenes for Use in the Classroom:**

- Introductory sequence where Gomez collects the five men who will each contribute to buy the suit.
- The scene in which the five men fantasize about the suit, its power, and its potential.
- Any or all of the five scenes where the men each wear the suit for the fulfillment of their dreams.
- Especially, the scene in which Gomez returns from the bus station with the suit.

**Questions for Discussion**

1. **How do these five men develop an intimate relationship? What is the real basis of their relationship?**

   The five men slowly develop their trust in each other, with Gomez being the slowest one to trust or be trustworthy. They even learn to trust Vamenos more quickly than Gomez, who has a reputation as a con artist. The suit is their conduit for disclosing their fantasies to each other, something that men are usually reluctant to do in an honest manner. The suit serves to unite the men in the sense that it gives them a formal ritualized way to signify the reality and special nature of their friendship. Each man has a special responsibility to preserve the suit.

2. **Why is this male-male relationship an intimate one?**

   The five men demonstrate a degree of trust in each other as they even let Vamenos wear the suit. They are ritualistically dedicated to the wearing of the suit. They each disclose something of their inner fantasies and dreams. There is even a level of warmth as they send each man off on his quest and joyfully welcome him back with a look that would make Charleton Heston's Moses seem less hallowed.

# *On the Stage*

## Edward Albee. (1962). Who's Afraid of Virginia Woolf

**Brief Summary:** Martha and George, a married couple, are unable to have children. Their coping with this fact has lead them to create a vicious, desperate, and mean-spirited relationship in which they both engage in games in order to hurt the other person. A young couple is drawn into their games one night after a dinner party.

**IPC Concepts:** Types of conflict, especially pseudo conflict, fact conflict, and ego conflict, games and conflict, intimate relationships, need for honesty, support, warmth, spousal relationships.

## Bernard Slade. Same Time Next Year.

**Brief Summary:** This play illustrates a rather unique type of relationship. A couple meets and begins an extramarital affair. Their assignations occur only once a year when they travel to the same meeting place. The total affair lasts for 26 years. We see them go through personal changes, changes in clothing styles, priorities, obsessions, personal phases and fads. They discuss their marriages and families. The two people reflect extraordinary trust and closeness, while they also realize that they have no real wish to marry. This play raises questions about the limits and functions of various types of relationships.

**IPC Concepts:** Types of relationships, needs and exchange theory, cycles, trust, support, disclosure, ethics.

## Tennessee Williams. (1947). Streetcar Named Desire

**Brief Summary:** This play is set in the apartment of Stanley and Stella Kowalski in the French Quarter of New Orleans. Two streetcars, one named Desire and the other named Cemetery, once rattled through this neighborhood. When Stella's sister, Blanche comes to visit unexpectedly, Stanley cannot cope with what he perceives to be an intruder and a liar in the middle of his marriage. His violent and manipulative handling of Blanche dramatizes the impact of such behavior on the lives of all involved.

**IPC Concepts:** Types of relationships, needs and exchange theory, cycles, trust, support, disclosure, ethics.

## *CNN*

**Recognizing Domestic Partners. (1:31). CNN Interpersonal Communication Today, 1999, Volume 2.**

This clip presents the situation of same-sex partners who are not permitted to be legally married. This case looks at Seattle's new Domestic Partners Ordinance, which gives a measure of recognition to the status of same-sex partners.

**Love at First Site, (: 58). CNN Interpersonal Communication Today, 1999, Volume 1.**

This clip is about a web site that offers a web site dating service. The site is called Love At First Site and offers clients an opportunity to see the person who is behind the ad with security from harassment if the meeting does not work out.

---

# *INTERPERSONAL COMMUNICATION THEORY IN LITERATURE AND ACADEMIC RESOURCES*

## *Theory Illustrated in Literature*

**Alice Walker. (1982). The Color Purple. New York: Harcourt Brace Jovanovich.**

**Brief Summary:** This is the story of a poor, used and abused African American woman, Celie. Her abusive father gives her into an abusive marriage. She suffers in silence until she discovers that her husband, Mister, has been hiding letters from her sister, Nettie, who had moved to Africa with Christian missionaries. Celie finds the letters and secretly reads them whenever she can steal a few minutes between chores, or by hiding them inside her Bible and reading them at church. The husband has other women but barely knows Celie. Mister's mistress, Shug, befriends Celie, and they develop their own love relationship. As her love grows with Shug, Celie develops more and more self-esteem and confidence. She is eventually able to stand up to Mister and move out on her own. She moves to Memphis with Shug where her life improves tremendously.

**<u>IPC Concepts</u>:** Self perception, self esteem, impact of significant others, Relationships – need for warmth and affection, trust and commitment, conflict, diversity, culture, gender, emotion, gender and intimacy.

### Ernest Hemingway. (1929). A Farewell To Arms.

**<u>Brief Summary</u>:** This is Hemingway's story about a tragic love affair set on the Italian front during WWI. The story is about an American, Lieutenant Frederic Henry, who volunteers as an ambulance driver, is wounded and falls in love with his nurse, Catherine Barkley – "Cat." The couple enjoys a wonderfully romantic year until Cat's tragic death.

**<u>IPC Concepts</u>:** Relationship and attraction, needs, disclosure, support.

### Carson McCullers. (1940). The Heart Is A Lonely Hunter. N.Y.: Modern Library.

**<u>Brief Summary</u>:** The heroine is a young girl named Mick Kelly. The story is set in a small, Southern town. The characters are all lonely, broken people, some of whom fight their loneliness with violence and depravity, and some with sex or alcohol. Mick searches for beauty. When John Singer shoots himself, the characters of the novel are left in an intense loneliness and with a feeling of having been cheated out of someone special.

**<u>IPC Concepts</u>:** Types of relationships, needs theory, handling of emotion, self esteem.

## *<u>Academic Resources</u>*

### Covington, Stephanie and Liana Beckett. (1988). *Leaving the Enchanted Forest: The Path From Relationship Addiction to Intimacy*. New York: Harper & Row Publishers.

**<u>Brief Summary</u>:** This a fascinating book on the pattern many people follow when they move from relationship to relationship. The authors offer the explanation that such behavior may be caused by our need for the relationship rush that one experiences when the relationship is new. As the relationship moves on, such a rush is more difficult to experience. Some people may develop a need for, or dependency on, this type of biochemical response to a relational partner.

**<u>IPC Concepts</u>:** Relationship patterns, addiction, gender differences.

**Harvey A. Hornstein. (1991). A Knight in Shining Armor: Understanding Men's Romantic Illusions. New York: William Morrow and Company, Inc.**

**Brief Summary:** This book is an interesting discussion of the emotional needs that many have when they initiate a relationship. Several paradigms are offered that describe patterns of male relational behavior. The author suggests that because of illusions regarding the nature of a relationship, it is difficult to really know the male partner because of the masks they feel compelled to wear.

**IPC Concepts:** Relationship types, needs and exchange theory, patterns of communicative behavior in relationships, gender.

**Donald Horton and R. Richard Wohl. (1956). Mass Communication and Parasocial Interaction: Observation on Intimacy at a Distance. Psychiatry, 19, 215-229.**

**Brief Summary:** This is a landmark article about the impact of television, and by present extension, of any form of media on the development of pseudo relationships between the viewer and the celebrity on the television/in the media. Horton and Wohl made some fascinating discoveries of how people feel about celebrities on television. Viewers not only refer to celebrities by their first name (Dan, Walter, Johnny, Jay, Dave, etc.), but they also feel as though they know the person and feel a sense of loss or abandonment when the celebrity does not appear when expected. This has been noted with soap opera viewing audiences.

**IPC Concepts:** Relationship types, needs theory.

**Barry L. Duncan and Joseph W. Rock. Saving Relationships: the Power of the Unpredictable. In *Psychology Today*, 26, 1, January/February 1993, 46-51, 86, 90.**

**Brief Summary:** An excellent discussion of problems faced by married couples, and the role of relational myths in contributing to such problems. The authors also suggest communication strategies that couples can employ to improve their relationships. The article stresses the interactive nature of relationships and the power of individual choice in interpreting the actions of the other partner.

**IPC Concepts:** Relationships – self-disclosure, commitment, trust, spouses.

**Barry Dym and Michael Glenn. Forecast For Couples. *Psychology Today*, 46, 4, July/August 1993, 54-57, 78, 81.**

**Brief Summary:** A practical discussion of relational stages. The authors posit a three-stage model: expansion and promise, contraction and betrayal, and resolution.

**IPC Concepts:** Relationships – self-disclosure, commitment, trust, spouses.

## *What's on the Web*

### Stepfamily Foundation
**http://www.stepfamily.org/**

**Brief Summary:** This web site is devoted to step relationships, and to providing counseling – on the telephone, worldwide, and in person – by Jeannette Lofas, and other Certified Stepfamily Foundation Counselors. Books, audio tapes and video tapes, Training Certified Stepfamily Foundation Counselors and Coaches, Free Information, Research, Corporate Programs to eliminate the negative spillover effects of divorce and remarriage.

**IPC Concepts:** Relationships – commitment, warmth, affection, trust.

### Committee for Children
**http://fyd.clemson.edu/famlife.htm**

**Brief Summary:** A site concerned with preventing youth violence and enhancing school safety. Clemson University sponsors this site. The purpose is twofold: First, to strengthen family and youth, and second, to help families cope during periods of crisis and change. They offer programs that teach youth and adults coping skills, effective communication skills, effective decision-making, and an appreciation of heritage. The "Building Family Strengths" program focuses on 10 characteristics for strong families.

**IPC Concepts:** Family relationships, commitment, support, trust, warmth.

### Love Test
**http://www.lovetest.com/**

**Brief Summary:** A fun and somewhat silly exercise that can put students in the mood or mindset to discuss various attraction variables in relationships.

**IPC Concepts:** Intimate relationships – commitment, compatibility, beliefs and expectations about relationships.

## Guidelines on Effective Communication, Healthy Relationships and Successful Living by Dr. Larry Alan Nadig
## http://www.DRNADIG.com/

**Brief Summary:** Dr. Nadig is a relationship counselor. The site includes guidelines on Effective Communication, Healthy Relationships, listening, and relational conflict.

**IPC Concepts:** Relationships.

## Mapping of Rules (Frederick R. Ford)
## http://home.pacbell.net/frccford/index.html

**Brief Summary:** This site features a list of rules followed by people in several different kinds of families. This site features a web based test (with online scoring that measures five family systems: Two Against the World, Children Come First, Share and Share Alike, Every Man for Himself, & Until Death Do Us Part. Links provide explanations and a bibliography.

**IPC Concepts:** Relationships and commitments, priorities, support, trust, caring.

# CHAPTER TWELVE
# Communication in Family Relationships

## Interpersonal Communication In Action

Chapter Twelve is a special chapter that looks at the family as a unique, critical social subsystem. The chapter illustrates the family as a network of intimate relationships within a unique context. The members are bound together by blood relationship, placed within close spatial relationship, and bound by rituals of its own creation. The family functions as a system whose communication is responsible for developing the self-concept of the children, providing recognition and support, and offering role models for appropriate behavior. The chapter notes barriers to effective communication and ways to improve family communication.

Six films will be presented that offer family dynamics from a multicultural perspective. *The Perez Family* and *My Family* present family dynamics from an Hispanic perspective. *Crooklyn* and *Boyz in the Hood* examine African American family dynamics. *Avalon* presents a multi-generational look at an immigrant family, starting with the first generation to migrate to the U.S. *Moonstruck* is a delightful look at a New York Italian-American family.

This is but a sampling of the many films that examine the family and its interpersonal dynamics. Others include the *Ice Storm,* the story of a highly dysfunctional family in the 1970s. *Now and Then*, the story of single moms and their children; *Parenthood*, the story of a large family and a multiple perspective look at the dynamics of being a parent; and *El Norte*, the story of a brother and sister in Guatemala who must struggle to leave the violence of their native land and try to make a life in the United States, in the north, el norte.

## LEARNING OBJECTIVES

- Increase student understanding of the nature of a family
- Increase student awareness of the power of communication on the family system
- Sensitize students to communication barriers and problems in families
- Increase student understanding of how to improve family communication

| In Classroom Assignments | For Homework |
|---|---|
| - Small Group Discussion | - Position Papers |
| - Whole class discussion | - Relationship Analysis Papers |
| - Role Play Exercises | - Web Exercises to supplement textbook and Instructor's Manual exercise |
| - Conversation exercises | - Journal Entries |

# *VISUALLY PRESENTED INTERPERSONAL COMMUNICATION THEORY*

## *IN MOVIES*

**The Perez Family, dir. Mira Nair. Marisa Tomei, Anjelica Huston, Alfred Molina, Chazz Palminteri, Trini Alvarado, Celia Cruz, Diego Wallraff, Trini Alvarado, 1995.**

**Brief Summary:** After 20 years of political imprisonment in Cuba, a former Cuban plantation owner, Juan Raul Perez, is released in 1980 as part of the massive prisoner release by Castro. He dreams of being reunited with his wife and family in Miami. He was imprisoned for burning his sugar cane fields rather than giving them to Fidel Castro. When he arrives in Florida in the company of a young fiery woman, Dorita, who claims to be his wife, he misses his brother-in-law who is looking for a single man. His real wife, Carmela, believes that he has not been released and grieves for him. The young woman, saddened by the reality of the immigration system, encourages Juan to find his wife. Along the way the unlikely pair meet many people with the name Perez. One immigration representative confides that his mother's name was Perez.

Juan is released alone after insisting that Dottie is not his wife. He searches for his wife's home in Coral Gables. When he arrives at her home, he shyly touches the door and sets off the new security system. In a panic he runs away. Returning to the migration center, he finds Dottie trying to create a family so that they can be released to a sponsor. She recruits an old man to be the grandfather, and a young boy, Felipe, to be the son.

Sneaking out to a disco with one of the security guards, Dottie encounters Carmela on a date with a policeman, Officer Pirella. The unlikely group slowly become a family. Juan so admires Dottie that he tells her, "you are so beautiful. You always know where you are." Their goal is to survive, learn how to deal with America, and try to find their place in it. They become interdependent and help each other deal with the constant changes in their lives. They give each other love and support. Even the silent Popi serves as the patriarch of the new Perez family and acts to support, and even to defend Juan and Dottie.

Juan finds his brother-in-law who refuses to acknowledge him. Juan visits his wife's home and finds her in the company of a local police officer with whom she is developing a relationship. Juan and Dottie begin to call each other mi amor. She mourns when Felipe seems to be lost. Eventually Juan is reunited with his wife, but they realize that they have grown away from each other. Each Perez Family is reestablished as the film closes.

**IPC Concepts:** Family as a social system, effective communication – illustrates family interdependence, environmental change, goals, and adaptation.

**Scenes for Use in the Classroom:**

- Dottie's efforts to create a family in order to escape the immigration center.
- The new Perez family's efforts to sell flowers.
- Juan's efforts to find Carmela, especially his discovery of Officer Pirella.
- Juan, Dottie, and Popi standing together to sell flowers and to defend against the brother-in-law.
- Juan returning to Dottie.
- Juan, Dottie, and Popi on the beach in the final scene.

**Questions for Discussion**

1. **How does the new Perez family constitute a family?**

   The new family group assumes traditional family roles. Popi is the grandfather; Juan, the father; Dottie, the mother; and Felipe, the son. They become almost instantly interdependent. Felipe even calls Dottie mother. They create family goals, and communicate frankly and openly about how to achieve them. They care about, and support each other.

2. **What events trigger a more cohesive spirit within the family?**

   The immigration camp fosters a kind of desperate need for family. It forces people to either work together or try to survive alone. The Perez family chooses to be interdependent. Once sponsored, they work together to sell flowers to make enough money to survive. As Juan struggles with the search for his wife and his feelings for his new family, everyone supports him and remains loyal to their new relationship. Popi accompanies Juan to try and meet his wife. When they see her with Pirella, Popi provides quiet support for Juan. Popi is also willing to be a human shield for Juan and any other member of the family who is threatened by another.

3. **How does communication function within the Perez family?**

   Both Juan and Dottie communicate openly with each other. They share their dreams and fears. Felipe keeps his secret to himself and it costs him his life. Popi doesn't speak, but his actions demonstrate his devotion and loyalty to his new family.

## My Family (mi familia), dir Gregory Nava. Jimmy Smits, Esai Morales, Edward James Olmos, Eduardo Lopez Rojas, Jenny Gago, Elpidia Carrillo, Jennifer Lopez, Mary Steenburgen, Scott Bakula, 1995.

**Brief Summary:** This is the multi-generational story of a family in L.A. The family consists of Jose Sanchez, the father; Maria, the mother; Chucho; Toni; Jimmy; Paco; Irene; and Memo.

The story begins in Mexico with the father making his way as a young man to L.A. on foot. He meets Maria, they marry and start a family. During the Depression, the authorities try to blame the bad economic conditions on Mexican workers, and they capture anyone who looks Mexican and deport them to Mexico. A pregnant Maria is among those deported. It takes her two years to return with her new son, Chucho.

The film jumps ahead to 1958 and the marriage of their oldest daughter, Irene. The family has now grown to six children. Olmos narrates that the wedding was one of the greatest days in the history of his family. During the celebration, the popular Toni announces that she wants to become a nun. Chucho confronts a rival gang and narrowly averts a violent encounter.

Chucho's involvement in gang activity brings about a violent argument between him and his father. Jose throws Chucho out of his home and stops communicating with him.

Chucho (Jesus) kills his gang rival and is sought by the police. On the day of the manhunt, Jose discloses his fear to Maria that he will never see his son again. Their son Paco and their daughter Toni both return home for the day from the navy and the convent, respectively. While being chased by the police, Chucho stops to look at his little brother Jimmy. Jimmy witnesses his brother shot in the head by the police. Maria believes that Chucho should have died in the river when he was a baby and she was trying to return to L.A.

Jimmy grows up angry and receives a sentence to prison for armed robbery. After his return home, his sister Toni returns home from the convent married to an ex-priest and a Gringo, David Ronconi (Scott Bakula).

Toni convinces Jimmy to marry a woman from El Salvador in order to protect her from deportation to a prison. After the "marriage," he tries to drive her away, but she wears him down and finally makes a connection with him while dancing in the street. Later he discloses his anger and fears to her and she reciprocates.

In one of the closing scenes, Paco closes his narration by saying that "my mother, she believed that everyone that lived in the house, we all left something behind. She believed the peace of our spirit stayed and lived in all the empty chairs."

**IPC Concepts:** Family interdependence, conflict, self-concept formation, change and adaptation.

**Scenes for Use in the Classroom:**

- Maria's return home to Jose.
- Jimmy watching Chucho get shot and die.
- Toni's return with her husband.
- Jimmy dancing with Isabel and their mutual disclosure scene.
- Jimmy and Carlito making their peace.

**Questions for Discussion**

1. **How does the family cope with tragedy and change?**

The family depends on its ties to one another. They show support models of behavior,

2. **What could the family have done differently (if anything) to help Chucho and Jimmy develop better self-esteem?**

Given the historical times, the ethnic bigotry, and the poverty, it would be difficult to demand more sophisticated behavior on the part of the parents. They are both hard working people who have done their best to cope with a very oppressive and difficult world and raise their family. On one hand, they have raised children to be hard working people, self-reliant, and devoted to their family. On the other, two of the sons have chosen to give into their anger.

3. **Could the family communicate better with less emotion in their conflict?**

One of the elements of culture is the learned behavior dealing with such factors as logic, passion, touching, space, etc. The Hispanic culture practices an openness with emotion that seems alien and often inappropriate to the white, western culture.

4. **Paco says that Jimmy contained all of the family's anger, and in a way, sacrificed himself for the greater good of the family. Discuss this claim.**

Because the family is so concerned about the welfare of Jimmy, they don't have the freedom to develop, indulge, or give into their own anger or frustration. They focus on the work to be done and on keeping the family together.

## Crooklyn, dir. Spike Lee. Alfre Woodard, Delroy Lindo, David Patrick Kelly, Zelda Harris, Carlton Williams, Sharif Rashed, Tse-Mach Washington, Spike Lee, 1994.

**Brief Summary**: This is the story of an African-American family in Brooklyn in the 1970s. Their strong willed mother, Carolyn, holds the family together despite extreme poverty, a free spirited unemployed father, Woody, and a sometimes dangerous, changing neighborhood. Their neighborhood has undergone tremendous change in terms of its racial and ethnic composition. This has fostered resentment between the groups.

The story centers around Troy, the only girl in the family. She is constantly harassed by two of her three brothers. She is fond of her third brother. She is especially close to her mother. She helps her mother with setting the table, etc.

While mother and father have domestic problems due to money, they both love their children. When family becomes a serious problem, they take Troy to spend the summer with her aunt in the south. Troy strikes up a friendship with her cousin, but longs for her home in Brooklyn. Upon her return, she learns that her mother has taken sick, very sick. Carolyn dies of cancer and the family is filled with insecurity as well as grief. Woody reassures Troy that no one will ever take her away from him. She had promised her mother that she would help make sure that the home ran properly. Her brother puts aside his animosity for her and becomes close to his sister as she takes up the role of housekeeper.

**IPC Concepts:** Family, sibling rivalry, conflict, communication between parents, between parents and children, role models, coping with change.

**Scenes for Use in the Classroom:**

- Carolyn yells at the boys for watching television.
- Carolyn talks to Troy about taking her brother's coin collection.
- Carolyn talks to Troy in the hospital about her responsibility for the family.
- Woody talks to Troy about the need for her to attend her mother's funeral.

**Questions for Discussion**

1. **How does the family handle conflict? There is a lot of yelling, but is there any real sign of caring?**

   This is the approach to conflict that very emotional families seem to take. The comedian Sinbad writes about this in his book Sinbad's Guide to Life because I know everything. He illustrates his family experience in which his mother and father would both lay into the children, especially him when they misbehaved. He explains that this was because thy loved him and didn't want him to mess up. He would support the yelling as caring theory. However, modern child rearing theory disputes this approach. This should make for a good topic for class discussion. Be prepared to play the role of referee.

2. **Carolyn yells at the sons, but talks softly to Troy. Troy is asked to do many things to help mom, while the boys seem to get off the hook. It seems that mom gives Troy more duties since she is able and willing. What would you do in this situation?**

   Parents will frequently turn to the path of least resistance when trying to get children to help with household chores. In this case, the three boys are resistant to help and inefficient when they do. Troy does a good job with chores and cherishes her mother's praise and camaraderie. The question deals with issues of developing responsibility in their children and of fairness to all of the children. It is a good question to stir up an excellent discussion in the class. I recommend having the class break into small groups for the first level of discussion and then opening it up to the whole class. Many students will have first hand experience with this issue.

3. **What kind of role models are the parents in this film?**

   Mother is responsible and caring. She is the cement that holds the home together. Her angry flare-ups are understandable to an adult observer, but difficult for the children to understand. She is seriously over stressed, which may have played a part in the development of her illness.

   The father is a loving and caring person. He is flexible, spontaneous, and full of laughter. He commands respect in the neighborhood, as a conversation with their goofy next-door neighbor demonstrates. However, he is irresponsible with money and selfish in his work. He will not sacrifice his own career satisfaction for the greater good of the family's financial needs.

4. **Does the family communication do enough to shape the self-concept of the children?**

Both mother and father need to spend more time and give more guidance to all of the children. The boys tend to run wild like small animals. They are yelled at, but they do not receive much instruction of how to behave. Consequently, they do not know how else to feel or behave. Troy is being taught to get her self-confidence from being a mother figure to the men in her life. *The Wendy Syndrome* discusses this tendency among many women who have been taught to get their self-esteem from care giving to the men in their lives. It parallels a companion volume, *The Peter Pan Complex*, which documents the tendency by many men to remain like little boys under their mother's care, rather than grow up and develop a sense of personal and familial responsibility.

## Boyz in the Hood, dir. John Singleton. Larry Fishburne, Ice Cube, Cuba Gooding Jr., Nia Long, Morris Chestnut, Tyra Ferrell, Angela Bassett, 1991.

**Brief Summary:** This is the story of the struggle to survive in the black section of south, central L.A. Fishburne plays Furious Styles who tries to give his son, Tre, the values that will help him to live a better life. The story begins with a young Tre getting into a fight at school and then moving in with his father so as to be given guidance, as his mother puts it, on "how to be a man." We follow him settling into the new home and watching his friend Doughboy being taken by the police for stealing.

After seven years, we rejoin the story with Tre attending a party welcoming Doughboy back from jail. Tre is trying to live according to his father's values amid the challenges of his the violence of his neighborhood. Ricky is trying to get into college to play football, while coping with the pressures of being a teenage father. The SAT test is a major challenge to his ability to achieve his goal. Furious, Tre's father is an advocate for community pride, integrity, and African-American culture.
An ongoing feud with a neighborhood gang leads to the shooting death of Ricky. In his rage, Tre wants to shoot the perpetrator, but his father intercepts him and talks him out of it for the moment. Tre sneaks out and joins Doughboy as they hunt for the killer. Tre opts out of the car, but Darren leads his other friends and kills three gang members. Doughboy talks to Tre about staying out of the violence. His overall mood and his obvious pain tell Tre that he found and killed the killer. Doughboy's disclosure takes place on a couple of levels as he and Tre become closer than ever. Doughboy only lives for another two weeks.

**IPC Concepts:** Family communication: father-son, mother-sons, barriers to effective communication, and the family as a social system.

**Scenes for Use in the Classroom:**

- Furious explaining the rules of living in his house to Tre when he moves in with his father.
- Doughboy trying to regain his brother's football from the street gang when they are small boys.
- Doughboy's mother yelling at him for getting caught trying to steal.
- Tre disclosing to his girlfriend after being harassed by the police.

**Questions for Discussion**

1. **Describe the relationship between Tre and his father, Furious. Why does it seem to work?**

   Tre respects and loves his father. Furious has been strict, yet caring with his son. He explains why he has high expectations of his son, and he is willing to disclose his own past in order to prove the wisdom of his advice to his son. Furious tries to be a role model for Tre. He practices what he preaches. He is involved in his son's life, knows what is going on, and is willing to listen to his son's feelings, fears, and problems. Furious knows what is going on in the neighborhood and he and Tre can communicate openly and candidly about just about any topic. Their discussion of the need to use a condom is a good illustration of this.

2. **What is life like in the home of Doughboy and Ricky? Is there any parental support?**

   Doughboy and Ricky's home is just about the opposite of Tre's home. Their mother tends to yell rather than sit down and talk to the boys or get involved in their day-to-day lives. She plays favorites by choosing Ricky over Doughboy at every turn. She yells at Doughboy when he is a little boy that he will never amount to anything. So much for helping with self-esteem. She constantly supports and encourages Ricky.

3. **Why does Tre finally disclose to his girl friend?**

   Tre has had a series of severe shocks. He has allowed a lot of anger to build up within him because he has not found a workable outlet for his frustrations. As a result he nearly loses his composure and balance when he visits her home. She lets him vent and then gives him support, caring, and gentle understanding. Given her empathy, he opens up his heart to her.

## Moonstruck, dir. Norman Jewison. Cher, Nicholas Cage, Vincent Gardenia, Olympia Dukakis, Danny Aiello, 1987.

**Brief Summary:** This film is a delightful look at Italian-American family dynamics. Cher plays Loretta, a young woman who agrees to marry Johnny, an older man (Aiello). This will be her second marriage, as her first husband died. Her father opposes the marriage on the grounds that since her first husband died, marriage must be unlucky for her. Her mother, Rose (Dukakis), asks if she loves him. When she answers no, her mother says, "that's good. When you love them they drive you crazy." Johnny must go to Italy to be with his dying mother. He asks Loretta to speak with Ronny, his estranged brother (Cage) in order to make peace and invite him to their wedding. Loretta meets and begins to fall in love with the younger brother Ronny. As the story unfolds, we see the conflicts, rituals, relationships, and interdependence of this family. When Johnny returns home, he asks Loretta not to marry him, not knowing she has already decided to marry his brother. When he asks to speak with her, she insists that it be at the breakfast table, because she needs her family around her. After an explosive exchange between Loretta and the two brothers, peace is established and the whole family, including the two brothers, celebrate the upcoming marriage.

**IPC Concepts:** Family and hierarchy, rules, change, cohesion, opening the lines of communication

**Scenes for Use in the Classroom:**

- Loretta talking to each parent about marrying Johnny.
- Rose talking to Perry, the professor, both, in the restaurant and on the walk home.
- The entire final setting with Loretta and the whole family, including Ronny and Johnny.

**Questions for Discussion**

1. **Mother tells the professor that she cannot go to his apartment because she knows her place. What does she mean by this?**

   The professor Perry is constantly looking for validation of his worth. He feels the aging process and fears the loss of his youth and virility. Rose, on the other hand, is very secure in her identity. Except for her husband's recent infidelity, she is happy and content with her life. She knows that she cannot start hopping in and out of a stranger's bed. She knows that her role in life is that of wife and mother. Her self-esteem gives her the strength and self-knowledge to live within these roles.

2. **How do mother and father handle the issue of the father running around with another woman?**

   Rose experiences tremendous pain from his cheating. He refuses to even acknowledge what is happening. When he comes in late from a date, she asks him where he has been. He exclaims, "I don't know where I've been or where I'm going." Eventually, mother simply confronts her husband at the breakfast table before the whole family. He sputters and pounds the table and then says that he will stop seeing her. He then says "mio amore" to show that he does have love for her. Mother is still hurt, but accepts his promise.

3. **Discuss Loretta's desire to have her conversation with Johnny in front of her entire family.**

   Loretta's family is the center of her world. They keep few secrets from each other. They are interdependent such that what affects one person is taken to affect everyone. Her family will serve to give her support and help as needed. By the end of the discussion, both brothers have been accepted as new members of the family. Even the grandfather tells Johnny to have some wine and celebrate with la famiglia.

## *CNN*

### Mom & Dad Versus Uncle Sam. (5:30). CNN Interpersonal Communication Today, 1999, Volume 2.

The clip is about the controversy surrounding the Parental Rights Bill before Congress. The issue is what role the family or schools and government should play in the overall sexual education of children.

### Sibling Rivalry, (7:24). CNN Interpersonal Communication Today, 1999, Volume 1.

This is a good segment to use in conjunction with scenes from the film, *Crooklyn*. This clip explores families and their methods of managing conflict between siblings. The siblings in *Crooklyn* are almost always bothering each other, especially between the boys and their sister. In this clip, parents and experts work with young children in an effort to help these children work through issues of jealously among siblings. Examples of older siblings are offered to give a picture of how siblings can get along as they move into their teens and young adult years. The clip describes the emotional tug of war between siblings as "love and anger, friendship and jealousy."

### Consequences of Divorce. (4:53). CNN Interpersonal Communication Today, 1999, Volume 2.

This clip describes the impact of divorce on the children. The clip presents examples of the pain experienced by children. Dr. Laura Schlesinger comments on the impact on children. The clip documents a program used in several states in which children of divorce speak to divorcing parents with children.

# *Interpersonal Communication Theory in Literature and Academic Resources*

## *Theory Illustrated in Literature*

**Alice Walker. (1982). The Color Purple. New York: Harcourt Brace Jovanovich.**

**Brief Summary:** This is the story of a poor, used and abused African American woman, Celie. She is given into an abusive marriage by her abusive father. She suffers in silence until she discovers that her husband, Mister, has been hiding letters from her sister, Nettie, who had moved to Africa with Christian missionaries. Celie finds the letters and secretly reads them whenever she can steal a few minutes between chores, or by hiding them inside her Bible and reading them at church. The husband has other women but barely knows Celie. Mister's mistress, Shug, befriends Celie, and they develop their own love relationship. As her love grows with Shug, Celie develops more and more self-esteem and confidence. She is eventually able to stand up to Mister and move out on her own. She moves to Memphis with Shug where her life improves tremendously.

**IPC Concepts:** Self perception, self esteem, impact of significant others, relationships – need for warmth and affection, trust and commitment, conflict, diversity, culture, gender, emotion, gender and intimacy.

## *Academic Resources*

**Covington, Stephanie and Liana Beckett. (1988). *Leaving the Enchanted Forest: The Path From Relationship Addiction to Intimacy*. New York: Harper & Row Publishers.**

**Brief Summary:** This a fascinating book on the pattern many people follow when they move from relationship to relationship. The authors offer the explanation that such behavior may be caused by our need for the relationship rush that one experiences when the relationship is new. As the relationship moves on, such a rush is more difficult to experience. Some people may develop a need for, or dependency on, this type of biochemical response to a relational partner.

**IPC Concepts:** Relationship patterns, addiction, gender differences

**Barry L. Duncan and Joseph W. Rock. Saving Relationships: the Power of the Unpredictable. In *Psychology Today*, 26, 1, January/February 1993, 46-51, 86, 90.**

**Brief Summary:** An excellent discussion of problems faced by married couples, and the role of relational myths in contributing to such problems. The authors also suggest communication strategies that couples can employ to improve their relationships. The article stresses the interactive nature of relationships and the power of individual choice in interpreting the actions of the other partner.

**IPC Concepts:** Relationships – self-disclosure, commitment, trust, spouses.

**Barry Dym and Michael Glenn. Forecast For Couples.. *Psychology Today*, 46, 4, July/August 1993, 54-57, 78, 81.**

**Brief Summary:** A practical discussion of relational stages. The authors posit a three-stage model: expansion and promise, contraction and betrayal, and resolution.

**IPC Concepts:** Relationships – self-disclosure, commitment, trust, spouses.

## *What's on the Web*

**Stepfamily Foundation**
**http://www.stepfamily.org/**

**Brief Summary:** This web site is devoted to step relationships, and to providing counseling – on the telephone, worldwide, and in person – by Jeannette Lofas, and other Certified Stepfamily Foundation Counselors. Books, audio tapes and video tapes, Training Certified Stepfamily Foundation Counselors and Coaches, Free Information, Research, Corporate Programs to eliminate the negative spillover effects of divorce and remarriage.

**IPC Concepts:** Relationships – commitment, warmth, affection, trust.

## Committee for Children
**http://fyd.clemson.edu/famlife.htm**

**Brief Summary:** A site concerned with preventing youth violence and enhancing school safety. Clemson University sponsors this site. The purpose is twofold: First, to strengthen family and youth, and second, to help families cope during periods of crisis and change. They offer programs that teach youth and adults coping skills, effective communication skills, effective decision-making, and an appreciation of heritage. The "Building Family Strengths" program focuses on 10 characteristics for strong families.

**IPC Concepts:** Family relationships, commitment, support, trust, warmth.

## Mapping of Rules (Frederick R. Ford)
**http://home.pacbell.net/frccford/index.html**

**Brief Summary:** This site features a list of rules followed by people in several different kinds of families. This site features a web based test (with online scoring that measures five family systems: Two Against the World, Children Come First, Share and Share Alike, Every Man for Himself, & Until Death Do Us Part. Links provide explanations and a bibliography.

**IPC Concepts:** Relationships and commitments, priorities, support, trust, caring.

## Love Test
**http://www.lovetest.com/**

**Brief Summary:** A fun and somewhat silly exercise that can put students in the mood or mindset to discuss various attraction variables in relationships.

**IPC Concepts:** Intimate relationships – commitment, compatibility, beliefs and expectations about relationships.

# CHAPTER THIRTEEN
# Communication in the Workplace

## INTERPERSONAL COMMUNICATION IN ACTION

Chapter Thirteen of Interact explores the role of communication in interpersonal relationships in the workplace. This chapter of the Media Guide will illustrate several different types of workplace relationships and several functions of such workplace communication. Films such as *Barbarians at the Gates*, *Nine to Five*, *Tin Men*, and *Wall Street* depict a wide variety of interpersonal communication situations in the workplace. While *Barbarians at the Gates* is essentially about the takeover attempts of R.J.R. Nabisco during the 1980s, it is the interpersonal dynamics behind the headlines that constitute the real story of the film. *Nine to Five* is an amusing, yet true to life look at sexism and exploitative behavior in the workplace. When we take away the silly scenes with the boss tied up and chained to the ceiling, the balance of the film shows the interpersonal networks and relationships at work behind the formal, official channels of command and power in any organization. From the mail room, to accounting, to personnel, the grapevine carries the real mail. Change is introduced that is humanistic and motivational for the workers. *Tin Men* shows the day to day lives and conversations of aluminum siding salesmen. *Wall Street*, like *Barbarians*, is ostensibly about the big wheelers and dealers of Wall Street during the 1980s, but again, it is the interpersonal dynamics behind the headlines that constitute the real story of the film.

## LEARNING OBJECTIVES

- Assist students in preparing for employment interviews.
- Improve student understanding of supervisor and co-worker communication.
- Increase student awareness and understanding of the nature and forms of workplace leadership.

| **In Classroom Assignments** | **For Homework** |
|---|---|
| - Small Group Discussion<br>- Whole class discussion<br>- Role Play Exercises<br>- Conversation exercises | - Position Papers<br>- Relationship Analysis Papers<br>- Web Exercises to supplement textbook and Instructor's Manual exercise<br>- Journal Entries |

## *Visually Presented Interpersonal Communication Theory*

## *In Movies*

### Barbarians At The Gate, dir. Glenn Jordan. With James Garner, Jonathan Pryce, Peter Riegert, Joanna Cassidy, 1993

Brief Summary: The story of the leveraged buyout of RJR-Nabisco during the Wall Street gone-crazy years of the 1980s. Garner, as F. Ross Johnson, is fascinating, as the down to earth, yet larger than life, CEO of RJR-Nabisco. His leadership style contrasts sharply with that of Henry Kravis, his primary competitor (Jonathan Pryce). The focus of the story is on Ross's attempt to takeover RJR-Nabisco, but the film does a good job of illustrating the dynamic leadership style of Ross. He has a larger than life, free wheeling style of communication.

**IPC Concepts:** Leadership, meeting, communication with peers, subordinates, customers, competitors.

**Scenes for Use in the Classroom:**

- Discussion in men's room prior to negotiations.
- Almost any scene prior to the takeover by Kravis between Ross and his management team.

**Questions for Discussion**

1. **What does Ross mean when he says to his lawyer: "I can talk to Kravis. I speak bullshit"?**

   Ross thinks he knows what the language of the takeover business is, but he finds out the hard way that he has not paid enough attention to the egos of the people involved in the process. Kravis plays the "game" more seriously than most, and he has no sense of humor. He cannot be sold in the same way that Ross has sold things all of his working life.

2. **How does Ross communicate with his staff? How does he motivate confidence, trust, and enthusiasm in them?**

   Ross speaks in plain, direct language. He describes his vision of the future, of what is possible, of what he believes everyone can accomplish in language and vocal tones that is inspiring to his staff. He reinforces their competence, their strengths, and their achievements, rather than attack them on their shortcomings, mistakes, or failures. In the terms of Blanchard's One Minute

Manager, he consistently practices one-minute praisings with his highly talented staff.

## Nine to Five, dir. Colin Higgins. With Jane Fonda, Dolly Parton, Lily Tomlin, Dabney Coleman, Sterling Hayden, 1980.

**Brief Summary:** This movie is virtually two films in one. The first film is a silly comedy, complete with fantasy sequences of revenge against the boss and accidental enactment of these fantasies. The second film is a terrific depiction of the workplace, with chain of command, channels, networks, Theory X and Y leadership, and sexism in the workplace.

The story is about the trials, adventures, and lives of three working women in a large corporation run by a sexist management hierarchy. Violet (Tomlin) is a department supervisor reporting to a department manager, Mr. Hart (Coleman). Violet is a highly talented, knowledgeable employee, one who has trained many men who have then been promoted over her, Hart included. She has just been passed over again for a promotion. She struggles as a widow to support her son. Dora Lee (Parton) is Hart's secretary whom he treats as his next sexual conquest. She struggles to keep him at a safe distance while doing a good job, and trying to make him behave himself. The office perceives her to be the local slut. Judy (Fonda) is the newest employee returning to the workforce after a divorce in which her husband ran off with his much younger secretary. She must learn the ropes of being back to work. Hart is a self-centered, thoughtless, chauvinist who only cares about his own personal advancement and pleasure.

The story moves to the enactment of progressive, participative management policies, complete with corresponding increases in employee satisfaction and productivity. The film accurately depicts the office's informal networks, the dishonest practices of Hart when he takes credit for one of Violet's innovations, and a pair of company spies. If you look past the slapstick material, the balance of the film shows a fantasy vision of what could possibly happen when a variety of pro-worker policies are implemented. The office climate opens up and is more supportive, the workplace is more user-friendly, and there are more monetary and non-monetary incentives.

**IPC Concepts**: Interviews, communicating with supervisor, worker, co-workers, customers, coaching, leadership and ethical issues.

**Scenes for Use in the Classroom:**

- Judy's first day on the job and her orientation by Violet. While not an actual interview, it does a terrific job of depicting the realities of the workplace.
- Mr. Hart discussing the job with Judy on her first day on the job.
- Violet telling Judy how to handle herself on the job at Consolidated.
- Violet being told she was passed over for the promotion.
- Dora Lee serving as gatekeeper for Mr. Hart.
- Scenes of the proactive changes implemented by Violet, Judy, and Dora Lee.

**Questions for Discussion**

1. **Violet is both a good coach and counselor as a supervisor. How practical is her advice to Judy?**

   Violet's advice is grounded in her experience in the company. She gives Judy advice on how to get her work done efficiently and how to survive at Consolidated. She warns her about Roz who serves as Hart's office spy in addition to working in personnel. She warns her about leaving any personal items in plain sight as they are prohibited from the work area. She also misadvises her on Dora Lee due to her superficial understanding of her relationship with Hart. In this area, Violet functions on the basis of stereotype.

2. **How do the changes implemented by Violet, Judy, and Dora Lee foster a more employee friendly environment? Do these changes foster a more productive interpersonal climate?**

   The changes all encourage employees to be human beings with individuality and personal warmth. They encourage the employees to be friendly, interactive, and self-motivated. The changes encourage employees to be more interactive with each other, share work, support each other in getting the job done, and helping employees to deal with personal problems that interfere with their job performance. The prime examples are the single mom who can now share a job with another employee, and the woman with the drinking problem.

3. **What kind of work climate does Mr. Hart create?**

   In organizational communication terms, Hart is a classic Theory X manager. He doesn't trust or respect people, believes people are lazy, and punishes and reprimands employees for any work error. He does not believe in positive feedback except for himself. The atmosphere is inhibiting, restrictive, defensive, and antagonistic. People will only work when they are being watched. No one will volunteer to go beyond the letter of their job description. Any extra work is likely to be taken for granted and not rewarded.

## Tin Men, dir. Barry Levinson. With Richard Dreyfuss, Danny DeVito, Barbara Hershey, John Mahoney, Jackie Gayle, Bruno Kirby, J.T. Walsh, 1987.

**Brief Summary:** The story is about a pair of aluminum salesmen in 1963 Baltimore, one who is always on the make, and the other is who is something of a loser. The film focuses on their dysfunctional lifestyles, their ethical sales tactics, and their general approach to work. This film offers a somewhat cynical view of one side of the world of sales.

**IPC Concepts:** Communication between co-workers, with customers, coaching others at work, ethical issues.

**Scenes for Use in the Classroom:**

- Life Magazine scam.
- Tin men talking to the new salesman as they explain the realities of the job.
- Two scenes in which the manager coaches DeVito on getting the job done, and how to do it.

**Questions for Discussion**

1. **How effective is DeVito's boss in coaching him to change his sales tactics? What else could he say?**

   DeVito's boss doesn't really counsel his salesman very well. He never makes it clear that this is something essential to do. His advice comes off as more of – do what you can or there might be trouble. He needs to recognize that he is talking to someone who is accustomed to talking his way out of trouble and talking people into doing something they would otherwise not do. DeVito tells his boss what he wants to hear and there is no follow-up after the conversations. The net result is that DeVito is sacrificed for the good of the whole sales force. His sales are down the most and his violations are among the worst, so he becomes the company fall guy.

2. **How do the tin men encourage unethical sales practices in their new salesman?**

   The new hire is enculturated with stories of the most gifted salesmen and their incredible con jobs. These stories serve to enlighten the new salesman as to what is not only expected on the job, but taken as perfectly normal behavior. Indeed, it is the goal to become like these giants of corporate legend. Studies in organizational culture by Pacanowsky and Trujillo document the quality and power of the corporate storyteller. This is the kind of dynamic that can make an excellent journal entry for students who either work at a company where such stories are told, or have family members who can retell such stories to them. Either way, these are powerful agencies of organizational enculturation.

3. **How do the tin men manipulate interpersonal trust to get a sale?**

   The scams that they employ are carefully constructed to set the customer up, get their trust, and then manipulate them into a sale. The five-dollar bill scheme is perfectly tailored to massage the customer's level of trust so that it can be exploited. So too, with the Life Magazine ploy, which makes the customer think that they have already been selected to be in Life and they now just have to buy aluminum siding in order to look good or better for their friends, families, and neighbors. Even DeVito's nervous breakdown scheme draws the customer into the desire for new siding with the promise of free siding, only to then make them feel guilty and responsible for the poor, sick salesman.

## Working Girl, dir. Mike Nichols. With Harrison Ford, Melanie Griffith, Sigourney Weaver, Alec Baldwin, Joan Cusack, Oliver Platt, Kevin Spacey, Olympia Dukakis, Ricki Lake, David Duchovny, 1988.

**Brief Summary:** This is a romantic comedy about Tess McGill (Griffith), a young woman who is trying to improve her life and get a better job. Although she knows she can do more, she interviews for a secretarial position with a woman, Katharine Parker (Weaver), as her boss, and quickly learns about corporate manipulation, betrayal, and deception. Her desire to improve herself enables her to pretend to be her boss when Parker breaks her leg skiing and is out on sick leave. She meets Jack Trainer (Harrison Ford) and they begin working together on a big and important project. While working with Trainer, she demonstrates her business acumen and earns his respect and affection. When Parker returns and tries to discredit her efforts, she and Trainer are able to turn the tables on her and win the day.

The film shows the workplace in a fairly realistic manner. Her interview with Parker is useful for a demonstration and analysis of an employment interview. Parker's response to her new idea for an advertising campaign serves as an example of coaching and manipulation. It shows how the role of mentor can easily be misused by the mentor and allow for the exploitation of the mentee.

**IPC Concepts:** Interviewing dynamics, workplace communication between supervisors and employees, co-workers, and with clients.

**Scenes for Use in the Classroom:**

- McGill's interview with Parker.
- First day on the new job.
- Conversation with Parker over McGill's new campaign idea.
- Meeting with Trainer where McGill pretends to have her boss' position.

**Questions for Discussion**

1. **Analyze McGill's job interview. Discuss Weaver's interviewing skills and McGill's answers. Would you hire her? Is there anything in Parker's communication that might tip her off to the future problems?**

   She communicates her desire to do a good job. She demonstrates that she can put forward a professional image. She indicates her willingness to be a team player and work for the greater good of the department and the company. She is eminently hirable.

   Focus the discussion on her specific communicative behaviors in order to demonstrate these behaviors in action, sort of operational definitions of good interviewing behavior.

2. **How realistic is McGill's first day on the job experience? What have your experiences been like on the first day on a new job?**

   McGill has two first day experiences. When she starts as Parker's secretary, she experiences a fairly typical first day for a clerical/administrative employee. She gets the "we're a team" speech, although in this situation, her boss does not mean it. When she begins for Trask's company, she has a most fantastic experience as she expects to be a secretary and slowly realizes that she is a boss.

3. **Analyze Parker's coaching session with McGill. Is there any hint of the coming betrayal? Have you ever had an experience where someone else took credit for your work or idea?**

   Parker is very convincing in the early days of the relationship. She knows what to say and has a reasonably sincere tone. With time, Tess would have been able to se through the phony facade that Parker so often uses to sway others.

## Wall Street, dir. Oliver Stone. With Michael Douglas, Charlie Sheen, Daryl Hannah, Hal Holbrook, Martin Sheen, Terence Stamp, Sean Young, Sylvia Miles, James Spader, 1987.

**<u>Brief Summary</u>:** A very loose adaptation of the Faustus story. Charlie Sheen sells his soul for a piece of the Wall Street pie. In so doing, he discovers the pleasures of making it big in the stock market very quickly, and what it can do to his friends, family and co-workers, and ultimately, to himself. His career is going nowhere when he manages to land an interview with Gordon Gekko (Douglas), one of the big, wheeler-dealers on Wall Street during the mid 1980s. Gekko's speech in the middle of the film that "greed, for lack of a better word, is good" captures the guiding business ethic of this type of investor. He extends the greed ethic into every aspect of his business and personal life. Sheen also adopts this ethic and reaps the rewards, until he must face his own conscience after betraying the trust of his father, and the people with whom he worked prior to coming to Wall Street. He must ultimately pay for his practice of insider trading and personal betrayal. This is an engrossing film that beautifully depicts the effects of the bottom-line ethic at work in corporations.

**<u>IPC Concepts</u>:** Interviewing; communication with management, co-workers, clients, counseling sessions, ethical questions on deception, cheating, greed.

**<u>Scenes for Use in the Classroom</u>:**

- Sheen's conversations with Gekko.
- Sheen's conversations in the office of his stock firm with his superiors, receiving coaching on how to do the job.
- Sheen's conversations in the office of his stock firm with his co-workers.
- Sheen conducting "sales" calls with clients

**<u>Questions for Discussion</u>**

1. **How does Gekko coach Sheen to succeed? Why is Gekko effective with this kind of advice?**

   Gekko works on Sheen's weaknesses, his desire to make a lot of money, his eagerness to do so as quickly as possible, and his willingness to take all kinds of short cuts. There is an old W.C. Fields movie called *You Can't Cheat An Honest Man*. This kind of sums up Sheen's character. He is already willing to sin and only needs a coach to show him what to do. Gekko also plays with Sheen. He does not take to him immediately. Rather, he plays a few games with him that serve to increase Sheen's ardor and eagerness. He rejects Sheen, makes him wait, tells him he has no chance, and then slowly implies that there might be a slim chance if he has what it takes. All of this makes Sheen want to prove himself to this mover and shaker.

2. **How effective are Sheen's superiors in his stock office in coaching him on his job? Why are they not effective with him?**

   Sheen's superiors are cautious, conservative men. They are true company men who believe in taking the slow, straight, legal approach to managing stocks, locating clients, and making money. They do not trust or sanction short cuts. They do not give him any incentives for this slow, cautious, low yield approach. Sheen is much too greedy and impatient for their advice to work.

3. **How does Sheen manipulate interpersonal dynamics to get business from his clients?**

   Sheen takes to playing games very quickly. He plays the big shot, suggesting his willing to share sacred, secret information if they will reciprocate. He offers vast quantities of money if only they will tarnish, if not sell their soul. He justifies this approach on the grounds that there is no one else in the room to hear what is going on, and that everyone is doing it. In order to gain some of this sacred, secret information, he is willing to engage in corporate spying by sneaking into private offices and copying confidential files. This information serves to impress Gekko and get an edge up with his clients.

## *CNN*

### Personal Relationships: Love on the Job. (1:58). CNN Interpersonal Communication Today, 1999, Volume 2.

The clip examines the practice of,, or problem with, developing romantic relationships on the job.

### Mitsubishi Lawsuit. (1:45). CNN Interpersonal Communication Today, 1999, Volume 1.

This segment examines the sexual harassment suit at the Mitsubishi Company. It specifies the constant, uncontrolled, and indiscriminate forms of harassment toward women. The segment also looks at the potential of the settlement.
This is a good segment to use in conjunction with the film *Disclosure* in Chapter 14. The Michael Douglas/Demi Moore film based on the novel by Michael Crichton examines the problem of sexual harassment in the workplace and gives it a new face, with the male harassed by his female superior.

### High-Tech Job Interviews. (1:47). CNN Human Communication Today, 1999, Volume 1

The segment examines the changing dynamics of interviewing in the 90s as a result of new video technology. CityBank donated a video conferencing system to over 30 universities. The bank used to spend about $1,000 per interview, due to expenses incurred while traveling to each campus. The video conferencing costs about $13 plus $60 per hour to run. Companies save $800-900 per interview.

### Selling Teamwork. (1:46). CNN Human Communication Today, 1999, Volume 1

The clip is about the selling of motivational paraphernalia in the form of posters, slogans, etc. The company is Successories located in shopping malls next door to major retail stores like J.C. Penneys. The posters that they sell can either be very successful or they can backfire if they are foisted onto employees, and if management does not live by the philosophy contained or advocated in the poster messages. The clip notes Scott Adams, writer of the comic strip Dilbert, who has mocked these types of posters in his comic strip.

## ***On the Stage***

### David Swift. (1967). How to Succeed in Business Without Really Trying.

**Brief Summary:** This play is about J. Pierpont Finch and his speedy rise to the boardroom of the company. He uses humor, a handbook, and charm to get to the top. A musical comedy, it contains some interesting observations on organizational dynamics.

**IPC Concepts:** Communication, interviewing, leadership, and influence.

---

# *INTERPERSONAL COMMUNICATION THEORY IN LITERATURE AND ACADEMIC RESOURCES*

## *Theory Illustrated in Literature*

**Michael Lewis. (1989). Liar's Poker: Rising through the Wreckage on Wall Street. New York: WW Norton & Company.**

**Brief Summary:** Though not a novel, this first-hand account of life in a stock brokerage firm during the 1980s is a fascinating look at the daily routines, corporate and communication culture of the brokerage houses, and the rituals, rites of passage, and overall quality of life of these people.

**IPC Concepts:** Workplace culture, workplace games, manipulation.

## *Academic Resources*

**Kroeger, Otto and Janet M. Thuesen. (1988). *Type Talk: The 16 Personality Types That Determine How We Live, Love, and Work.* New York: Tilden Press.**

**Brief Summary:** This book discusses the Myers-Briggs Personality Assessment approach and how to use it in the workplace. There are examples of each personality type, what type of work may suit the type, and how to interact with people of all types. A practical, easy to understand summary and application of this popular approach to personality.

**IPC Concepts:** Communication, work, and different types of people.

**Goleman, Daniel. (1998).** ***Working with Emotional Intelligence.*** **New York: Bantam Books.**

**Brief Summary:** This is an extension of Goleman's original work on the concept of emotional intelligence. The theory explains why people with tremendous talent, IQ, and skill sometimes do not rise above fairly menial jobs, while those with seemingly less talent, etc. go very far in the workplace. Goleman does a good job of showing how and why development and management of our emotions is so vitally important to well balanced people and success at work.

**IPC Concepts:** Communication, relationships, workplace, emotion, motivation.

## *What's on the Web*

**Howard Sambol. (1999). Ten Secrets of Effective Communication in the Workplace.**
**http://www.careercraft.com/comm.html**

**Brief Summary:** This site is a general discussion of the above communication concepts adapted for the workplace. Some good illustrations are included that help make the theoretical concepts understandable. The site is clearly written and practical.

**IPC Concepts:** Reflective listening, disclosure, "I" messages, rapport, authenticity, feedback, self-awareness.

**Interviewing (for job, job candidates, by media, exit interviews, etc.) assembled by Carter McNamara, PhD. This site is sponsored by The Management Assistance Program for Nonprofits.**
**http://www.mapnp.org/library/commskls/intrvews/intrvews.htm**

**Brief Summary:** This site contains a treasure-chest of information on interviewing and many other topics in interpersonal communication, conflict, listening, etc. There are numerous links to information on these topics, library resources, and exercises. Categories of information include: Various Types of Interviews, Related Library Links, On-Line Discussion Groups, Being Interviewed by the Media, Exit Interviews, General Guidelines for Conducting Interviews, Interviewing for a Job, Interviewing Job Candidates.

**IPC Concepts:** Employment interviewing, interpersonal skill, conflict management, mediation.

## The Interview
## A career services web site maintained by Virginia Tech.
## http://ei.cs.vt.edu/~cs3604/careers/interview.html

**Brief Summary:** This site includes links to articles on: Types of Interviews, Frequently Asked Interview Questions, Questions to Ask, Lawful and Unlawful Interview Questions, The On-Campus Interviewing Program, Business Etiquette, Attire, and links other college placement and career sites with information about interviewing.

**IPC Concepts:** Employment interviewing, getting the interview, preparing and taking part in the interview.

## Virtual Resume Interview Information Resources.
## http://www.virtualresume.com/interviewing.html

**Brief Summary:** The site provides links to practical articles on job interviewing and links to other sites with information about interviewing. It offers articles on interviewing, tips on how to interview in a traditional employment interview and in behavioral interviews. The latter category focuses on the applicant's behavior in order to establish the applicant's competency for the job in question. A sample question is "Give me a specific example of a time when you had to address an angry customer. What was the problem and what was the outcome?" Traditional interview aids include suggestions for resumes, using recruiters, internet site searches, common mistakes made during interviews, guide to successful interviewing, elements of a successful interview, preparing for interviews, guerilla interviewing, a headhunter's interview secrets, the telephone interview, and favorite interviewing questions. This is an excellent site for supplementary material on employment interviewing.

**IPC Concepts:** Employment interviewing, getting the interview, preparing and taking part in the interview.

# CHAPTER FOURTEEN
# Electronically Mediated Communication

## INTERPERSONAL COMMUNICATION IN ACTION

Chapter Fourteen of Interact is a new one for the textbook. It introduces the student to the dynamics of interpersonal communication via the world-wide-web. With the incredible explosion of web-based communication, students need an introduction to the communication dynamics that occur, and that can occur on the web.

This chapter of the Media Guide will illustrate some the interpersonal dynamics of web-based relationships. *Disclosure* examines an organization that is immersed in electronic communication technology. E-mail plays a critical role in setting up the story and helping to resolve the conspiracy. *Outland* is a science fiction story that illustrates the near future in which we will use various forms of video/voice mail. *You've Got Mail* looks at the world of today in which it is possible to meet people via the net, sometimes not really knowing who the other person really is. The film *Mother* is another film that you might want to use briefly to illustrate the difficulties with adapting to new technologies. Mother has problems using call waiting on her phone. When her younger, technology savvy son gives her a video phone, her attempt to position herself in front of the camera is both amusing and probably too close to the truth for many novice video phone users.

## LEARNING OBJECTIVES

- Increase student understanding of the nature of interpersonal communication on the internet.
- Increase student awareness of the dangers of developing relationships purely via the internet.
- Increase student awareness of the need to develop interpersonal skills appropriate to electronic communication media.

| **In Classroom Assignments** | **For Homework** |
|---|---|
| - Small Group Discussion<br>- Whole class discussion<br>- Role Play Exercises<br>- Conversation exercises | - Position Papers<br>- Relationship Analysis Papers<br>- Web Exercises to supplement textbook and Instructor's Manual exercise<br>- Journal Entries |

# *Visually Presented Interpersonal Communication Theory*

## *In Movies*

**Disclosure, dir. Barry Levinson. With Michael Douglas, Demi Moore, Donald Sutherland, Caroline Goodall, Dylan Baker, Roma Maffia, Dennis Miller, 1994.**

**Brief Summary:** Based on the Michael Crichton novel, this film utilizes e-mail in order to show how people can communicate about others in both positive and hurtful ways. The central character, Tom Sanders (Douglas) is wrongfully accused of sexual harassment by an old flame and co-worker, Meredith Johnson (Moore), and his entire career and personal life are thrown into turmoil. Johnson also assumes the position of his new superior in the company. E-mail comes into play both as a way to smear his reputation and later, as an anonymous way for someone to help in clearing his name. The film depicts the hurtful manner in which a large number of e-mail messages can assault a person's integrity and psyche. Similarly, it shows how secret information can be channeled around an organization or a social system in order to foster change in that system. The film also illustrates the use of videophone calls via video linkups. We are very close to implementing this type of technology on a broad scale. Indeed, computers are slowly being equipped with digital video cameras for two-way video communication. Disclosure also illustrates the informal flow of information via networking.

**IPC Concepts:** Electronically mediated communication via e-mail, phone recorder, fax, and video linkup, in addition to virtual reality technology.

**Scenes for Use in the Classroom:**

- Sanders' videophone conversations with co-workers around the country.
- The scene in which the cell phone is left on while the receiving part's voice mail is recording.
- The scene in which hateful, accusatory e-mails are being read by Sanders.
- The scene in which Sanders receives help via e-mail.
- The scene in which the voice mail recording helps to clear his name.

**Questions for Discussion**

1. **Discuss the impact of high tech recording and monitoring equipment on interpersonal communication and relationships in the workplace and in society in general.**

   This application of technology is already a burgeoning area of conflict. Some employers have taken to monitoring the behavior of their employees in terms of productivity and their time spent on various technology (i.e. keystrokes, number of personal e-mail messages, etc.). In addition, some employers have used monitoring technology, such as cameras and audio recording devices, to monitor employee behavior in order to uncover any illegal activity on the premises. Similarly, a few communities have installed video cameras, not only in private and/or high security areas, but also on public streets and shopping malls.

The question becomes one of how much we want to have our normal behavior monitored, recorded, and then used to correct our behavior. Locker rooms in factories, rest rooms, and break rooms have traditionally been designated as places of relaxation and time for a few moments of private space and time. In Disclosure, Sanders is monitored in a variety of ways.

2. **Discuss how you handle claims made about people and events made via e-mail. What steps can/should you take to protect yourself and others about false claims made via e-mail?**

   Claims made via e-mail can be viewed as rumors. The analogy is a useful one. Rumor studies done in organizational communication and sociology theory suggest very reliable guidelines for their responsible handling. Verify the rumor. Seek outside sources of confirmation. Check to see if the rumor makes any sense.

3. **How can e-mail initiate, develop, and maintain relationships?**

   E-mail is a most effective way to remain in touch with people that you cannot see often due to schedule conflicts or separation due to distance. It allows you to let the person know something current in your life without any real fuss or even having to communicate directly to the person. You do not have to reach the person when you have the desire to communicate, nor do you have to make the message document fancy or worry about accurate postage. It allows for a form of instant gratification on the urge to contact someone you miss.

## Outland, dir. Peter Hyams. With Sean Connery, Peter Boyle, Frances Sternhagen, James B. Sikking, Keeka Markham, Clarke Peters, John Ratzenberger, 1981.

**Brief Summary:** While this is essentially a remake of *High Noon* on a small, mining space station, the story is frequently advanced through the use of electronically mediated communication. Connery, in charge of security for the space station, communicates with his wife via visual phone messages, even recorded visual messages. His wife informs via one such recorded video that she can no longer take life on a space station and is leaving for earth with their son. He keeps tabs on things and events on the station via visual monitoring screens.

**IPC Concepts:** Futuristic video phones, relational turning points.

**Scenes for Use in the Classroom:**

- Connery's communication with his wife both to receive her message on video recorder to announce her departure and to notify her that he would be joining her soon. These take place early in the film and at the end of the film.
- It is also useful to see the video intercom setup by which Connery communicates with his junior officers and monitors activities on the station. There are several scenes in which this occurs.

**Questions for Discussion**

1. **Discuss the impact of high tech recording and monitoring equipment on interpersonal communication and relationships in the workplace and in society in general.**

   The set for this film is a space station in orbit over a mining planet in space. Most public areas are under surveillance by video cameras. These monitors enable the law enforcement on the station to be able to keep track of any criminal activity on the station. The people on the station are completely accustomed to being monitored. The interesting point about this depiction is that it addresses Orwell's vision of the future with people becoming so accustomed to constant monitoring, that they are virtually unaware of it. This dynamic does not justify or make the monitoring right, but it could be a justification by those elements in authority or reactionary elements of society who wish to justify such totalitarian tactics.

2. **How can e-mail initiate, develop, and maintain relationships?**

   In this film, video mail is being used to keep each party informed of what is occurring. The marshals on the station keep each other informed about what is happening on each shift. Connery's wife tells him of her plans to leave for earth and asks that he join them so that they can continue their life together under more livable conditions.

   E-mail gives us the ability to communicate over great distances, without having to be available at the same time, with a minimum of cost and preparation. Such communication allows us to maintain a connection with those who are important to us on one level or another.

## You've Got Mail, dir. Nora Ephron. With Tom Hanks, Meg Ryan, Parker Posey, Greg Kinnear, Jean Stapleton, 1998.

**Brief Summary**: The story is about a modern e-mail relationship that is tested due to the real world pressure of business. This is a remake of The *Shop Around the Corner*, which used letters instead of e-mail. The two central characters Joe Fox (Hanks) and Kathleen Kelly (Ryan) must sort out their electronic relationship and their roles as business competitors.

**IPC Concepts:** E-mail, relational development, strength, and trust of the on-line relationship.

**Scenes for Use in the Classroom:**

- The first chat room scene is very useful to set up their enthusiasm about the relationship.
- Chat room scenes in which Joe gives Kathleen advice on her business and on her relationships.
- The two scenes (back to back) in which Joe asks Kathleen to forgive him for putting her out of business, and when she meets NY152 (Joe) in the park with Brinkley, the dog.

**Questions for Discussion**

1. **How does the anonymity of the web chat rooms help to foster relational development and honesty?**

   When the parties involved are responsible and honest, the chat room gives them an opportunity to be open and candid without fear of a face-to-face rejection or negative reaction. The parties can take risks in order to let their inner fears or feelings come out. They can feel free to ask for help or state an honest opinion. Joe and Kathleen certainly exhibit this dynamic. Their initial chat room meetings give them a basis for a relationship because they did not have to go through the initial awkwardness of most meetings.

2. **How can e-mail initiate, develop, and maintain relationships?**

   Chat rooms can be a potentially safe place in which to meet other people. Joe and Kathleen meet in a chat room for singles. They know that they have at least one thing in common when they start to talk to each other. They can maintain the relationship because they can talk to each other fairly often and at their own convenience by simply sending a message. Parties can share a lot of information without having to worry about sharing the conversation time. Their message can be lengthy, knowing that the other person can read at their leisure and respond to whatever they choose. They can ask for and receive advice, support, etc.

3. **What are the dangers of web based relationships?**

   Web relationships are unusual relationships due to the degree of anonymity. Cases emerge in the news now and then of people who were totally fooled by a web partner who had pretended to be someone completely different from the real person. Some people role-play or assume the persona of a different gender, age, racial, ethnic group, etc. The motivations are varied, but the reality is that you cannot be absolutely certain of whom you are communicating with until you actually see the person. Joe and Kathleen tease about this problem in a couple of scenes in the last portion of the story. Joe, in particular, teases Kathleen that her web partner might be 152 years old, have had 152 victims, have 152 pock marks on his face, be married, etc. It is humorous in the film because we already know the answer, but it can be devastating in real life. This is especially true when children are using the web and a very troubled or sick adult tries to manipulate the child.

## *CNN*

**Gulf War Forces Use of Email, (2:02). CNN Interpersonal Communication Today, 1999, Volume 1.**

The Gulf War introduced a new era of communication during wartime. This clip examines the use of e-mail during the conflict, and the impact on the interpersonal relationships of our soldiers. It notes that this was the first war in which soldiers and their families could be in daily communication even from the battlefield.

**Love at First Site, (:58). CNN Interpersonal Communication Today, 1999, Volume 1.**

This clip looks at dating services on the web. It raises questions regarding the role of the internet in intimate relationships. The site discussed is an on line dating service which offers private, secure introductions to other people who are looking for someone to meet and possibly date. It offers photos of the client without giving out any unauthorized personal information.

**Valentines' Day On-Line, (1:15). CNN Interpersonal Communication Today, 1999, Volume 1.**

This clip takes a look at the efforts on the web to help people satisfy their need for love and inclusion. The segment notes a variety of sites whose services range from cyber cards, to help in creating love messages, to valentine dating services, to cyber kisses for Valentine's Day.

# *INTERPERSONAL COMMUNICATION THEORY IN LITERATURE AND ACADEMIC RESOURCES*

## *Theory Illustrated in Literature*

In an age of electronic communication, it is worthwhile to remember how people initiated and sustained interpersonal relationships via letters. These two books are an excellent way to examine the reality of corresponding with a close friend or family member, and the art of letter writing that could be of use in internet corresponding.

### David Sobel. (1999). Galileo's Daughter: a historical memoir of science, faith, and love. New York: Walker & Company.

**Brief Summary:** This collection of letters is a fascinating look into a very close relationship. The letters, although written in an archaic form, nonetheless show depth of caring, affection, and concern for both parties. This is an excellent way to see how correspondence via print media can be important and repeated today via electronic media.

**IPC Concepts:** Interpersonal communication mediated by writing.

### Lisa Grunwald and Stephen J. Adler Eds. (1999). Letters of the Century: America 1900-1999. New York: Random House, Inc.

**Brief Summary:** Grunwald and Adler have selected 423 letters from the 20th century to illustrate the power of the written word in social interaction. The collection includes letters from some of the most influential and colorful personalities of the last one hundred years, including Jonas Salk, Mark Twain, and JFK. Reading these letters is a wonderful experience that might be compared to knowing the words to a song, and hearing it sung. The letters are organized by decade, with helpful annotations.

**IPC Concepts:** Interpersonal communication mediated by writing.

## *Academic Resources*

### Barbara K. Kaye and Norman J. Medoff. (1999). The World Wide Web: A Mass Communication Perspective. London: Mayfield Publishing Company.

**Brief Summary:** Especially good in chapter 8 – on the social implications of web use, and chapter 12 – on career opportunities via the web.

**IPC Concepts:** Introduction to web technology, terminology, types of e-mail, even legal and ethical concerns.

## *What's on the Web*

**The Dark Side of Cyber Relationships**
http://www.chowk.com/Chaathouse/OffWall/jdugal_aug1098.html

**Brief Summary:** Essentially an anecdotal opinion on the risks of cyber relationships. The author refers to a friend's experience with a cyber-relationship turning dark in real life. The person receives 50 harassing phone calls per day. The statement warns the reader of the risks of giving real information to someone whom you cannot see or properly assess as you can in a face-to-face meeting.

**IPC Concepts:** Relational development, stalking.

**Friendship and intimacy in the digital age. By Timothy Bickmore.**
**http://www.media.mit.edu/~bickmore/Mas714/finalReport.html]**

**Brief Summary:** A final paper presented in MIT course, Systems & Self. This a web article on the nature of on-line relationships. The article examines the acceptance of issues and implications of computer-based intimate friends. The article is based on interviews and a review of the psychological literature on interpersonal relationships. There is also a discussion of the disadvantages of such relationships.

**IPC Concepts:** Development of relationships, trust and strength of cyber-relationships.

**Revenge of the Introverts. By Jeb Livingood, (1995). Computer-Mediated Communication Magazine, 2(4), 1 April 1995, p. 8. Online:**
**http://metalab.unc.edu/cmc/mag/1995/apr/livingood.html**

**Brief Summary:** Short article with a thesis that the Internet is an introvert friendly environment. This is a good site to have students visit in order to set up a discussion of self-concept, shyness, personality/temperament, and the web.

**IPC Concepts:** Personality, relationship development.

**Researching Personal Relationships What's on the Web" by Malcolm Parks (U of Washington) and Joseph Walther (Rensselaer Polytechnic Institute), originally presented at the INPR meeting in Seattle in 1997.**
**http://www.rpi.edu/~walthj/inpr96/sld001.htm**

**Brief Summary**: Originally presented at the INPR meeting in Seattle in 1997. This is a rich 72-slide presentation about the impact of computer-aided communication (e-mail, moos, etc.) on interpersonal relationships. However, because it is set up in small slide segments, you have to be very patient to get through all of them. Joseph Walther has a large bibliography of computer-mediated communication that supports "Researching Personal Relationships in Cyberspace." You will need to go to his personal web page and click on "CMC Bib." The file is in rtf (rich text format, readable by most word processors).

**IPC Concepts:** Nature of on-line relationships, how they develop, relational issues.

## Personal web site for Joseph Walther
**http://www.rpi.edu/~walthj/**

## Sheclicks.com
**http://www.sheclicks.com/**

**Brief Summary:** This is a web site created for women to make the web more user friendly for women. The introduction states, "Welcome to SheClicks.com! We've worked like mad to be sure that each one of the colorful buttons on our Home Page leads somewhere interesting and fun. We hope you'll enjoy the site, and if you have suggestions…" "SheClicks.com is devoted to helping women master online life—and build a healthy attitude toward the Internet that says, "Hey! We own this pile of hardware, it doesn't own us."

**IPC CONCEPTS:** Gender and the web.

# APPENDIX

---

## MOVIES CITED

A Few Good Men, dir. Rob Reiner. Jack Nicholson, Demi Moore, Kevin Bacon, Kevin Pollak, 1992.

As Good As It Gets, dir. James L. Brooks. With Jack Nicholson, Helen Hunt, Greg Kinnear, Cuba Gooding, Jr., Shirley Knight, 1997.

Barbarians At The Gate, dir. Glenn Jordan. With James Garner, Jonathan Pryce, Peter Riegert, Joanna Cassidy, 1993

Being There. Hal Ashby, dir. With Peter Sellers, Shirley Maclaine, Melvyn Douglas, Jack Warden, Richard Dysart, 1979.

Big Chill, dir. Lawrence Kasdan. With Tom Berenger, Glenn Close, Jeff Goldblum, William Hurt, Kevin Kline, Mary Kay Place, Meg Tilly, JoBeth Williams, Don Galloway, 1983.

Blade Runner, dir. Ridley Scott. With Harrison Ford, Rutger Hauer, Sean Young, Edward James Olmos, Darryl Hannah, Joanna Cassidy, 1982.

Boyz in the Hood, dir. John Singleton. Larry Fishburne, Ice Cube, Cuba Gooding Jr., Nia Long, Morris Chestnut, Tyra Ferrell, Angela Bassett, 1991.

Breakfast Club: dir. John Hughes. With Emilio Estevez, Judd Nelson, Molly Ringwald, Anthony Michael Hall, Ally Sheedy, Paul Gleason, 1985.

Christmas Story (The). Bob Clark, dir. With Peter Billingsley, Darren McGavin, 1983.

Color Purple (The), dir. Steven Spielberg. With Danny Glover, Whoopi Goldberg, Margaret Avery, Oprah Winfrey, Akosua Busia, Rae Dawn Chong, Larry Fishburne, 1985.

Crooklyn, dir. Spike Lee. Alfre Woodard, Delroy Lindo, David Patrick Kelly, Zelda Harris, Carlton Williams, Sharif Rashed, Tse-Mach Washington, Spike Lee, 1994.

Diner, dir. Barry Levinson. With Steve Guttenberg, Daniel Stern Mickey Rourke, Kevin Bacon, Timothy Daly, Ellen Barkin, Paul Reiser, 1982.

Disclosure, dir. Barry Levinson. With Michael Douglas, Demi Moore, Donald Sutherland, Caroline Goodall, Dylan Baker, Roma Maffia, Dennis Miller, 1994.

Do The Right Thing, dir. Spike Lee. With Spike Lee, Danny Aiello, Ossie Davis, Ruby Lee, Richard Edson, Rosie Perez, John Torturro, 1989.

Doctor (The), dir. Randa Haines. With William Hurt, Christine Lahti, Elizabeth Perkins, Mandy Patinkin, Adam Arkin, 1991.

Driving Miss Daisy (1989), dir. Bruce Beresford. Morgan Freeman, Jessica Tandy, Dan Ackroyd, Patti Lupone, Esther Rolle.

E.T. The Extra-Terrestrial. Steven Spielberg, dir. With Dee Wallace, Henry Thomas, Peter Coyote, Robert MacNaughton, Drew Barrymore, Tom (C. Thomas) Howell, 1982.

Educating Rita (1983), dir. Lewis Gilbert. Michael Caine, Julie Walters, Michael Williams, Maureen Lipman, Jeananne Crowley, Malcolm Douglas.

Fried Green Tomatoes, dir. Jon Avnet, with Kathy Bates, Jessica Tandy, Mary Stuart Masterson, Mary-Louise Parker, Cicely Tyson, Chris O'Donnell and Stan Shaw, 1991.

George Carlin: Doin' It Again. 1990.

Guess Who's Coming To Dinner, dir. Stanley Kramer. With Spencer Tracy, Katharine Hepburn, Sidney Poitier, 1967.

How to Make an American Quilt, dir. Jocelyn Moorehouse. With Winona Ryder, Ellen Burstyn, Anne Bancroft, Maya Angelou, Kate Nelligan, Jean Simmons, Alfre Woodard, Kate Capshaw, Claire Danes, 1995.

I Never Sang For My Father, dir. Gilbert Cates. Melvyn Douglas, Gene Hackman, Dorothy Stickney, Estelle Parsons, Elizabeth Hubbard, Lovelady Powell, 1970 .

Moonstruck, dir. Norman Jewison. Cher, Nicholas Cage, Vincent Gardenia, Olympia Dukakis, Danny Aiello, 1987.

Mother, dir. Albert Brooks. With Albert Brooks, Debbie Reynolds, Rob Morrow, Lisa Kudrow, 1996.

Mrs. Doubtfire, dir. Chris Columbus. With Robin Williams, Sally Field, Pierce Brosnan, Harvey Fierstein, Polly Holiday, 1993.

My Dinner with Andre, dir. Louis Malle. With Andre Gregory, Wallace Shawn, 1981.

My Fair Lady, dir. George Cukor. Rex Harrison, Audrey Hepburn, Stanley Holloway, Wilfrid Hyde-White, Gladys Cooper, Jeremy Brett, Theodore Bikel, Henry Daniel, Mona Washbourne, Isobel Elsom, 1964.

My Family (mi familia), dir Gregory Nava. Jimmy Smits, Esai Morales, Edward James Olmos, Eduardo Lopez Rojas, Jenny Gago, Elpidia Carrillo, Jennifer Lopez, Mary Steenburgen, Scott Bakula, 1995.

Nine to Five, dir. Colin Higgins. With Jane Fonda, Dolly Parton, Lily Tomlin, Dabney Coleman, Sterling Hayden, 1980.

Nothing in Common, dir. Garry Marshall with Tom Hanks, Jackie Gleason, Eva Marie Saint, Hector Elizondo, Sela Ward, 1986.

On Golden Pond, dir. Mark Rydell. Henry Fonda, Katherine Hepburn, Jane Fonda, Doug McKeon, and Dabney Coleman, 1981.

Ordinary People: dir. Robert Redford. With Donald Sutherland, Mary Tyler Moore, Judd Hirsch, Timothy Hutton, Elizabeth McGovern, 1980.

Outland, dir. Peter Hyams. With Sean Connery, Peter Boyle, Frances Sternhagen, James B. Sikking, Keeka Markham, Clarke Peters, John Ratzenberger, 1981.

Perez Family (The), dir. Mira Nair. Marisa Tomei, Anjelica Huston, Alfred Molina, Chazz Palminteri, Trini Alvarado, Celia Cruz, Diego Wallraff, Trini Alvarado, 1995.

Pygmalion, dir. Anthony Asquith and Leslie Howard. Leslie Howard, Wendy Hiller, Wilfrid Lawson, Marie Lohr, David Tree, 1938.

Quantum Leap, Television series, presently in syndication.

Ship of Fools, dir. Stanley Kramer. Vivien Leigh, Oskar Werner, Simone Signet, Jose Ferrer, Lee Marvin, Jose Greco, and Michael Dunn, 1965.

Simon Birch, dir. Mark Stevenson Johnson, with Ian Michael Smith, Joseph Mazzello, Ashley Judd, Oliver Platt, David Straithairn, Dana Ivey, Beatrice Winde, Jan Hooks, Jim Carrey, 1998.

Steel Magnolias, dir. Herbert Ross. With Sally Field, Dolly Parton, Shirley MacLaine, Darryl Hannah, Olympia Dukakis, Julia Roberts, Tom Skerritt, Sam Shepard, 1989.

Switch, dir. Blake Edwards. With Ellen Barkin, Jimmy Smits, JoBeth Williams, Lorraine Bracco, Tony Roberts, Perry King, 1991.

Terms of Endearment, dir. James L. Brooks. Shirley MacLaine, Debra Winger, Jack Nicholson, John Lithgow, Jeff Daniels, Danny DeVito, 1983.

Tin Men, dir. Barry Levinson. With Richard Dreyfuss, Danny DeVito, Barbara Hershey, John Mahoney, Jackie Gayle, Bruno Kirby, J.T. Walsh, 1987.

To Kill A Mockingbird, dir. Robert Mulligan. Gregory Peck, Mary Badham, Philip Alford, John Megna, Brock Peters, Robert Duvall, Frank Overton, Rosemary Murphy, Paul Fix, Collin Wilcox, Alice Ghostley, William Windom; narrated by Kim Stanley, 1962.

Tootsie, dir. Sydney Pollack. With Dustin Hoffman, Jessica Lange, Teri Garr, Dabney Coleman, Charles Durning, Bill Murray, Sydney Pollack, Geena Davis, Estelle Getty, 1982.

Torch Song Trilogy, dir. Paul Bogart. With Anne Bancroft, Matthew Broderick, Harvey Fierstein, Brian Kerwin, Karen Young, Charles Pierce, 1988.

Trading Places, dir. John Landis. With Eddie Murphy, Dan Ackroyd, Ralph Bellamy, Don Ameche, Denholm Elliot, Jamie Lee Curtis, 1983.

Twelve Angry Men, dir. Sidney Lumet. With Henry Fonda, Lee J. Cobb, Ed Begley, E.G. Marshall, Jack Klugman, Jack Warden, Martin Balsam, John Fielder, George Voskovec, Robert Webber, Edward Binns, Joseph Sweeney, 1957.

Victor/Victoria, dir. Blake Edwards. Julie Andrews, James Garner, Robert Preston, Leslie Ann Warren, Alex Karras and John Rhys-Davies, 1982.

Wall Street, dir. Oliver Stone. With Michael Douglas, Charlie Sheen, Daryl Hannah, Hal Holbrook, Martin Sheen, Terence Stamp, Sean Young, Sylvia Miles, James Spader, 1987.

War of the Roses, dir. Danny DeVito. With Michael Douglas, Kathleen Turner, Danny DeVito, 1989.

Who's On First in *Naughty Nineties*. Jean Yarbrough, dir. With Bud Abbott and Lou Costello. 1945.

Wonderful Ice Cream Suit (The), dir. Stuart Gordon, with Joe Montegna, Esai Morales, Edward James Olmos, Clifton Gonzales, Liz Torres, Sid Caesar, and Howard Morris, 1998.

Working Girl, dir. Mike Nichols. With Harrison Ford, Melanie Griffith, Sigourney Weaver, Alec Baldwin, Joan Cusack, Oliver Platt, Kevin Spacey, Olympia Dukakis, Ricki Lake, David Duchovny, 1988.

You've Got Mail, dir. Nora Ephron. With Tom Hanks, Meg Ryan, Oarker Posey, Greg Kinnear, Jean Stapleton, 1998.

# PLAYS CITED


Albee, Edward. (1962). Who's Afraid of Virginia Woolf.

Boublil, Alain and Claude-Michel Schonberg, Lyrics by Herbert Kretzmer. (1985). Les Miserables.

Coward, Noel. (1925). Easy Virtue.

Lane, Burton and E.Y. Harburg. (1960). Finian's Rainbow.

Lapine, James and Stephen Sondheim. (1985). Sunday in the Park with George.

Lerner, Alan Jay and Frederick Loewe. (1956). My Fair Lady.

Schaeffer, Anthony. Sleuth.

Shakespeare, William. A Mid Summer's Night Dream.

Shakespeare, William. Romeo and Juliet.

Shakespeare, William. The Tempest.

Shaw, G.B. (1913). Pygmalion

Shaw, G.B. (1939). In Good King Charles' Golden Days.

Slade, Bernard. Same Time Next Year.

Styron, William. (1979). Sophie's Choice. New York: Random House.

Swift, David. (1967). How to Succeed in Business Without Really Trying.

Uhry, Alfred. (1987). Driving Miss Daisy.

Williams, Tennessee. (1947). Streetcar Named Desire.

# CNN CITED


"Eating Disorders." (2:09). CNN Interpersonal Communication Today, 1999, Volume 2.

"The Ugly Bill: Hobbit House in Manila." (2:18). CNN Interpersonal Communication Today, 1999, Volume 2.

"Weight Hate: Tipping the Scales." (5:25). CNN Interpersonal Communication Today, 1999, Volume 2.

Baby's First Words. (2:44). CNN Interpersonal Communication Today, 1999, Volume 2.

Bilingual Storyteller, (3:41), CNN Interpersonal Communication Today, 1999, Volume 1.

Black English, (2:32). CNN Interpersonal Communication Today, 1999, Volume 1.

Consequences of Divorce. (4:53). CNN Interpersonal Communication Today, 1999, Volume 2.

Domestic Violence, (4:30). CNN Interpersonal Communication Today, 1999, Volume 1.

Eating Disorders, (2:09), CNN Interpersonal Communication Today, 1999, Volume 1.

Gulf War Forces Use of Email, (2:02). CNN Interpersonal Communication Today, 1999, Volume 1.

High-Tech Job Interviews. (1:47). CNN Human Communication Today, 1999, Volume 1.

Inner City Teens Talk. (2:12). CNN Interpersonal Communication Today, 1999, Volume 2.

Latch-key Kids, (2:23), CNN Interpersonal Communication Today, 1999, Volume 1.

Lost Language, (2:11). CNN Interpersonal Communication Today, 1999, Volume 1.

Love at First Site, (: 58). CNN Interpersonal Communication Today, 1999, Volume 1.

Love at First Site, (:58). CNN Interpersonal Communication Today, 1999, Volume 1.

Mitsubishi Lawsuit. (1:45). CNN Interpersonal Communication Today, 1999, Volume 1.

Mom & Dad Versus Uncle Sam. (5:30). CNN Interpersonal Communication Today, 1999, Volume 2.

Personal Relationships: Love on the Job. (1:58). CNN Interpersonal Communication Today, 1999, Volume 2.

Prozac For PMS, (1:38). CNN Interpersonal Communication Today, 1999, Volume 1.

Recognizing Domestic Partners. (1:31). CNN Interpersonal Communication Today, 1999, Volume 2.

Selling Teamwork. (1:46). CNN Human Communication Today, 1999, Volume 1

Sibling Rivalry. (7:24). CNN Interpersonal Communication Today, 1999, Volume 1.

Social Contact Cures Colds, (1:55), Human Communication Today Video, 1999 Volume 1.

Teen Roundtable. (4:32). CNN Interpersonal Communication Today, 1999, Volume 1.

US Reaction to Princess Diana's Funeral, (1:55).

Valentines' Day On-Line, (1:15). CNN Interpersonal Communication Today, 1999, Volume 1.

---

## LITERATURE CITED

Albom, Mitch. (1997). Tuesdays with Morrie: an old man, a young man, and life's greatest lesson. New York: Doubleday.

Baldwin, James. (1963). Go Tell It On The Mountain. New York: Dial Press.

Griffin, John Howard. (1976). Black Like Me. Updated with epilogue for the author. New York: New American Library.

Grunwald, Lisa and Stephen J. Adler Eds. (1999). Letters of the Century: America 1900-1999. New York: Random House, Inc.

Hammett, Dashiel. (1965). The Maltese Falcon. New York: Knopf.

Hemingway, Ernest. (1929). A Farewell To Arms.

Hemingway, Ernest. (1952). The Old Man and The Sea. New York: Scribner.

Huxley, Aldous. (1965). Brave New World & Brave New World Revisited. New York: Harper & Row, Publisher, Incorporated. (Original work published in 1932).

Irving, John (1989) *A Prayer For Owen Meany.* N.Y.: Ballantine Books.

Lee, Harper. (1960). To Kill A Mockingbird. New York: Harper Collins Publishers.

Lewis, Michael. (1989). Liar's Poker: Rising through the Wreckage on Wall Street. New York: WW Norton & Company.

McCullers, Carson. (1940). The Heart Is A Lonely Hunter. N.Y.: Modern Library.

O'Brien, Tim. (1991). "The Things They Carried." *In Lives & Moments: An Introduction To Short Fiction*, Ed by Hans Ostrom. Fort Worth: Holt, Rinehart and Winston, Inc. pp. 583-596.

Orwell, George. (1946). Animal Farm. New York: New American Library.

Orwell, George. (1949). 1984. New York: Harcourt, Brace.

Sobel, David. (1999). Galileo's Daughter: a historical memoir of science, faith, and love. New York: Walker & Company.

Tolkien, J.R. (1966). *The Hobbit.* Boston: Houghton Mifflin Company. See Chapter V, "Riddles in the Dark."

Turkel, Studs. (1980). *American Dreams: Lost & Found.* New York: Ballantine Books.

Walker, Alice. (1982). The Color Purple. New York: Harcourt Brace Jovanovich.

---

## ACADEMIC RESOURCES CITED

Arnett, Ronald C. and Pat Arneson. (1999). *Dialogic Civility in a Cynical Age: Community, Hope, and Interpersonal Relationships.* N.Y.: SUNY Press.

Bloch, Douglas. (1991). *Listening to Your Inner Voice: Discover the Truth Within You And Let It Guide Your Way.* Minneapolis: CompCare Publishers.

Borysenko, Joan. (1987). *Minding the Body, Mending the Mind.* Toronto: Bantam Books.

Buber, Martin. (1958). *I and Thou.* Trans. Ronald Gregor Smith, 2nd Ed. N.Y.: Scribners.

Cameron-Bandler, Leslie and Michael Lebeau. (1986). *The Emotional Hostage: Rescuing Your Emotional Life.* San Rafael, CA: FuturePace Inc.

Cissna, Kenneth N. and Rob Anderson. "The Contributions of Carl R. Rogers to a Philosophical Praxis of Dialogue," *Western Journal of Speech Communication*, 54, 2 (Spring 1990): 125-147.

Covington, Stephanie and Liana Beckett. (1988). *Leaving the Enchanted Forest: The Path From Relationship Addiction to Intimacy.* New York: Harper & Row Publishers.

Csikszentmihalyi, Mihaly. (1990). *Flow: The Psychology of Optimal Experience.* N.Y.: Harper Perennial.

Csikszentmihalyi, Mihaly. Finding Flow. Psychology Today, 30, 4, July/August 1997, 46-48, 70-71.

Duncan, Barry L. and Joseph W. Rock. Saving Relationships: the Power of the Unpredictable. In *Psychology Today*, 26, 1, January/February 1993, 46-51, 86, 90.

Dym, Barry and Michael Glenn. Forecast For Couples.. *Psychology Today*, 46, 4, July/August 1993, 54-57, 78, 81.

Ellis, Albert and Arthur Lange. (1995). *How To Keep People From Pushing Your Buttons.* N.Y.: Citadel Press Book.

Garner, Alan. (1980). Conversationally Speaking: Tested New Ways to Increase Your Personal and Social Effectiveness. N.Y.: McGraw-Hill Book Company.

Goleman, Daniel. (1995). Emotional Intelligence: Why It Can Matter More Than IQ. New York: Bantam Books, 1995.

Goleman, Daniel. (1998). Working With Emotional Intelligence. New York: Bantam Books, 1998.

Goleman, Daniel. (1998). *Working with Emotional Intelligence.* New York: Bantam Books.

Graham, Elizabeth E., Michael J. Papa and Gordon P. Brooks. (1992). Functions of humor in conversation: conceptualization and measurement. Western Journal of Communication, 56, 2, 161-183.

Hall, Edward. (1966). The Hidden Dimension. Garden City, NY: Doubleday & Company.

Hornstein, Harvey A. (1991). A Knight in Shining Armor: Understanding Men's Romantic Illusions. New York: William Morrow and Company, Inc.

Horton, Donald and R. Richard Wohl. (1956). Mass Communication and Parasocial Interaction: Observation on Intimacy at a Distance. Psychiatry, 19, 215-229.

Howe, Reuel L. (1963 ). *The Miracle of Dialogue.* N.Y.: The Seabury Press.

Hugenberg, Lawrence W., Sr. and Mark J. Schaefermeyer. (1983). Soliloquy as Self-Disclosure. The Quarterly Journal of Speech, 69, 2, 187-187.

Kaye, Barbara K. and Norman J. Medoff. (1999). The World Wide Web: A Mass Communication Perspective. London: Mayfield Publishing Company.

Keirsey, David and Marilyn Bates. (1984). *Please Understand Me: Character & Temperament Types.* Del Mar, CA: Prometheus Nemesis Book Company.

Kroeger, Otto and Janet M. Thuesen. (1988). Type Talk: The 16 Personality Types That Determine How We Live, Love, and Work. New York: Tilden Press.

Kroeger, Otto and Janet M. Thuesen. Type Talk: The 16 Personality Types That Determine How We Live, Love, and Work. New York: Tilden Press, 1988.

Lakoff, George and Mark Johnson. (1980). *Metaphors We Live By.* Chicago: University of Chicago Press.

Leathers, Dale G. and Ted H. Emigh. Decoding facial expressions: a new test with decoding norms. The Quarterly Journal of Speech, 66, 4, 1980. 418-436.

Leathers, Dale. (1997). Successful Nonverbal Communication: Principles and Applications. 3rd. ed Allyn & Bacon.

LeCompte, Andrew. (1999). Creating Harmonious Relationships: A Practical Guide to the Power of True Empathy.

Lutz, William. (1981). Double-Speak: From "Revenue Enhancement" To "Terminal Living." N.Y.: HarperCollins Publishers.

Lynch, James J. (1985). *The Language of the Heart: The Human Body in Dialogue.* New York: Basic Books Inc., Publishers.

Merrill, David and Roger Reid. (1983). Personal Styles and Effective Performance: Make Your Style Work For You. N.Y.: St. Lucie Press.

Paul, Annie Murphy. Where Bias Begins: The Truth About Stereotypes. Psychology Today, 31, 3, May/June 1998, 52-55, 82.

Redmond, Mark V. (1985). The Relationship between perceived communication competence and perceived empathy. Communication Monographs, 52, 4, 377-382.

Roberts, Charles V. and Kittie W. Watson, eds. (1989). *Intrapersonal Communciation Processes: Original Essays*. New Orleans: Spectra Incorporated, Publishers and Scottsdale, AZ: Gorsuch Scarisbrick, Publishers.

Solomon, Muriel. (1990). *Working with Difficult People.* Englewood Heights, New Jersey: Prentice Hall.

Tannen, Deborah. (1990). You just don't understand: women and men in conversation. New York: William Morrow and Company, Inc.

Wolvin, Andrew and Carolyn Gwynn Coakley. (1996). Listening 5th Edition. Boston: McGraw-Hill.

Zimbardo, Philip G. (1977). *Shyness: What It Is. What To Do About It.* NY: Addison-Wesley Publishing Co.

---

## WEB SITES CITED

The Active Listening Exercise was prepared by the New England Regional Leadership Program.
http://crs.uvm.edu/gopher/nerl/personal/comm/e.html

All Media Guide.
http://www.allmovie.com

A Great Stereotype Breaker
http://www.suite101.com/discussion.cfm/relationships/25876
Annenberg CPB Project – Personality, Thoughts and Feelings: What Makes Us Who We Are?
http://www.learner.org/exhibits/personality/thoughts.html

Annenberg CPB Project: Sincerity and Deception: How You Present Yourself
http://www.learner.org/exhibits/personality/thoughts_sub.html

Assertiveness prepared by Organizational Development and Training, Department of Human Resources, Tufts University.
http://www.tufts.edu/hr/tips/assert.html

Association for Psychological Type,
http://www.aptcentral.org/

COMFLE.
http://commfaculty.fullerton.edu/jreinard/internet.htm#INTERPER

The Center for Nonverbal Studies (CNS).
http://members.aol.com/nonverbal2center.htm#Center for Nonverbal Studies
http://members.aol.com/doder1/bodymov1.htm

Committee for Children
http://fyd.clemson.edu/famlife.htm

Conflict Resolution Resources at The School of Social and Systemic Studies
http://www.nova.edu/ssss/DR/

Constructive Love: The Lesson by Thom Rutledge
http://www2.scescape.com/support/lesson.htm

The Dark Side of Cyber Relationships
http://www.chowk.com/Chaathouse/OffWall/jdugal_aug1098.html

Empathy
http://www.utexas.edu/ftp/courses/kincaid/ddye/empath.html

Empathy: Deepening your relationships
http://www.igc.apc.org/PeacePark/tslskc03.html

Four Principles of Interpersonal Communication
http://www2.pstcc.cc.tn.us/%7edking/interpr.htm

Friendship and intimacy in the digital age. By Timothy Bickmore.
http://www.media.mit.edu/~bickmore/Mas714/finalReport.html]

Gender differences in nonverbal cues
http://www2.pstcc.cc.tn.us/~dking/nvcom2.htm

Great Ideas in Personality
http://galton.psych.nwu.edu/greatideas.html

Guidelines on Effective Communication, Healthy Relationships and Successful Living by Dr. Larry Alan Nadig
http://www.DRNADIG.com/

Harmonious Assertive Communication.
http://front.csulb.edu/tstevens/c14-lisn.htm

How To Express Difficult Feelings
http://www.DRNADIG.com/feelings.htm

Howard Sambol. (1999). Ten Secrets of Effective Communication in the Workplace. http://www.careercraft.com/comm.html

Human Communication Research Centre
http://www.hcrc.ed.ac.uk/Site/site_home.html

Interpersonal Communication articles web site
http://www.pertinent.com/pertinfo/business/communication/index.html

Interpersonal Communication: Interpersonal Conflict by Tim Borchers, Moorhead State University
http://www.abacon.com/commstudies/interpersonal/inconflict.html

Interpersonal Communication: Self-Disclosure by Tim Borchers, Moorhead State University
http://www.abacon.com/commstudies/interpersonal/indisclosure.html

The Interview
A career services web site maintained by Virginia Tech.
http://ei.cs.vt.edu/~cs3604/careers/interview.html

Interviewing (for job, job candidates, by media, exit interviews, etc.) assembled by Carter McNamara, PhD. This site is sponsored by The Management Assistance Program for Nonprofits.
http://www.mapnp.org/library/commskls/intrvews/intrvews.htm

Jere Moorman (1999). The person centered approach to conflict transformation. Center for Studies of the Person.
http://users.powernet.co.uk/pctmk/papers/conflict.htm

Kiersey Bates Temperament Sorter, version 2
www.kiersey.com

Love Test
http://www.lovetest.com/

Mapping of Rules (Frederick R. Ford)
http://home.pacbell.net/frccford/index.html

The Marriage Toolbox
http://www.marriagetools.com/betweenus/index.htm
Paul Michael, Publisher

Nonverbal Behaviour Nonverbal Communication
http://zen.sunderland.ac.uk/~hb5jma/1stbersn.htm

Nonverbal Communication.
http://cctr.umkc.edu/user/jaitken/nonverbhome.html

Notes on 'The Gaze.' Chandler, Daniel (1998).
http://www.aber.ac.uk/~dgc/gaze.html

Perception web site
http://www.perceptionweb.com/percsup.html

Personal web site for Joseph Walther
http://www.rpi.edu/~walthj/

Personality Tests
http://www.personality.com/test.htm

Researching Personal Relationships What's on the Web" by Malcolm Parks (U of Washington) and Joseph Walther (Rensselaer Polytechnic Institute), originally presented at the INPR meeting in Seattle in 1997.
http://www.rpi.edu/~walthj/inpr96/sld001.htm

Revenge of the Introverts. By Jeb Livingood, (1995). Computer-Mediated Communication Magazine, 2(4), 1 April 1995, p. 8. Online:
http://metalab.unc.edu/cmc/mag/1995/apr/livingood.html

Self-Disclosure of HIV Infection to Sexual Partners after Repeated Counseling. Perry, S. W., C. A. L. Card, et al. AIDS Education & Prevention 1994; 6(5): 403-411.
http://hivinsite.ucsf.edu/topics/testing/2098.366e.html

Sheclicks.com
http://www.sheclicks.com/

The Six Steps To Self-Disclosure: A Guide For The Sender, by Marty Crouch, Pastoral Counselor.
http://www.martycrouch.com/Disclosure.html

Stepfamily Foundation
http://www.stepfamily.org/

Tips on Effective Listening
http://www.DRNADIG.com/listening.htm

VanDruff, Dean & VanDruff, Marshall (1995), Conversational Terrorism: How Not to Talk http://www.vandruff.com/art_converse.html

Virtual Resume Interview Information Resources.
http://www.virtualresume.com/interviewing.html

# Correlation Guide: Media Guide and Wadsworth's Interpersonal Communication Textbooks

| Apple, *Media Guide for Interpersonal Communication* | Verderber & Verderber, *Inter-Act: Interpersonal Communication: Concepts, Skills and Contexts 9/e* | Wood, *Interpersonal Communication: Everyday Encounters 2/e* | Trenholm & Jensen, *Interpersonal Communication, 4/e* |
|---|---|---|---|
| **1.** An Orientation to Interpersonal Communication. | **1.** An Orientation to Interpersonal Communication. | **1.** A First Look at Interpersonal Communication. | 1. Introduction: Communication and Competence.<br>2. Interpersonal Communication: Building Relationships. |
| **2.** Self | **2.** Forming and Using Social Perceptions. | **2.** Communication and the Creation of Self. | **7.** Role Competence: Adapting to Social Expectations.<br>**8.** Self Competence: Establishing Identities. |
| **3.** Forming and Using Social Perceptions. | **3.** Communication in Relationships: Basic Concepts. | **3.** Perception and Communication. | **6.** Interpretive Competence: How We Perceive Individuals, Relationships, and Social Events. |
| **4.** Using Language to Construct Messages. | **4.** Using Language to Construct Messages. | **4.** The World of Words. | **4.** Verbal Competence. |
| **5.** Communicating through Nonverbal Behaviors. | **5.** Communicating through Nonverbal Behaviors. | **5.** The World Beyond Words | **3.** Nonverbal Competence. |
| **6.** Holding Effective Conversations. | **6.** Holding Effective Conversations. | **8.** Communication Climate. | **5.** Relational Competence.<br>**9.** Goal Competence: Interpersonal Influence. |
| **7.** Listening Effectively. | **7.** Listening Effectively.<br>**8.** Responding with Empathy and Understanding. | **6.** Mindful Listening. | |
| **8.** Interpersonal Communication and Emotion | | **7.** Emotions and Communication | |
| **9.** Communication Climate: Self-Disclosure and Feedback. | **9.** Sharing Personal Information: Self-Disclosure and Feedback. | | |
| **10.** Conflict Management | **10.** Using Interpersonal Influence Ethically.<br>**11.** Managing Conflict. | **9.** Managing Conflict In Relationships. | |
| **11.**Communication in Intimate Relationships | **12.** Communicating in Intimate Relationships: Friends, Spouses, And Family. | **11.** Committed Romantic Relationships.<br>**10.** Friendship In Our Lives | **11.** Intimate Relationships: Creating Dyadic Identities. |
| **12.** Communication in Family Relationships | **12.** Communicating in Intimate Relationships: Friends, Spouses, And Family. | | **10.** Family Interaction Patterns. |
| **13.** Communicating in the Workplace | **13.** Communicating in the Workplace | | **12.** Professional Relationships: Communicating with and Other Strangers. |
| **14.** Electronically Mediated Communication | **14.** Electronically Mediated Interpersonal Communication. | | |
| | | | **13.** Cultural and Historical Influences: Communication Competence in Context. |